BIGLAW: How to Survive the First Two Years of Practice in a Mega-Firm, or, The Art of Doc Review

BIGLAW: How to Survive the First Two Years of Practice in a Mega-Firm, or, The Art of Doc Review

Sarah Powell

Carolina Academic Press
Durham, North Carolina

Copyright © 2013
Sarah Powell
All Rights Reserved

Library of Congress Cataloging-in-Publication Data

Powell, Sarah.
  Biglaw : how to survive the first two years of practice in a mega-firm, or, the art of doc review / Sarah Powell.
       p. cm.
  Includes bibliographical references and index.
  ISBN 978-1-61163-304-7 (alk. paper)
  1. Practice of law--United States--Popular works. 2. Law firm associates--Job satisfaction--United States--Popular works. 3. Law firms--United States--Social aspects. 4. Law firm associates--United States--Handbooks, manuals, etc. 5. Law--Vocational guidance--United States. I. Title.

KF300.P69 2013
340.023'73--dc23

2012038570

Carolina Academic Press
700 Kent Street
Durham, NC 27701
Telephone: 919-489-7486
Fax: 919-493-5668
www.cap-press.com

Printed in the United States of America

To Jeff, for showing me what love is,

and Zoe, for making my life music.

Table of Contents

Foreword	xi
Introduction	3
Chapter One • Life in the Fast Lane, or, Anything Can Be Done at Any Time, for a Price and at a Cost	13
Rule Number One: Your Life Is Not Your Own	13
Rule Number Two: Respect the Hierarchy	15
Chapter Two • Reputation and Trust	21
Associate Life: Valuable Feedback is Sparse. Appreciation is Non-Existent.	25
Chapter Three • Know Your Place but Don't Let it Bring You Down	33
Understand Your Place in Biglaw: A Feudal System in a Meritocratic Universe	37
Chapter Four • Document Production and its Discontents	49
A. Witness Prep	54
B. The Priv Log	59
C. Resistance Is Futile	61
D. Biglaw Side Effects	62
E. Biglaw Benefits	64
Chapter Five • Compensation, or, Why Would You Do This to Yourself?	65
Flexibility	69
Training	70
Pro Bono	74

CONTENTS

Chapter Six • Judgment, Prudence, Precision, Diligence, or, Professionalism and the Billable Hour (The Devil You Don't Know)   79
    The Billable Hour   84

Chapter Seven • Email Etiquette, or, How Not to Flame Out on Your First Friday   97
    A. Think Before You Email   97
        1. Do not reply to all   98
        2. The copy conundrum   98
        3. Listserves that do not serve   99
        4. Ridiculously abbreviated language   100
    B. Don't Put Anything Bad in an Email, Ever   100
    C. Save Emails With Positive Feedback in a Permanent File   102
    D. Put Down Your Blackberry   102

Chapter Eight • Making Your Way — It Really Is Who You Know   105
    A. Early On: Figuring Out Who Is Who   105
    B. Beginning to Make Choices: Evaluating Partners and Teams   107
    C. Mobility and Stability Within the Firm: Learning How to Get Where You Want to Go, Hold On Where You're Happy and Still Diversify   108
    D. The Flip Side of Finding Access to Work: Setting Boundaries on the Work You Find   111
    E. Access to Work as the Key to Survival: How to Escape the "Toxic Team"   112
    F. When the Empire Strikes Back: How to Avoid Getting Sucked Back by Your "Toxic Team"   114
    G. Identifying the Toxic Team: How to Know When Getting Out is Essential   116

Chapter Nine • Information Mastery and Preparation, or, What Is Doc Review Anyway?   121
    A. Nuts and Bolts   123
    B. Pitfalls to Avoid   130

Chapter Ten • Mistakes   137
    A. The Blame Game   139
    B. Mistakes Will Be Made   143
    C. Avoiding Mistakes   143

D. Mitigating the Damage	165
E. When and How to Push Back	166

Chapter Eleven • Have a Life — 169
- A. Strip Down — 170
- B. Balance — 172
- C. Draw Lines — 174
- D. Be Kind — 179

Index — 183

Foreword

This book is the product of my experiences as a junior associate. It wasn't just that much that I had to do was unpleasant or that I made mistakes (or at least what I was told were mistakes), but that I couldn't see how it made sense, or how I could exercise any control over my life in the firm. Over time, however, I began to see how the small details of an associate's life fit into a bigger picture — indeed I realized that the often oppressive details are simply the flip side of what appears glamorous and exciting about the world of Biglaw practice. In this book I try to unveil some of the mystery of that world. I show the relationship between the work (and the burdens!) of a Biglaw associate and the nature of the large, elite firm, but I don't do so in theory or through abstractions but by keeping my focus on what actually happens in the first two or three years in Biglaw . . . and what the associate can do about it to maintain her sanity and chart her own course.

I want to thank the many Biglaw associates and friends who shared their daily cringes, mishaps, and small victories with me over the years – especially my friend Wells Bennett, for trudging through the draft and providing invaluable input and enthusiasm as another associate in the ranks. I want to acknowledge, with love and gratitude, my parents Janet and John Sharp, for their love and support, and, in particular, their excitement and enthusiasm for this book. I am deeply grateful to my editor, Elisabeth Lewis Corley, for her wise advice and her painstaking work on this book. Elisabeth brought to the project professional expertise, passion, and a genuine understanding of what I want to communicate.

I'm grateful for my beautiful daughter, Zoe, whose bright and happy spirit gives me hope and joy every day and who is the reason I had to find a humane path on my journey through Biglaw. And this book wouldn't have happened without my husband and sweetheart, Jeff, who always believed I had something valuable to say. His wild romanticism about the law and his unbowed belief in true love still take my breath away.

Finally, for the legions of unnamed senior associates and partners who drove me to write with a passion and a vengeance every morning before work for months at a time as this little book took shape over the past couple of years, I am grateful for all that I have learned, for the many engaging and brilliant people I have met along the way, and that I will likely never be one of you.

BIGLAW: How to Survive the First Two Years of Practice in a Mega-Firm, or, The Art of Doc Review

Introduction

I am a mid-level associate at a top-ten law firm.[1] Nothing in law school prepared me for "Biglaw" practice and it hit me like a ton of bricks. I entered a bizzaro world in which I struggled to keep my head above water for most of the first two years, repeatedly stunned by the sometimes nonsensical reality of a large law firm and confused about what was expected of me, and how to succeed (or at least not get canned). I was not alone. Over the years I have seen a staggering number of junior associates battered by Biglaw. Colleagues regularly call me up in tears or at the end of their ropes, detailing the latest outrage and wanting to walk away, this time for real. I have watched glum, stony-faced junior associates biting back tears or a stream of sputtering obscenities and anger or silently swallowing yet another mindless assignment or a torrent of petty criticism in stoic silence and I have lived that silent despair more often than I care to recall.

But I have learned how to survive and occasionally thrive in this world over the years from my own experiences and the shared wisdom of many colleagues and close friends. And most importantly, I have been able to use my experience to gain valuable skills and expertise that will serve my clients throughout my career. I do not regret my choice to work in Biglaw. I just wish I had had this information years ago. I would have spent a lot less time in the early years confused, indignant, anxious, frustrated, bitter, fearing imminent firing – and crying in my car. I want to share what I have learned. There are many books about law practice, some written by partners, ex-partners, career guidance writers, and people who have not suffered in the trenches as an associate in Biglaw in decades, if ever. There are things about surviving Biglaw that a partner will never be able to tell you. I do not know why. Maybe they include a vow of silence and for-

---

1. According to Vault.com. "Biglaw" is commonly understood to include any United States law firm listed in the Vault.com top one hundred or *American Lawyer* top one hundred law firms.

getting with the partnership agreement. And you will never hear the truth in on-campus interviews. I have no magic bullet and this book does not come with a guarantee. I do not believe there are any easy answers or a key to immediate success with no pain. There will be pain if you decide to enter Biglaw. But I have made it work and learned some valuable lessons in the process and I want my experiences to make it easier for you if you are considering entering this field. What I have to offer is candor about what the first few years are really like for a junior associate, a candor that has often been sorely lacking in our industry.

My practice areas are complex civil litigation and white-collar criminal defense, but the guidance in this book will be useful to every new associate, to anyone considering Biglaw as a career and even to those considering entering law school and still weighing their options. I have had experience in two Biglaw firms and have learned enough about other firms from friends and colleagues to know that new associates will face similar challenges wherever they go. That is not to say that every law firm is the same – they are not. Your quality of life and much of your sanity over the first few years will depend almost entirely on the partners and senior associates with whom you work directly, the culture, environment and support of your firm and how successfully you navigate the political and practical demands of the organization. But the general expectations, assignments and perspectives you will face are inherent in the world of Biglaw, and are much the same anywhere.

While some discussion of cruel or hilariously unstable partners is probably unavoidable (and occasionally entertaining) I did not set out to mock or to propagate more exposés of the seedy extravagance of big law firms and their powerful clients. I believe the perspective of someone inside, who has made her peace with the Biglaw ethos, is more useful to those considering this path than someone on a crusade to end the system. Not that a good case could not be made for such a crusade. The system *is* inhumane, corrupt, broken, makes life hell for many young associates and leaves too many bitter and jaded ex-lawyers in its wake. In the interest of full disclosure, I confess I think my firm offers the best of Biglaw, that, if you want to work in Biglaw, my firm is the place to be and, personally, I would like to stay here. So this will not be a vengeful hatchet job. It is simply an insider's view.

The keys to surviving Biglaw are understanding the world you are entering and knowing with utter clarity and focus what you want from the experience. At times, keeping this focus will be your only armor against despair. This book will help you do this. I will give as clear a picture as I can of the world of Biglaw. Less the high-spending, wining and dining, sexy world of Biglaw you might see on television or read about in novels – I have not seen that side in a while – and more the day-to-day, real world that I live in every day. I will spend a considerable amount of time on the practical skills, habits and knowledge necessary to survive in that world. And throughout I will be urging you to ask yourself what you want and what you are and are not willing to do to get it.

 I am writing this book because too many of my colleagues and friends in Biglaw firms all over the country are miserable. All of the stories I tell here are based on personal experience. I have changed details in places to protect the privacy of those who have shared their stories with me, but as modified to ensure confidentiality, the events described took place and none of them is unusual. Too many young associates are miserable and too many go through months of gripping anxiety, depressed and alone, raging inside, or hopeless, wondering how they got through law school in the first place if they were so stupid and incompetent and thinking everyone else knows how it ought to be done. They spend too much of their time harried, unhappy, unfulfilled professionally and personally, certain they are about to be fired. More regularly than we go out to lunch together or grab a coffee, too many mid-level associates cry in my office, about partners with whom they seem to be caught in some kind of textbook abusive emotional relationship, or about the endless drudgery and the lack of substantive responsibility or development of any real skills, endless months of quality checking witness preparation binders and supervising contract attorneys with no other duties that even vaguely resemble the practice of law, or the fact that they are quickly approaching thirty and have no time to date and no hope of a serious relationship. Too many senior associates call to say they have to get out, that they cannot live this way anymore, they cannot believe they have actually become the typical, micromanaging, obsessive, senior associate they once hated, but have no idea what to do to change the pattern.

 If you imagine that life in Biglaw will be a series of prestigious, high-flying cases, in which you cross-examine the lead witnesses and pull off stunning victory after stunning victory, or glamorous cocktail parties with influential politicians, NFL players and celebrities, you will be bitterly let down. It is that for some, certainly, but not the first-year associate. If you hang around long enough, if you stick it out, persevere, network and do your time, you may reach a point in Biglaw in which you are an integral part of exciting cases, getting major assignments and making real decisions and serious contributions. But that point will come, if it does, sometimes rather automatically, as a result of surviving seven or eight years of something closely resembling most people's vision of hell. You might think elevation to equity participation or even to more interesting cases and greater responsibility would come as a result of merit or effort and sometimes it is but it is also about sheer tenaciousness and the ability to stick it out. Biglaw may be prestigious and lucrative, but it is not fun, glamorous, exciting or often even marginally satisfying in the early years. For a junior associate it is grueling, frantic, exhausting, tedious, mind-numbing, isolating, lonely and unbelievably frustrating.

 If you are still reading at this point there may be hope. If the main reason you are entering Biglaw is that you cannot figure out anything else to do with your life after law school, it will not be worth it. You need to find a reason that makes sense to you so that your decision will not seem completely crazy when you are at your wit's end (for the fourth time in a single week). You need to think hard about what you want and why you have chosen this path. There are plenty of reasonable personal approaches and requirements but it is important to know where you stand going in. Do you want to put in two years for student loan payments and résumé gold and then get out? Do you want to stay five years, pay down your student loans and then leave for the Department of Justice or some other public interest job? Do you want to make partner, or some other version of more-permanent senior associate (of counsel, special counsel)? Do you want to work a few years, socking away money and then move to Indiana and open a locavore barbeque?

Of course you will not know every curve and nuance of your career path, no one can. You may not even be certain what area of law you hope to concentrate on, or whether you want to stay in law at all, and certainly your goals may change over time, but you need to have a strong, unshakeable sense of why you made the choice to enter Biglaw and what you hope to get out of it. If you do not have this focus to motivate you, drive you on through rough times, give you solid, achievable goals or at least a purpose, Biglaw is perfectly capable of crushing the soul out of you and leaving you broken and bitter by the side of the road. I have seen it too often.

Most young associates simply cannot clearly say why they chose Biglaw. It is the default choice for many from top law schools and on-campus interviewing makes it an easy default choice. That will not help you. Whatever your reason is, it has to be strong enough that you can cling to it at three in the morning when the partner you are working for has torn apart your long, substantive and brilliantly-researched memo, in which you made the fatal mistake of failing to include the correct space in your abbreviations of your Federal Supplement citations (F. Supp., people!) among other mortal sins and insisted you have it redone and on his desk by nine in the morning after which he will proceed to ignore it completely for the next two weeks until he then comes streaming into your office with his hair on fire with last minute edits, swallowing up the next twelve hours of your life.

If you do not have a firm reason for subjecting yourself to this constant torrent of other people's often-invisible agendas, Biglaw will make you miserable, over and over again. The question, "What the hell am I doing here?" will torment you. If you do have a clear understanding of what you want from Biglaw, why you want to be here, and perhaps roughly how long you expect to stay and when you will decide to leave (with any luck, on your own terms), it can be the only life preserver you have at times, but it will be all you will need. Having this understanding will not necessarily make your life in Biglaw happy or enriching – but with it you will be able to survive.

Some young attorneys decide to go into Biglaw dreaming of becoming a top partner – always in the news, handling those cutting edge cases we all read about, stunning the public with her brilliance. Some might even think their own lives will resemble the legal dramas they have seen on television. Many – and I was one – did not see any other option after law school, with crushing student loan debt and no real marketable experience. While I entered law school hoping to go into public service and change the world, I quickly realized that I would not be hired for the best public interest jobs right out of law school, and that somehow I had to find a way, as a single-parent, to pay that three-thousand-dollar-a-month student loan bill, support myself and my young daughter and ensure a secure and independent financial future for us both. For many, Biglaw may seem like the only option. That is not a good enough reason to enter the fray. Biglaw can be a valuable stepping stone: government and public interest employers are more interested in people after they have been in Biglaw for a few years and have been well trained. However, I was not sufficiently clear on my objective when I went in to Biglaw to spare myself the dark nights of the soul from which I hope to spare you.

I have heard stories about the good old days of large law firms, when a young associate joined a firm and could expect to stay there and make partner if he did everything that was expected of him, put in the hours and did decent work. Associates were mentored and worked closely with great senior partners. There was mutual commitment and loyalty. You gave your all to your firm, and your firm, in turn, gave you training, responsibility and eventually partnership. You must understand that those days are gone. You will hear a lot about commitment and loyalty in on-campus interviews. Partners and the associates they bring along will talk about the commitment the firm will have to giving you real, substantive experience, regular feedback, the ability to work closely with partners and have individualized experiences. This is rarely the case any more.

Today, the likelihood of making partner at the firm you joined right out of law school is close to zero. And the culture of mentoring and shaping young attorneys is gone, too. Legions of young associates are needed to staff massive, bet-the-company cases. They are hired, with little expectation that they will stick around more than two or three years. There is no commitment or loyalty to those associates. Many associates do leave after they have gotten whatever they wanted from Biglaw, offering no loyalty or commitment of their own, spending their time at the firm trying to float under the radar and, whenever possible, giving less than one hundred percent. To get anything useful out of Biglaw, you have to go after it yourself. Biglaw will throw money at you, for a time, and much more than in decades past, but it has no long-term interest in your career. Developing your skills and shaping your career will be your responsibility. You must decide what you want out of Biglaw, and then go about actively seeking the experiences and assignments that will help you get what you want.

If, when I started at my first firm, I had begun with the settled intention of staying no more than two or three years, doing my time, paying down my debt with the huge year-end bonuses (it was a great economy when I graduated from law school), and then getting out and going to work for the Civil Rights division of the Department of Justice or some other life-affirming job, then those first years might have been easier. I had some such notion, much like many young associates I have known, and the goal is reasonable and achievable. But, like many associates, I did not always have a clear, settled vision pulling me through the dark hours, days, weeks and months. And I really had very little idea what I was in for. It does not matter why you want to go into Biglaw, only that you have a clear, definite reason and that you understand what your life will be like for the first few years. Without such understandings, the tedious assignments, frantic pace, chronic exhaustion, constant criticism and hellish micromanaging of senior associates and partners, will not be worth it. If you know what you are in for and you know why you are there, you will be able to get what you want from Biglaw. This book will help you with the first part but the second must be your job.

You will not have any control over a lot of what happens to you in Biglaw, but if you simply let it blow you about, you will find yourself hopeless and hating life. If you do have a clear purpose, instead of being thrown about helplessly, you will be able to focus your efforts proactively and get something of real value. If you want to explore as many practice areas as possible before choosing an area in which to specialize, that goal will guide all the decisions you make about assignments you accept (or try to get), with whom you would like to try to work, even how long you remain at the firm. If your goal is to make partner at your current firm or another one day, that will dramatically affect the choices you make politically, inter-personally and in terms of assignments you seek. If you want to develop certain legal skills (get actual trial experience, develop criminal defense skills, take depositions et cetera), you will choose *pro bono* assignments with those skills in mind and focus your energy on finding billable work that will give you hours practicing the skills you want to master.

You may want to go into Biglaw for four years or so to sock away money for a down payment on a house, or drastically pay down your student loan debt and then move on to a more humane career path. You will want to keep your head down and slide by with the minimum of effort. You can do that. It will not be pleasant but it is possible. You may have a passion for insurance litigation (or SEC filings, or whatever) and want to do the most sophisticated work with the biggest clients. So you will seek out those partners and groups that are busy doing what you want to do. You may be single, in your mid-twenties and tickled by the idea of free dinners and cab rides home when you work after eight in the evening, and plenty of money to blow on new Wii games. These are all perfectly legitimate reasons to go into Biglaw but each has a different shelf life. What matters is that you spend the time and develop the self-reflection to find your own reason and understand how much time is associated with each choice. Without a clear picture and time-line, none of this makes sense, none of this is worth it, and it will only make you crazy or miserable. You must always have a ready answer to the question, "why am I doing this to myself?" even if the answer changes over time.

Finally, there is one other seldom-acknowledged path in Biglaw. If you choose it, this book will be of little use to you. I cannot recommend it, but I want to give you all the information you need to make your own choices about your Biglaw experience. Here it is: it is possible to slack off completely, screw up, do a half-assed job with as little effort as possible, make multiple mistakes, blow everything off, and get away with it – for about two years.[2] I do not mean floating under the radar for a few years, not making waves, doing as little as you can get away with, which many associates do with varying degrees of success. I mean a complete blowout. It should go without saying that there are, of course, limits; but those limits should be well outside the behavioral and ethical norms of anyone considering a career in the law. I am not talking about malicious mischief or any action that would be a violation of any law or regulation. But I do mean utterly useless. I have seen people get away with it for as many as two years. Never more than that. Maybe it is not a bad idea if you have no commitment to staying at the firm, going to another firm, or remaining in the practice of law in the same city. It is probably a better choice if you are writing the Great American Novel when you are blowing off work. You will need something to do when you are found out, as eventually you will be. I have seen associates come in, sock money away hand over fist, do almost nothing and then happily move on to what they really want to do with their lives.

I suspect that I am detailing this as an "option" more because I would like to provide comfort to new associates living in fear that their heads are on the chopping block than because I see merit in this choice. If someone who is not even trying can hang on for two years, then someone who *is* trying need not be in constant fear of firing from his first glaring mistake to his last day in Biglaw. But, for some, this do-nothing plan can work – for approximately two years.

I first heard associates talking about this possibility during an irredeemably bad document review to which I was assigned early on in my career. After making a fairly egregious mistake that I feared was the last straw, I was told, "Don't worry, you can totally screw up and get away with it for about two years before

---

2. Crucial caveat: this is true in just about every economy, however, in recessions as severe as the one beginning in the fall of 2008, this course of action is not recommended. During this recession, firms were even letting go first years for supposed "performance" reasons, when first years cannot possibly have much of anything upon which to base a performance evaluation. It would be foolish, at best, to pursue this short-term nihilistic approach to your career during a recession. However, in any other economic condition, it seems to work quite well.

you'll get fired." I did not believe it at first, but it turns out to be true. I have watched junior associates follow this path over the years and I now believe, unless he screws up in unbelievably epic ways, a sufficiently brazen associate can walk that path with relative impunity. Even in the worst economies, if you have received an offer from a Biglaw firm and have been fortunate enough to be allowed to start work there, the firm has already invested a huge amount of money, time and other resources in you. Even if you repeatedly turn in horrible assignments, regularly leave the office in the middle of the day for a few hours, bill only barely acceptable hours (one hundred forty or below usually) for months on end, it is not in the firm's interest quickly to fire you and go through recruiting and training another associate. The amount of time a firm can allow you to be unproductive will vary widely depending on the economy, but if the firm has allowed you to begin working, it needs you and needs to get a certain amount of return from your employment. Recruiters often get twenty-five to thirty percent of an associate's starting salary in fees, so recruiting new junior associates is time-intensive and expensive. No firm wants to pay a headhunter $50,000 for a lateral hire so soon after hiring a new associate. Bottom line: if all you want from your firm is two years of paychecks, you will probably be able to coast for that long. I do not think this is any way to approach your legal career, or even two years of your life, but I have seen it happen. You will leave with some money, but not much else: no reputation, no network, no references, possibly no future in that city, but it can work, if you are certain the short-term money is all you want. Even in large cities, the legal world is much smaller than you think. Your reputation may follow you wherever you go.

If that is your definitive and exclusive goal, you will have accomplished the first prong of what we have established as what you need to survive Biglaw: to know exactly what you want to get out of it. And, the second prong, knowing what it is and how it works will not much matter. You will be in control of your career and your choices will be your own. You will be able to coast through the turmoil and not let the common frustrations, irritations and injustices get you down. But make sure embarking on this path is a *conscious* decision on your part. Make sure it is what you want and that it is your intentional course of action. You should enter into it knowing all the costs, knowing what the consequences will be and with a firm decision to accept all that this choice will bring.

Often young associates seem to find themselves on a nihilistic path by default and get stuck on a destructive collision course without any understanding or decision of their own. This path chooses them and they seem powerless to avoid impending disaster. They hate Biglaw. They cannot handle the stress, the tedium, the ridiculous demands, constant criticism with no positive recognition, complete lack of useful feedback on their work and having their lives taken over by the demands of maniacal partners and mismanaging senior associates. They had no idea it would be this way. They cannot change the way Biglaw works, the broken, inhumane system, or the injustice and they become frustrated, angry and bitter. Resentment and helplessness build day after day until they cannot face another mountain of documents to review and code with baroque subject matter codes, or some unbelievably asinine exercise in futility that will waste yet another week of their lives, driving up their blood pressure to record levels yet again – not and maintain any slim grasp on their sanity. So instead of making conscious choices about what they want in life and where they want to go, or where they hope to end up, and taking positive action to get there, these associates screw up repeatedly in their assignments, want to kill themselves, do shoddy, half-assed and unprofessional work, slack off whenever they can get away with it, resent the firm and the partners and senior associates and make it almost impossible for the firm to keep them on. Then they usually end up leaving (or being encouraged to leave) after two miserable years with nowhere to go and almost nothing valuable to show for their misery.

This is not the way to control the direction of your life and your career. It will make you more miserable than just about any other Biglaw experience you could have. You must go about your career with good judgment, deliberation and conscious action. If you want to slack off, party hard, not grow up and then leave after a couple years – fine. Go at it with all abandon. But make everything you do, in Biglaw, and throughout your career, a conscious and careful choice. Do not let Biglaw run over you like a furious, crazed steamroller. Know the world you are entering and know what you want from it.

Whatever your reasons for entering the field, many times you will feel – and you will be – powerless over what happens to you in Biglaw. But you cannot let it make you hopeless and you do not have to take it all lying down. You can, for example, if you know where you want to go, steer towards it. Right after I started work at my first firm after graduation I was "given" to the international trade group. They had been promised a new associate and I was chosen, which meant that all of my assignments for the foreseeable future would come from international trade. I had no interest in international trade work, which did very little litigation at that firm. If I had simply gone with the flow and done nothing, I would probably be in that group today. With such a highly specialized, niche practice, I would have become stuck. But I realized quickly that that was not the path I wanted to be on in the long run and I chose to act. I did all that I could to find new opportunities for work. I volunteered for projects with other groups, even though my time was already filled with the trade group work. I voiced my interest to other partners at the firm who were practicing in areas I was interested in, and delicately expressed my desire to the managing partner and others not to be caught in a narrow niche practice so early on in my career. It was slow to happen, but eventually I was able to remove myself completely from the trade group with very little in the way of serious bridges burned. You can make choices in Biglaw that affect where you go, how satisfying your work is and how happy your life is in the long and short term.

We will talk a great deal more in the course of this book about some important lessons you can learn early on in your legal career: to take charge of your career and take ownership of your work. Biglaw may seem to leave no room for individual choice and action, but that is far from reality. You can think about your career and make choices about assignments you agree to work on, people with whom you try to work, skills you want to focus on developing. You can choose to maximize your experience and you will leave with highly valuable skills. You can decide how your career will take shape and the kind of lawyer you will become. Do not let Biglaw act on you. Take the time to find out what it is you want and what is important to you and take steps from there to get where you want to go.

Of course, I cannot know whether Biglaw is right for you, or for anyone for that matter. I have come to my own conclusions about Biglaw from writing this book – but they need not be your conclusions. I know that it takes too much from my own life and those of my colleagues to be sustainable for most over any length of time. On balance, the bad of Biglaw may far outweigh the good. But my own view on that shifts according to the day, depending on what is going on. My goal here is simply to give you the information you need to make a wise, informed choice, and the knowledge and skills to arm yourself if you do decide Biglaw is for you. If you choose to go into Biglaw, you should go with eyes wide open. Brush away the illusions and false expectations and think about what it is you want from Biglaw and whether it is right for you. This is the way it is.

Chapter One

Life in the Fast Lane, or, Anything Can Be Done at Any Time, for a Price and at a Cost

Rule Number One: Your Life Is Not Your Own

So what is Biglaw? We are talking about the top one hundred or so law firms that among them scoop up the lion's share of the most sophisticated and high-stakes legal business in this country. For journalists and novelists and daydreaming law students, Biglaw represents glamour, prestige, money, famous lawyers and front-page cases. But for the junior associate in his or her first couple of years, it can all too easily feel like Dante's *Inferno* as re-written by Kafka: sheer torture gleefully administered by criminally insane jailors. The good news is that although the feelings are understandable, and a great deal of the unpleasantness unavoidable, Biglaw practice is not as absurd and senseless as it may first appear and if you understand why it is the way it is, you can make your experiences in Biglaw a lot less oppressive from the very beginning.

The first time I had to cancel my vacation for an urgent matter, I found myself sitting in a room with eight other junior associates, enduring endless Neil Diamond ballads on the communal iPod amid piles of stale Chinese takeout boxes, while we reviewed antitrust-related documents for trial. A partner with whom I worked chortled, "Well, that's life in the fast lane. That's life in the big city!" And this was a partner who was kind, generous and generally respectful of his associates, someone with whom I thoroughly enjoyed working. He did not intend his words to be cruel. He was just humorously affirming the truth of the matter: if you work in Biglaw, your life is not your own.

His little phrase became a mantra during my first year – the longest and darkest of the doc review period for Biglaw associates – sometimes repeated in disgust, sometimes with gallows humor, sometimes in raw and exhausted bitterness. It is the great Biglaw inside joke. Why do you think you are paid all that money? Your private time, your personal life, your marriage, family, hobbies and pets – all of these are subservient to the demands of your firm and, thus, the partners and senior associates with whom you work. You will cancel dinner plans with college roommates ten minutes before you are expected, repeatedly. You will miss Mother's Day. You will be heading out the door at seven o'clock on a Friday night and a partner will stream into your office with an urgent assignment that he has been sitting on for a month but is now due Monday morning and you will kiss your weekend goodbye and forget about sleep except for that quick nap on the couch in your friend's office – because your office does not have a couch – yet. That's life in the fast lane.

The first time it happens you could be in shock. *How dare they!?!? What disrespectful, insensitive, self-absorbed lunacy makes them think that they can ask – no, just assume – that I will be available at any time for any useless, mind-numbing, duplicative task that can be dreamed up in the mind of an overzealous, über-anal, ego-maniac of a partner?* (But you will not be because you will have read this book.) That's life in the fast lane. By the hundredth time it happens, no one even thinks about it. The fight in every new associate has been silenced. You find yourself mumbling a lame apology to your brother over the phone, promising to see him and his new baby soon, taking a deep breath and turning back to review the 858th document in your batch of 2500. Every plan you make, every date or invitation you accept from now until you leave Biglaw will come with the sheepish caveat: *I am so sorry, I never know what might come up at my firm and I may have to cancel at any time.* It is often said that Biglaw will take ninety percent of your life most of the time and you will have to learn how to cram everything else that matters to you into the remaining ten percent. That's life in the fast lane.

It seems so cute the first day of work in Biglaw, when the firm issues you a little card to carry in your wallet with emergency contact information – the firm's. It is not cute. The firm expects to take precedence over your next of kin whenever it chooses and it wants to know at all times if you are suddenly out of commission or if you happen to show up dead somewhere, so that it can quickly get someone else to take your place. I know of one associate at a Biglaw firm who was in a serious car accident and disappeared for a couple days while in intensive care. Her boyfriend worked at the same firm and was hounded by the partners she worked with for days. He was asked to turn in her assignments and even get information from her for a case while she was in the hospital. I have seen associates work from hospital beds or drag themselves into the office deathly ill or injured. One woman I know slipped on an icy sidewalk and broke her ankle on the way to work. Faced with a crucial deadline, she limped into the office, worked all day and into the night with buckets of ice on her leg and then took a taxi to the hospital when she finished work, at two o'clock in the morning. I have received emails from senior associates who were on maternity leave, days after delivery. I have called into team meetings from the beach in Hawaii, the Rocky Mountains and one funeral. Hey, at least I got to go.

Biglaw can do anything. This is how Biglaw is able to offer the best legal services that are humanly achievable, why it handles the most sophisticated and sexy legal matters and high profile clients and why it pays sky-high salaries to people just out of law school with no more relevant experience, knowledge or skill than a ten-year-old child. It can examine every angle, chase down every alternative possibility, hunt through millions of documents to find that one bad email that will cost an adversary company billions, come up with unlimited strategies and alternative scenarios, analyze every probable outcome and prepare for any eventuality. It has the resources, money and time to throw itself with abandon into serving the needs of the client. And it will accomplish all this on the backs of legions of highly-paid, incredibly intelligent and virtually indentured young associates.

You are expected to give one hundred percent all the time, no matter how silly, futile, duplicative or menial the task. To succeed in Biglaw you must become a true professional in every thing you do. There are plenty of "lifestyle" firms that advertise their respect for the life balance of associates, claiming they encourage associates to live their lives. And this can be (relatively) true. My own firm is incredibly humane. But when things hit the fan at any firm in Biglaw, you should know that no one is going to ask you if perhaps you might be available to stay late.

Rule Number Two: Respect the Hierarchy

The second most glaring reality to be quickly absorbed and accepted is the rigid hierarchy in place in Biglaw. You will find that this controls your work life in ways that might surprise you. Even more relaxed, "lifestyle" firms will have a strict hierarchy that you must respect. Seniority is crucial. Naturally, there is a great divide between partners and associates. But you will find that associates are further divided depending on the year of graduation from law school. Junior associates have been at the firm one to two years. Mid-level associates typically have three to five years of experience. And senior associates have generally been practicing for six or more years. All of your assignments will depend on your level. Your salary and bonus will be determined by your year. In a later chapter we will focus on the various permutations of the compensation structures and how they are affected by the market, but begin now to understand how important and rigid the hierarchy will be. It determines the kind of work you will be assigned, the amount of compensation you will receive and who goes first at the water cooler.

Hierarchy is everywhere. It is a comically frequent occurrence for me to receive team emails with the email recipients carefully listed in hierarchical order: senior partner first, then junior partners and of counsel, then senior associates, mid-levels, then second years and, finally, the first years. On an email. In fact, it is so common that I take note if an email has been addressed alphabetically or simply in some random fashion and wonder if the sender is trying to make some subconscious populist point against the privileged elite. By now it should be clear that Biglaw is no egalitarian democracy and junior associates are all-too-easily replaceable cogs in the vast Biglaw machine. Times may be changing in some places, but traditional Biglaw attorneys still respect the lines of hierarchy, even in addressing an email.

It is dangerous to forget your function in Biglaw and your place in the hierarchy. I have attended so-called community building seminars, sponsored occasionally by the firm, seminars intended to improve quality of life, consciousness, or to nurture partner/associate relations – or at least to give the appearance that the firm might be interested in that kind of thing. Firms may want in the recruitment process to make you think they are Kumbaya-singing, life-affirming, diverse and supportive places. But do not be fooled. I have listened to partners expressing how much they really wanted to understand how associates were feeling about the firm and their interactions with partners. They seemed to feel a certain amount of regret that associates were expressing unhappiness, say, in the latest *American Lawyer* survey. So they would get us all together for workshops on associate/partner relations. I have then watched young associates who challenged partners or asked prodding and uncomfortable questions about compensation, work allocation or other touchy subjects completely cut off overnight and given no further work from the partner whom they challenged. On at least two of those occasions, the associate in question was unable to log enough billable hours and ended up being "encouraged" to look for opportunities elsewhere within a year.

The further down the chain of hierarchy you are, the less important you are and the easier it will always be to replace you from an endlessly renewable supply of other willing young associates. Your assignments will be more tedious and you will find less forgiveness for your mistakes. Sloppiness, carelessness or letting exhaustion affect the quality of your work will kill you. If a junior associate were to be given a sophisticated task or a plum opportunity, there would be resentment from more senior associates. First years are often thrown dismal doc review assignment after doc review assignment, without even the briefest explanation of the case or where the document review sits in the larger picture of the case. Pity the first year who wants to know what "doc review" is. Document review, "doc review" is about to become your world. The means of review change – actual pieces of paper may morph into digital data, cages full of boxes may be less likely than external hard drives – but the need for someone to review and code those documents appears to be eternal. It simply has to be done and the newest attorneys have the honor. Or, if you get a break from doc review, you might be assigned a research topic and never told anything about its intended use. A summary judgment motion? Presentation to the client? No telling.

It is an unspoken truth that advancement to the more interesting tasks and greater responsibility is almost solely dependent on your year. Cases are staffed according to your billing rate, which is determined fairly strictly by your year of seniority. If a task is cost efficient and appropriate at your rate, it will be assigned to you, without the slightest consideration for your ability, your talents, experience or interests, and certainly not for your need to develop skills in any given area. The only thing that matters is the year you graduated from law school. After years of doing nothing but doc review and legal research, all at once the curtain seems to rise at the dawning of your third or fourth (or fifth) year and you are suddenly given more responsibility for cases, treated with more respect and basic kindness and even forgiven more quickly for oversights and mistakes.

Because cases are staffed primarily by seniority, you will often find yourself working solely with a handful of mid-level or senior associates, rather than working directly with a partner. And unfortunately, in many cases, you may find yourself interacting most directly with attorneys who have only two or three years more experience than you do. Granted, two or three years can account for a world of difference in the practice of law, but you cannot possibly learn all you need to know from a person who graduated two years before you. That is one of the reasons it is important for you to try to work directly for partners when you can. This will be difficult to accomplish and it can be risky: it will expose your many silly errors directly to an equity participant, instead of possibly-more-forgiving senior associates. But it is crucial for your professional development that you find opportunities to work with partners, and let them become familiar with your work and abilities, so that you can increase the likelihood of the more varied and demanding assignments necessary to developing the skills and experience you need to move to the next level. Close collaboration with senior, experienced lawyers will be good for you intellectually, professionally and politically within the firm, but Biglaw is *not* organized to help you develop as an attorney.

Hierarchy is an omnipresent force in Biglaw, like gravity and, while it operates primarily on the basis of seniority there are other forces at work as well. Not only do firms segregate associates by year of graduation, but firms very often divide into sub-groups of attorneys who always work together and have a loyalty that goes beyond their commitment to the firm – the international trade group, for example, or the group that works only on Partner X's cases and who came with him from his former firm. These groups can be incredibly insular, cliquish and rigid. If Partner X is a big rainmaker, his associates will get plum assignments and bigger bonuses, be made of counsel earlier, escape more easily the taint of their oversights and omissions. If you are staffed on a case that one of these tight-knit groups is handling, brace yourself. You will always be the outsider; you will always be handed the more menial tasks; you will get blamed first for mistakes; and you will watch as the exciting depositions, arbitration meetings, minor pretrial motions that could be argued by an associate are taken away from you and given to a more junior associate in the "in" group, who has no knowledge on a specific, crucial topic on which you have been concentrating for months. This may sound like a violation of rule number two: "respect the hierarchy" but it is not. While seniority is a fundamental and programmatic part of the hierarchy, personal relationships and access to power – be that access to partners or belonging to a well-connected sub-group within the firm – are always hierarchically significant.

The hierarchy goes all the way up the chain. You receive your assignments and are supervised directly by a third or fourth year associate. They, in turn, are supervised by a more senior associate, who is ultimately supervised by a partner at the very highest level. If you are assigned to the largest cases, you might not work directly for a partner your entire first year at the firm. You could fail to recognize the senior attorney if you passed her in the hall. Senior associates seem like pagan deities. You never know when you will incur their favor or their wrath. You are made to jump through any number of hoops for them in an effort to satisfy their unquenchable desires for perfection. Their expectations seem arbitrary and unfathomable. But they must please the even more mysterious and demanding god: the partner. Your assignments are funneled down the chain and you will try your damnedest to get your work product, the valuable case information you have gleaned from thousands of documents, for example, or the key legal analysis, up the chain to the partner. I will say more, later, about why doing that is both your ethical responsibility and something you will want to do for your own sake, but for now, the point is that you should be prepared for it to be a frustrating and difficult challenge.

If the legal world is one governed by prestige and hierarchy, and I believe it is, Biglaw exemplifies this more completely than any other area of the law. No one gets a job in Biglaw these days without doing acceptably well at one of the top law schools (as ranked by *U.S. News and World Report*), or being at the top of his or her class at another first-tier law school, and not without a clerkship, position on law review or other equally prestigious accomplishments or accolades. So your colleagues at Biglaw will be some of the brightest and most accomplished individuals you have ever encountered and, once you are there, the rankings do not end. It will matter, at least to some of the partners, where you went to law school and whether or not you were on law review. Similarly, it will matter to your future career opportunities and prospects whether you were hired at a Vault top ten or Vault top seventy-five firm. This will be true especially early in your career, when no one has much else with which to judge your abilities. There will even be clear hierarchical distinctions among partners at the firm. The rainmaker partners will be more important than the others. They will get away with worse behavior and rudeness. The associates who always work with rainmaker partners will also be given more esteem, more leeway and better opportunities for assignments. These distinctions may often seem ridiculous, but there is no escaping the hierarchies in the legal industry and they reach the *reductio ad absurdum* in the world of Biglaw.

    Some of what at first may seem absurd is actually quite reasonable. The amount of money the firm can bill a client for an attorney's time increases with experience. A junior associate's time is based at one rate, a mid-level associate at a higher rate, a senior associate, still higher, a junior partner higher and so on up the chain to the senior partners. It would serve no client to pay four hundred and fifty dollars an hour to have a senior partner sitting in a windowless room coding documents for discovery. And it just isn't done. From the moment you walk in the door to the time you leave your entire purpose in life will always be to do the tasks for which more senior attorneys are too highly paid. Making the distribution of work economically palatable for the firm's clients determines the work flow. That is really the essence of Biglaw practice. So early on, your work will necessarily be the most monotonous, repetitive and time-consuming in the firm. This is not done to torture you and to break you down but to provide the most cost effective service to the client. The reason I, as a mid-level associate, still spend so much of my time managing and supervising discovery and document production is because the more senior associates are off doing interviews, depositions and other more complex work. Supervising discovery is the cost appropriate task for my level. I am too expensive to do a lot of heavy-slogging doc review anymore, but my tasks are still quite repetitive. The junior associates have to be supervised by somebody and the mid-level associate must take it on because it would be a waste of the senior attorneys' time. Mid-levels often get frustrated because we end up supervising document productions for what can seem like eternity, without the chance to develop more advanced skills. In a later chapter we will go into more detail about *pro bono* work and how those assignments can provide opportunities for professional growth.

    We will also talk more about strategies for avoiding certain traps that the hierarchy sets for the unwary but it would be best, I think, to get it into your head right away that there are consequences for your options as a mid-level and senior associate if you let yourself be trapped in one area too soon and for too long. If you get too expensive to do the least complex work in another practice group to which you would like to move, you have no way of developing the skills you would need to have in order to change your specialty, do something new or work with new partners. It is not impossible to make changes at mid-level, and certainly some people manage it, but it gets harder and harder as your billing rate increases. You need to plan from the beginning that by the mid-level years you will be pretty much set in your general practice area. You will want to be an established part of the team with a work-generating partner, lest you find yourself as a senior associate priced out of the work you know how to do. Because it is rare for partners to work with senior associates with whom they have no prior experience, you want the partners in the areas you want to pursue to know your work. That is one of the reasons you should try to work for as many partners as possible in the early years. If you are going to want to switch from litigation to corporate practice, it is best to figure that out early, when junior associates can pretty freely move around or change direction. If, as a fifth year, I decided I wanted to practice environmental and regulatory law, I think it would be nearly impossible at my firm. Again, taking on *pro bono* assignments could be a way to open some new doors and work with new people. I will have more to say about that later.

You will be ahead of the game if you know going in that your life is not your own, that anything can be done for a price and no one is valuing you very highly in your first year and if you understand that a far-reaching hierarchy based on seniority, access to power and money and sometimes absurd attachments to prestigious associations, will govern every move you are able to make. In a way, it is a game, and there will be times it may not hurt to think of it that way. You now have some resources that could help you see a move or two further ahead than you might otherwise have been able.

Chapter Two

Reputation and Trust

> *"You don't build a reputation on what you are going to do."*
>
> Henry Ford (1863–1947)

Let us take the position that you are now armed with some basic definitions and rules about what Biglaw is and what your life as an entering associate will be like and that you are taking it on. You are there. You have to survive. What is job one? All legal careers are exercises in control of reputations and the building of trust. In a big law firm, this is simply exaggerated. Your reputation and the trust you build will make or break your career in Biglaw. You will get no real responsibilities or interesting assignments until you begin to develop the trust of the senior attorneys and partners on your cases. However, this is something of a Catch-22 in Biglaw, since getting the attention of anyone up the chain of hierarchy is difficult. It is not, however, impossible. You walk in the door at zero, with no presumption whatsoever of being trustworthy or competent. Whenever you begin work for a new partner or senior associate, you start basically at zero with them. And when you screw up, which is inevitable, especially as a young associate – even on a minor project – you will find yourself hurtling back to zero at dizzying speed.

A first-year associate is presumed to know absolutely nothing – and this is often a fair assumption. We learn very little about success in the *practice* of law in law school. There are partners who refuse to staff first-year associates on their cases because they feel first years are completely useless. Everything you do, every piece of work product you deliver, will be dissected, criticized, torn apart and double checked (or "QC'd," that is, checked for quality control) and returned to you for redo after redo. If you are given a research assignment and spend ten hours on it with no good results, you will be grilled on the searches you ran, the databases you checked, the treatises you read, whether you contacted the firm librarians or senior associates for additional suggestions on searches, whether you looked through other case resources for search terms. This means not only doing the work but also keeping a clear trail and documentation of what you have done. Only after you satisfy the senior attorney that you did a meticulous, accurate and exhaustive job, will your work be considered complete.

You have to be prepared to stand behind and defend everything you do – no matter how mundane. It is not just the glamorous assignments you need to ace. (There will be times you will understand with blinding intensity that it is a *good thing* you will not have many of those in the beginning.) You need to ace the spreadsheet you were asked to set up to track the progress of the staff attorneys' document review by custodian and status of the various production work streams. You must ace the two PowerPoint slides containing numbers of criminal white collar prosecutions over the past ten years you were asked to create for a client presentation, two slides that took you a full ten hours to finish and double check. And when you are handed back the five heretofore identical binders you have meticulously shepherded to completion and told to conform four copies to the one a partner has now heavily highlighted, flagged and annotated, you must ace that. Ditto the three hundred exhibits you have carefully arranged, as instructed, in date order when they now want them arranged by subject matter. You must ace everything and give your absolute best on every project, no matter how lame and seemingly pointless.

You must learn to think of everything, scrutinize every nuance and detail, anticipate any and all questions, find the holes in the arguments and problems with the strategies and, again, carefully document and track everything you do: every search you run, every database you check, everything. You are expected to bring your full intellect, complete attention and dedication to everything you do and you are expected to be able to account for your work product down to the last detail and the precise tenth of an hour. These are skills that take some time and patience to master. I was only able to make some progress after I finally silenced the voice of dissent within me that would rise up in revolt each time I received a new assignment even more stupid (in my junior associate mind) than the one just completed. None of what you do is rocket science, but it must be done as perfectly as humanly accomplishable given its time and economic constraints. Nothing you do should be mechanical. If your job were easy, the firm would hire a monkey or get a computer to do it instead of paying you all that money. Understanding this, really making your peace with it, is a crucial first step towards attaining the level of professionalism expected in Biglaw. Without it you cannot expect to begin to build your reputation or engender trust.

If senior attorneys cannot trust your work to be accurate, professional and exhaustive, they do not want to see it. They will ask someone else to do it over and leave you behind in the dust. This is not because they are all just jerks. You should understand their perspective. Partners and senior associates utterly depend on the work of younger associates and risk their careers and reputations by making statements every day based solely on their work, knowing that even with the most exhaustive QC in the world, no one has checked everything every junior associate has done. Partners need to be able to walk into court and assert facts or statements about the law that they cannot have had time to prepare and research fully on their own. When they submit a motion saying that there is no evidence of X, or there is rampant evidence of Y, or abundant legal support for Z, they need to be dead certain that the cases you found are the only relevant cases on point and that you found (or did not find) all of the relevant documents, and that there is nothing bad out there looming that will be thrown in their faces. Who spends a month of his or her life immersed in a million documents in several different databases, trying to prove that there is absolutely no evidence, whatsoever, in your case that X occurred or did not occur? You. The partners cannot possibly do all the research required for complete preparation and read all of the thousands of relevant case documents. Their careers and reputations depend on you and that kind of trust does not come easily. It can vanish in a heartbeat.

As a junior associate, your most important "clients" are the partners and senior associates with whom you work. Your first task is to build your reputation in their eyes and gain their trust. And it may be a very long time before your work is not double and triple checked, duplicated by more senior associates, scrutinized, questioned, examined with a microscope and rejected over and over; or before your ideas and suggestions are not dismissed out of hand, if not sneered at. Do not, ever, do a half-assed job (unless you are determined to follow the nihilist career path mentioned briefly in the Introduction). Your work product should pass through several levels of scrutiny before it leaves your hands, even if it is a rough, rough draft. At a bare minimum you need to reread for typos and ensure a professional appearance. It should be almost perfect – as perfect as you are able to make it on your own in the time allowed, before you send it anywhere, even as a mere first draft.

Try not to draw conclusions as you communicate what you have learned. You do not have sufficient perspective or understanding of the law to draw conclusions early on. Get really good at communicating what you have found in important documents – what the documents say, not what you think they mean; what a key case held, what the facts were and what the reasoning was, not your interpretation of what it means in your case. Time and time again as a young associate I ran to senior attorneys with what I saw as a very bad document, only to be told that, actually, this was incredibly useful for the case. No one will be interested in your conclusions. The better you get at synthesizing and summarizing information and giving your superiors comprehensive and useful facts, the happier they will be.

Do not be surprised or discouraged when your work product is returned to you. Handing in an assignment may be the end in law school but not in Biglaw.

You will feel like the work is done – the best you could do, the most you could find. You will be certain you have looked at the issue for so long you will gouge your eyes out if you have to think about it another second. But senior attorneys will always have follow-up questions: new issues will have come up since the work was assigned, preferences for style and format might have changed, some sections might have become moot, more depth of discussion might be needed in some areas. It will not serve you to get defensive and bristle when it happens – it will always happen and not just to you. And you should expect that everything you do will be checked. Your rate of review will be noted: how many docs you get through per hour or per day. Your accuracy of review will be measured: how often your superiors agree with your coding. The thoroughness of your research will be checked. Part of learning the professionalism you need to survive Biglaw is understanding right up front that your work will never be perfect or even acceptable on the first go around and it will be picked to death by several other levels of attorneys. The same brief that might garner beaming smiles of appreciation and a commendation from a supervisor in a government legal department would quite likely be ripped to shreds by Biglaw partners and senior associates. Nonetheless, you must strive to make your work as complete and perfect as you are able. For everything, check it, double check it and then read through it again and even have someone else read through it if they have the time and are allowed to bill on your matter. Do not let yourself slack off, get lazy, cut corners or dash off a half-assed attempt. It will be obvious to senior attorneys and can get you cut from a team and blacklisted, not exactly the kind of reputation you are looking for.

There is another kind of trust that you will need to cultivate as well and that is belief in yourself. This may sound self-evident and simplistic – or even contradictory, given the demands for perfection and the certainty of error – but it will not serve you to go quaking into new tasks and experiences thinking that a single mistake will get you fired. You have to remember how you got where you are and you have to cultivate a certainty that you would not have done so had you not been greatly skilled at absorbing new information and learning from your mistakes. The likelihood of losing the job you have worked so hard to secure without some kind of warning (in a non-horrific economy) is de minimis. The firm will give pretty clear signals that you are not meeting their standards. So, in the meantime, do your best, pay attention and do not allow your mistakes to cripple you. Learn from them and move on.

Knowing that there is a reason Biglaw seems to demand impossibly high levels of perfection will not make the demand easier to meet, but it can make the burden sustainable. Biglaw firms have their own reputations on the line. They get the complex cases and the plum retainers because they have the reputation for success and for their ability routinely to accomplish the improbable. You are getting paid to sustain that reputation and that influx of cash. In the frantic rush of Biglaw, mistakes will surely be made. Errors and oversights from exhaustion or lack of time will always occur. That one horrible privileged document will make it out the door and have to be clawed back. You will have forgotten to check for subsequent history on one key case that gets noticed by the partner on the eve of oral argument. Everyone understands all you have to do and all that is on your plate. But those mistakes will be forgiven only if you have done everything in your power to do a thorough, careful and accurate job and a history of taking pains and successfully meeting demands will help. If you slack off, get burned out and allow your eyes to glaze over for the last half of your document batch or try to skate by with a halfhearted attempt, your reputation is dead. You must carefully build your reputation and tend it. It is really all we have as attorneys, and it is your career at stake.

Associate Life: Valuable Feedback is Sparse. Appreciation is Non-Existent.

So how do you go about building this all-important good reputation and trust in what can feel like a vacuum? While no two individuals have precisely the same experience, there are sufficient similarities in Biglaw practice for you to learn from my mistakes and those of other associates. Enter the doc review from hell. For the first two years of practice in Biglaw, I went through several extended periods in which I honestly had no idea where I stood with the firm. I could have been doing just fine. But I often feared I was hurtling to impending destruction and could be fired at any moment. After a series of stupid mistakes and a period in which I allowed myself to fall into cycles of resentment at my uninspiring assignments, I went through a couple of months mired in a burned-out refusal to spend any more concentration than I could fake while immersed in documents and I became convinced I had burned my last bridge and would soon be asked to find work elsewhere.

It had not been my fault entirely. I was staffed on a doc review supervised by a senior associate who had been away from Biglaw practice for a few years while she had a child. She was "old school," clueless about the technological advances that made massive electronic discovery more manageable and cared nothing about balancing law firm demands with having a life outside the firm. Believing electronic review was less reliable, she originally had thousands of documents printed out, so that we could really get a "feel" for the documents we reviewed and "see" the context better – costing the client tens of thousands of extra dollars in vendor costs. She devised cumbersome, duplicative coding systems for us to follow, in which the junior associate had to staple a yellow cover page to each document and fill in more than thirty check boxes for the various issues for which we were reviewing each document, then write by hand on the cover the custodial information, the date of the document, the author, etc. and then move to the next document. This took an incredible amount of time and was maddening, especially since she had staffed only two junior associates on a doc review of hundreds of thousands of documents with a too-tight production deadline. Eventually, even she realized this was crazy and we moved to electronic review and coding, which is light years faster, but only after the team had turned dangerously mutinous. And then she dictated search terms on the document universe that generated massive quantities of false positives – so that we were getting mountains and mountains of completely irrelevant documents to our case, way, way more than would be acceptable in any reasonable doc review. Ordinarily there are clear document review guidelines, usually compiled in a binder giving the reviewer the needed facts, background and context of the case, outlining the legal issues, giving examples of important or privileged documents to help guide the review. In this case, we had a crazy short deadline, were provided no guidelines and our supervisor insisted that we bill only eight hours a day because the client did not want to pay for more. This created an impossible situation, heading for a train wreck. It should have surprised no one that the other associate and I made plenty of ridiculous mistakes. My biggest mistake during this fiasco was that I allowed my attitude to slip further and further until I had no sense of ownership in my work product. This may have been understandable given the unreasonable demands placed upon us but it was not acceptable and served neither the client nor me. We were throwing documents around so fast we could not possibly get things right and I gave up trying.

If I had had more experience, I would have gone immediately to partners whom I trusted and let them know about the impossible conditions. They would have known that the senior associate's expectations were impossible, but, as a junior associate, I had no idea that doc reviews were not supposed to go this way and so I trudged on every day for over six months of absolute hell. Unsurprisingly, our supervisor was not pleased with our work, and I received a scathing evaluation from her that year. Had I not had solid evaluations from the previous year and from other attorneys to give me a little cushion I do not know what would have happened, but she made sure I never worked with her group again. I moved on and tried to work with other groups within the firm, with whom I felt more comfortable. But, by the end of that case, I had gone through over a year of misery that could have been avoided had I understood how to take control of my career in Biglaw.

What I did not realize until later was that many of my fellow junior associates felt exactly the same way and had similar experiences during their first years. A friend in the intellectual property group of a firm in a large mid-western city made some naïve and silly errors on an agreement he was told to draft. The lead partner never mentioned a thing about his performance to him, but wrote a harshly critical email about him to another partner, complete with sarcastic comments and pretty serious conclusions about his fitness to practice law. Then the partner accidentally included the junior associate on a later part of the email chain days later, and he read it all. Horrified, he went to talk with the partner and got it resolved after some discussion, but he spent months after that gripped by fears that they were putting him down behind his back and that he might be fired. We have all gone through this and, unfortunately, we usually go through it thinking we are completely alone and that all the other associates get it while we are completely incompetent, but I have now seen it often enough to know that all new associates are in the same, junior associate boat. We just did not know it. You will. One is much less likely to give in to despair when one does not feel isolated and alone and you cannot build the kind of reputation that will sustain a successful career if you are operating in a vacuum in despair.

Too often young associates are like horses with blinders. We work and work on a case, trudging along spending countless hours of our lives for weeks and months, and in the end we often have no idea where things fit into the bigger picture of the case or how our work has been received. We sift through documents, we churn out information. For a section of a summary judgment motion we turn in a memo on which we have spent the last forty hours slaving and never hear whether the partner thought it was brilliant or simply chucked it in the trash. We are never told how the oral argument went, what key information was learned in the latest deposition, or briefed on the new theory of the case the government is pursuing in its criminal investigation of our client. No one has time to keep us in the loop. We find it impossible to do better on the next assignment, because we have no idea what we did right, if anything, in the previous ones, or how we might possibly improve. This frustration can be paralyzing.

There often seems to be a disconnect in Biglaw. Your work seems to fall into a void. You turn in a memo and hear not one word about it for three weeks until the partner has time to breeze through it on the subway, after which he peppers you with irritated questions, comments and concerns in an unpleasant early morning email. It may feel like someone is always there to blindside you with your inconsistencies, the holes in your approach or your findings, the sloppiness of your citations, the follow-up needed, the ignorance or illogic in your reasoning. But often you will not be able to be certain your work got any attention at all. You may not even receive the briefest email, "thx," acknowledging that your work was at least received. You will constantly labor to get your work, your insights and information, key documents you have found or issues you have recognized up the chain to senior associates and partners. Either they have no time to read your memos or they will ignore your work product on the assumption that you could not have found anything of value that had not already been found. Getting them to focus on the important points, main themes and conclusions, will be your daily struggle, one in which you will wholeheartedly engage or your work will be lost in the void of Biglaw flurry. Giving in to frustration and falling into despair will only guarantee that you will fail to develop a reputation for the kind of work of which you know you are capable and which will sustain your professional growth.

If our error is sufficiently egregious, we learn with certainty that we have made a mistake or not lived up to partner expectations, by dint of harsh and swift retribution. But in between massive mistakes we flit along in a daze without any clue who has read our work, how it was used or how successful we were at the assignment. So we stumble along, constantly anxious, always exhausted, often at our wits' end, from one assignment to the next, with very little means of judging our development or improvement over time, if any. Add to that the likelihood that the kind of work product that is absolutely perfect for one partner for whom you work might be completely rejected by another and you have a recipe for madness. Most people learn best with regular feedback and positive reinforcement. You will have to learn that silence cannot be interpreted either positively or negatively. The only thing you have to steer by is the often belittling and callous rejection of your work.

As I try to stress throughout this book, there are reasons for the madness. Remember that Biglaw is rigidly hierarchical, which means that if you are at the bottom, you will not see much of how things look from the top of the pyramid. It isn't personal. No one has time to think about nurturing young associates and building an environment that is warm and fuzzy when the stakes are as high as they are and the demands of clients are as never-ending. Being low on the Biglaw totem pole means you seldom get much of a view. It also means you almost never get credit or compliments for your work. You will stand quietly by as senior associates trot out theories of the case that you came up with and shared with them and as they eagerly reveal to partners important "hot" docs that you found after eleven straight hours of focused searches, all without a word about your work. The system doles out rewards the way it does responsibilities, slowly and hierarchically. You will be expected to give one hundred ten percent of your time, intellect and attention, but no one will ever appreciate or recognize you for it. Know that you are not alone in taking abuse and getting no credit for what you do. Here is an example of a typical exchange between a partner and senior associate. And, yes, something very much like this happened. I cannot make this stuff up.

A partner sends an email to a senior associate saying, in effect, "Can you put together the bios of Partners C, D, E, F and G in the antitrust group for a client presentation?"

The senior associate replies, "Sure, how about Partners H, I, and J, as well?"

The partner hurls back, "I have already given you *all* of the partners that we need to include, everyone who might possibly be involved in antitrust matters for this client. Add Partners H and I, but not J."

You see what happened here? The senior associate made a valuable contribution and the partner accepted two out of three of his suggestions. And, yet, the irate partner still had to make sure the senior associate understood these were the partner's ideas and that the senior associate's ideas were useless. Could the partner simply have said, "Great idea! Yes, thanks, do, please, include H and I, but not J."? Certainly. But not in Biglaw. And this was a *senior* associate, someone who had presumably earned the right to a little respect and instead had to accept abuse for making a constructive suggestion.

You will certainly be reamed if you screw up, but you will rarely hear a single word to let you know someone was happy with your work. No one will appreciate that you put together a binder of key documents in an unbelievably short period of time, incorporating all of the most recently discovered information in a hectic scramble to meet a crazy deadline imposed on you. But they will notice that you have a typo on the index, that the dates are formatted inconsistently or that you had one document out of fifty out of chronological order. Forget that you have been frantic for hours to get this rush project done, that you were given no warning or time to complete it and that you actually managed to pull it off when it should have been impossible. Partners are so busy and preoccupied, senior associates so swamped and stressed, that no one has time to sit with you and praise your writing ability or the document you found that will cripple the other side's argument, or your efficient management of the staff attorney document production. You get that filing out of the way, that deposition, that monumental research assignment and you move quickly to the next upcoming deadline or fire drill.

The true extent of the utter lack of any appreciation in Biglaw was driven home for me one day when I had lunch with a friend who worked for the Department of Justice ("DOJ"). He told me about filing a minor motion in a case and making his boss so happy that she gave him a plaque in recognition of his fine work. At first what he told me seemed too surreal to be believed and then it hit me: this *was* his reality, just not mine. My heart sank lower and lower as he talked about his work because I suddenly realized that his experience was utterly alien to me. He had a consistent sense that he was appreciated and valued at his job – that he was making a difference. After two years in Biglaw, I would have fainted if a partner had walked into my office and spent five seconds praising my work or thanked me for cancelling yet another vacation. It does not happen in Biglaw. I can think of only a single example in those first two years of someone telling me that I had done a good job. Of course, I worried at first that this awful silence was speaking to the quality of my work, but eventually I learned that this is true for all junior associates.

I had been so constantly frantic during those first two years, so anxious and in such a fog moving from one assignment to the next, that I had not even seen what was missing until my friend's experience gave me a slap. He was trusted and relied upon, treated with respect and appreciation, he felt secure in his position and his boss raved about him. He was given real responsibility of his cases. Wow. Not in Biglaw where rejection is routine, trust takes slow, painstaking years to earn and seconds to lose and junior associates are one hundred percent fungible. My friend's experience hit me like a vision of some alternate universe of fairyland fancy. That was the first time I realized how hard the first two years had been. I was so encompassed by anxiety that I could not even see how stressed, how exhausted, how depressed I had become or how profoundly unhealthy the environment was in which I lived and breathed. Being under constant pressure to prove yourself and never knowing where you stand can be toxic.

Early on I went for months at a time in a bleak, grey fog of one witness preparation binder after another, one document review assignment after the next, one legal research task after another with nothing at all for feedback, feeling on the verge of being fired for months at a time. I had no understanding of how my work fit into the big picture, no knowledge if my work was valuable at all or even received by senior attorneys on the case. I learned to assume everything was acceptable if I didn't get yelled at, but that is nothing close to appreciation. Living this way for months, even years, is soul killing. So don't. You will be forearmed. I am not telling you all of this so that you will be able to change the system. You won't. The lack of feedback and partner support stems directly from the unchangeable facts that Biglaw can do anything and that Biglaw is a hierarchy. Partners and senior associates are even busier and more frantic than you are. When you do an assignment right, no one notices (because you did it right and they are quickly moving to the next crisis). When you do it wrong, your life will be hell or you will simply be summarily dumped from the assignment or case. You know this now. And you are forewarned. You will know how to parse the signals.

While silence is not necessarily positive, you will safely be able to assume that it is positive if you continue to get work from the same people. If they ask you for more and more, or someone new wants you for an urgent assignment at the drop of a hat, you should take that as a clear sign that you are beginning to be trusted and someone up the chain believes that you will do the job right. You will be able to gauge the level of senior associate happiness with you by the amount of micromanaging you receive. They are inversely proportional. The happier they are with you, the less you will hear from them and you will know you are beginning to establish a good reputation that will sustain you over the rough spots. If your supervising attorney is on you like glue, checking your every minor assignment, running your searches to check the results and breathing down your neck, it is probably because you screwed up the last assignment, blew a deadline or otherwise demonstrated a weakness that shook their confidence.

But if you understand the reality of Biglaw, you can arm yourself with that understanding and with the knowledge that this long, painful apprenticeship will end. One way or the other, it does have a guaranteed end point. You can decide Biglaw is not for you and leave or you can gird your loins and hang in knowing that – if you survive that long – somewhere around the third or fourth year, people will begin to presume a certain amount of competence from you. You will see the criticism lighten, you will see your work accepted with less scrutiny. Some of it may be that your work has actually gotten better, but a lot of it is just that people start to treat you with more respect. Maybe there is some strange, rough fairness in that. No one cares if you are brilliant on your first day but if you demonstrate an ability to do that over long periods of time under grueling conditions, well, that is truly valuable and can be relied upon. But you must give your all. Nothing less will be accepted.

No matter what happens, do not let anyone convince you that you cannot succeed in Biglaw. You can. You made it through the door – you met the minimum requirements and have the credentials. You have to be smart and ambitious and able to do the job to get hired in Biglaw. Now, whether you *want* to succeed is completely up to you.

Chapter Three

Know Your Place but Don't Let it Bring You Down

Now that you are in the door and understand the basic Biglaw hierarchical structure and some rules for survival, your next challenge is to fight the endless string of demotivators – constant fire drills, last minute crunches, long hours, horrific management styles, mind-numbingly tedious assignments and the lack of feedback unless it is withering criticism – which conspire to affect the quality of your work. How do you remain engaged, vigilant, careful, giving one hundred percent one hundred percent of the time, when you are up against so many things that sap your will to live?

The drudgery, combined with constant criticism and micromanaging, long and erratic hours, the stress of impossible deadlines and the terror of making mistakes, will take their toll if you let them. By now you know: whenever there is not someone breathing over your shoulder to point out inconsistencies, holes in your approach or your findings, the sloppiness of your citations, the follow-up needed, the ignorance or stupidity in your reasoning, there will be an invisible someone ready to chuck your work in the trash and ask another associate to do the assignment, with never a word to you about how to get it right the next time. Your work will almost never be acceptable the first time. It will never be thorough enough, accurate enough, professional enough or insightful enough. It will sometimes be only grudgingly accepted after several rounds of drafts, several discussions with partners and senior associates and many more attempts. And if you are not around to accomplish whatever hundredth eleventh hour iteration of the task it is, you will be passed by and never missed. Even with all of this conspiring to drain your energy you must never lose your motivation to do a good job or your quality of work will inevitably slip, you will become unreliable and a liability on your team and, as we have seen, once your reputation suffers you will find yourself in the precarious position of not having enough work, which will lead to your Biglaw end, one way or another. So, what do you do?

As a junior associate, and throughout your Biglaw career, you will be juggling two powerful and opposing forces: it must be done perfectly; it must be done now. You know by now that you will be dealing with senior associates and partners who are even busier than you. They have no time to plan ahead or manage their cases in an organized fashion, would consider a time management or personnel management course beneath them and seem never able or willing to give you all the information you need to understand any given assignment. It is a road map to hell.

Partners are not deliberately cruel, well, most of the time most of them aren't. They are not setting out to make your life miserable. But they do it remarkably effectively because they are so often up in the clouds focusing on the highest levels of several high-stakes, bet-the-company cases at once that they have no recollection – if they ever knew – the amount of time required to accomplish tasks to their satisfaction. They have no idea how to communicate what they want or expect clearly. After a month of a ten-hour day, six-day week doc review a partner will say out of the blue, "Why haven't you been coding docs for X topic?"

The real answer, one you will *never* voice, is, "Because you never mentioned that was relevant to the case and with my miniscule experience with this case prior to beginning the review, I could never have figured that one out on my own."

The correct answer, however, will always be, "Okay. I'll go back through the 18,000 documents I've already coded and look for that issue." And depending on how important the partner thinks that issue is and whether it is worth the time and expense to duplicate the work, that is exactly what you will do. This is but one example. There are infinite ways that you will misunderstand, not hear, not divine, not read a partner's mind correctly.

And that is when you have the luxury of incurring the ire of a partner. Senior associates seem to specialize in passive aggression. You hand over your exhaustive witness interview binder and your supervising attorney says, "How fascinating that you thought it was okay to put this binder in chronological order, instead of broken into issues. We have never done this before. That is, except for those last two binders, but then those didn't count." Don't fight it. This will happen to you every day in one way or another. Just get on with it. One key to survival in Biglaw is being ready to take the verbal lashing and turn back to the horrid project, whatever it may be, and do it all over again.

And many partners are clueless about how to organize and manage their many cases, deadlines and workloads in an efficient and humane manner. There will be "old school" partners who came up through the associate ranks a decade or more ago. If they had to live shackled to their desks, taking any verbal abuse that was doled out by the partners, why shouldn't you? They had to lock themselves in a doc review room for months at a time in some dismal location going through boxes stacked to the ceiling with hardcopy documents. And you want to review documents electronically (and from home on the weekends?!?!) on some new-fangled litigation management database? Old school partners mistrust technological advances and life-balancing fancies intensely.

But even the most reasonable and decent partners struggle with communicating their needs and allowing for the possibility that others might have needs as well. Their perspective on practicing law is at such a high level that they have forgotten how many staff attorneys are needed to review and produce 800,000 documents in a one-month time period. They have no idea, and no patience for being told, that a seemingly simple research assignment will require five hours of background reading, and have any number of angles and twists to ferret out, requiring double the time they are allowing. They seem incapable of realizing that we cannot read their minds, and did not actually know that this time they wanted their deposition preparation binder in order of key topics instead of chronological order, reversing a pattern that held for the previous five binders. So we waste eight hours undoing all that we just wasted two days doing. Or that they prefer Bates numbers to be stamped on the lower left side of the page, with custodial information on the right and they want privileged documents printed in pink (and removed from a witness's copy of the binder!). Or that they wanted one highlighted/flagged copy of the binder for their use and the other copies clean for the witnesses to use. How would you have known that? The binders could just as easily have been for review by senior partners. And why ever did they not simply tell you before you spent ten hours doing it another way? These are the frustrating realities of a young associate's life. Maybe if I keep describing these things over and over they will start to sound funny and when they happen to you a part of you can laugh – silently, of course.

Partners and senior associates learned nothing in law school about being efficient supervisors, the importance of people skills, winning friends and influencing people, managing workloads and communicating with others. Given their own stressful and overloaded lives, they are not about to embark on a course of self-improvement now. They made it through the junior associate slog and so must you.

In addition to the frantic pace and sheer volume of work, a young associate will have to deal with the fact that the vast majority of assignments in the first two years in Biglaw will be utterly mind-numbing. Most will also be futile, stupid, duplicative fantasies dreamed up by obsessive-compulsive senior associates zealously attempting to chase down every last possibility – and a complete waste of your time. Nowhere else will you spend an entire month generating a privilege log – a perfectly formatted, triple QC'd, exquisitely detailed, five-hundred page privilege log – that is never actually served or used in any way. (Prepare for more about priv logs in the next chapter.) Clients of small law firms would never pay what it costs to produce the most pristine and gorgeous priv log known to man. But Biglaw clients can and they expect perfection. Many of the tasks you devote your heart and soul to for significant periods of time will go unused and unread entirely because new information will have come to light before your task is complete and the issue will have become moot. Other assignments will seem to have no purpose, other than to speed your own slip into madness.

You are forewarned: half of what you do will never even see the light of day. It will be prepared for trial and then a partner will decide she does not want to use it. It will be prepared in anticipation of the other side's motion and then their motion will be silent on the issue. It will be prepared to produce to the government and the case will settle. It will be prepared to brief a senior partner on an important issue and that issue will become moot or the partner will learn enough from a helpful corporate witness to consider wading through your research a waste of time. It is hard to stay motivated to give your all at all times when so often your hard work flies non-stop from your desk into someone else's recycle bin. Of course it hurts. You want to spend your time doing things that actually matter. It feels as exhausting and debilitating as throwing oneself into preparing for the Olympics, over and over again, only to have the games cancelled at the last moment, or to be left behind while your nemesis competes and wins the gold. Why bother?

This is where you will have to return again and again to that original motive we discussed: why did you choose to go down this road? What do you expect to get out of it? What is your plan? Remember that you are doing this with your eyes open and you always have alternatives. If you chose to stay you must never allow yourself to flirt with the seductive, soul-sucking, resentment-spawning practice of believing your assignments are rational, useful and valuable in the greater scheme of things. Eighty percent of your work will be a complete waste of time, your assignments the inefficient, duplicative, asinine fancies of an absurdly over-compensated partner. You still have to do them, and you have to do them perfectly and within the time allowed. You must always balance between making it perfect – knowing that there will be no forgiveness for error – and getting it done immediately. Just don't expect it to mean anything. The task may be reading through thousands of pages to check the work of a paralegal or staff attorney before a set of twenty binders goes out the door to a client. You know that in the time allowed all you can do is skim the pages with your reputation on the line. How senior associates and partners view you will depend on how successfully you handle each Sisyphean task you are given. And on this will depend the quality and sanity of your life. Who said this was a good idea?

Somehow you have to find a way of doing each job well. There are plenty of paths here but perhaps the strongest and most sustaining might be because doing it well is a reflection of your best self. So make it beautiful, not because it will mean anything to anyone else, not because you will be praised for it, not even to avoid the inevitable abuse if you fall short of perfection, but for the craft, for the history of the law, if you can, out of respect for the profession. Whatever your motivation is you will have the most support in times of deep frustration if you have found a reason to do well, just for the sake of doing well. You must give your best effort in all you do in order to make it to the place where you have an opportunity to do meaningful work that can make a difference. It takes years, but you will get there if you persevere.

As a young associate your life will often be a cycle of crazy busy months followed by a month or two of uncomfortable slowness, during which you begin to wonder if you are earning your keep at the firm as you eye your sad billable hours for the week and feel an ever-increasing dread that you may never have a billable assignment again. When you are preparing for trial, for an important filing, or whatever large assignment is eating your life at the time, you will have no time to breathe, much less have a life outside of the firm. It will feel like a full-out sprint, one that might go on for months. Then suddenly you will have nothing to do for a month or even two while one case winds down and another revs up. Learning how to balance these times and survive the highs and lows, each of which can be difficult in its own way, is key. You can never assume that because you have had a slow day you can make plans or give priority or inflexible attention to matters outside the firm. Remember rule number one: your life is not your own.

Because of the frantic pace of Biglaw practice, partners and senior associates compulsively need to know where you are at all times. They will get very nervous if you disappear for lunch with no Blackberry contact. And nervous partners and senior associates can make your life miserable. They will not be happy if they call your office in the evening, when most associates will still be at the office, and find that you have left for the day since you had a slow afternoon. Until you have developed your reputation with them, until they are able to trust you somewhat, it will make them unhappy if they cannot find you immediately when they want something from you, which could happen at any time. Some partners expect to be able to walk into your office at nine o'clock in the evening and find you there, ready to read through a thirty-page draft memo with them and to sit and watch while they edit it for the next three hours. You should never consider the weekends your own. If you plan to be away for the weekend during a busy time in your case, let them know long in advance. That's life in the fast lane.

Understand Your Place in Biglaw: A Feudal System in a Meritocratic Universe

Biglaw is a feudal system at heart. The partners are kings. The of-counsel and senior associates are barons and knights. You get where I'm going with this:

junior associates are peasants. The partners have the clients, cases and all of the work. They give the task of managing the nuts and bolts of their cases to senior associates with whom they may have worked exclusively for years and whom they trust implicitly to run their cases. The senior attorneys manage the cases, devise sometimes sadistic work streams to accomplish the various tasks of discovery and fact development within required deadlines and they give assignments and lesser roles to the mid-level and junior associates. If they like you, trust you, come to rely on your work, they will give you more. If not, you will find yourself cut off. The senior associates control the assignments and they dole them out as they see fit.

That is one reason that in a bad economy some junior associates do get squeezed out – but not without warning. You can see this coming. When senior level associates do not have enough work of their own, they hoard it, often performing tasks that they would normally give to junior associates and for which they really should not be billing the client at a senior associate's rate. In a good economy, when there is more than enough work to go around, they get the plum assignments and you get lots of grunt work, but it puts food on your table. When there is more than enough work to go around times are good for junior associates, because, although too busy, you are desperately needed by multiple partners simultaneously, so you have more choice over whom you end up working for and whom you would rather avoid.

Feudal it may be but it is also a meritocracy because if you do reasonably well, if you don't screw up horribly, if you trudge along and do your best, you will eventually move up the chain. You do not have to be the most brilliant or charismatic attorney of your year. You simply have to hang in there and do a good job, and wait for time to take care of your advancement. You may not be able to make partner by being merely competent, and the meritocracy may not hold in the face of the politics and economic pressures at that level, but you should be able to make it to the senior associate level on your merits.

As a junior associate, you are, fortunately or unfortunately, depending on the perspective and the economic climate, the cheapest associate labor pool around – not the cheapest attorney but the cheapest *associate*, more on that below. As we have seen, it would not do for a senior associate to spend eight to ten hours a day for eight weeks reviewing and coding documents for an initial review for a document production – or to strenuously QC every page of the 243 exhibits that will be submitted at trial. You are the only logical source for that kind of slogging work. And there will be times, when there is not enough work to go around, that you will feel lucky to get it. If you are very lucky, you will work for a firm with a staff attorney program, or one that uses outside contract attorneys (also known as project attorneys) for the massive doc review projects, which means you will be saved from the most tedious, first-line responsiveness reviews. Then the documents you see will have already been coded for various subjects relevant to your case and narrowed down somewhat and you will have fewer irrelevant documents to wade through.

While it would always be better to have associates reviewing documents, on voluminous reviews that kind of expense could not possibly be justified. So firms turn to other attorneys even further down the chain than you. Staff attorneys are permanent employees of a firm but they are not considered associates and are not on a partner track. Their billing rate is much lower than that for associates, in the vicinity of $180 an hour, rather than $350 an hour and up. So they do a lot of doc review and, less frequently, some privilege reviews. Because they are normally not allowed to bill for things like "legal analysis," they are rarely used for drafting legal memoranda or the like. Not all firms have staff attorneys and some that did in the past now do not. During the economic crisis of 2007 to 2009, some firms fired all the staff attorneys and gradually allowed some to return as contract attorneys. Contract attorneys are not employees of the firm but instead are contracted with outside vendor legal staffing companies. For the fired staff attorneys this means less pay, no benefits and being hired on a job-to-job basis, not permanently.

Contract attorneys work for various vendors and legal staffing companies. Robert Half Legal is one of the largest and most aggressive in pricing. Some law firms have made a good business out of supplying and managing contract attorneys. Morgan, Lewis & Bockius has an eData practice with which some clients work exclusively in all of their litigations, even when they are not otherwise represented by Morgan Lewis. They do doc review as well, often at rates even lower than those for staff attorneys. Sometimes my firm uses both contract attorneys and staff attorneys. The contract attorneys do the first, rough slog through millions of docs and data gathered from a client. Then the staff attorneys do second line coding for more complicated issues or privilege, manage and QC the contract attorneys and then we manage the staff attorneys.

Treating staff attorneys as fungible has costs. When firms fire their staff attorneys they throw away decades of institutional experience and often really solid employees, sometimes people who have been on cases with firm clients for years and have invaluable knowledge of clients' businesses and products. Staff attorneys often know as much or more about the nuts and bolts of a client's business as associates know more than partners. All that institutional memory that could have been brought to a document review is lost, along with commitment and loyalty. It is very hard to get good work product out of contract attorneys. They quit at a moment's notice, they show up late, they surf the web and zone out, they do "Ctrl F" searches in documents instead of reading them. And who can blame them? They are often in dingy, windowless rooms on the wrong side of town, with no working air conditioning doing a horrendous, monotonous job with no hope for anything better and getting yelled at repeatedly by junior associates with much less experience for failing to interpret nuanced and cryptic review guidelines perfectly. Staff attorneys can have their issues, too, with a longer string of demotivators than associates and even less reward. No attorney doing document review at any level gets off easy.

Your most common assignment for the first two years (and often beyond) will be: binder-making. You will make binders of documents useful to the preparation of witnesses to be interviewed or deposed, binders to brief attorneys who will interview or depose witnesses for the other side, binders creating a case chronology, binders compiling all of the key documents of a case, binders summarizing an endless number of targeted issues, binders creating exhibits for depositions. A good friend at another firm calls this the land of Binderia, and you will go there often, you will live there, make it your home.

You will also spend endless hours reviewing documents for accuracy or proofing drafts (especially if you are a corporate attorney); doing QC of the work of staff attorneys and legal assistants; doing legal research; handling case and workflow management tasks such as creating, maintaining and updating spreadsheets and other documents to track case assignments or projects; drafting small portions of a brief or other filing; drafting memoranda summarizing a meeting, interview, or telephone conference or summarizing and analyzing key case documents and creating chronologies of a case. Occasionally you might be asked to second chair a less important witness interview or deposition or assist in witness preparation. As with everything I have stated so categorically, there will be exceptions. Perhaps you will be asked to accompany a partner to India (or at least Indianapolis) to assist in a foreign document collection for a patent infringement case. Do not let the rare exceptions fool you into believing that there is no rule. And remember your place.

Tedious assignments will be your reality for most of the first years you practice in Biglaw and certainly they will be a part of your life in law well beyond those first years. The amount of responsibility with which you will be entrusted and the complexity of the work assigned to you will depend, as we have seen, on the reputation you are able to establish and on the partners with whom you work and how they choose to staff their cases. Some partners prefer a very "lean" case – a couple of junior associates, one senior associate and them. This is a great scenario for the ambitious junior associate because you will get more responsibility and visibility. Other partners, and partners handling massive cases, will have a huge team in which you are a mere cog in the machine laboring amongst perhaps twenty or more staff or contract attorneys doing first line review, eight junior associates, two or three senior associates or of counsel attorneys and two or more partners. This scenario is called "leverage" in Biglaw. Partners with massive cases must leverage their time and delegate their work to many other attorneys. The more massive the case, unfortunately, the less interesting will be the assignments that trickle down the chain. You will be far, far removed from the strategic sessions, client contact opportunities or interesting legal analyses, but you will be protected by your anonymity and steady billable hours.

CHAPTER 3 · KNOW YOUR PLACE

In my first year, my crowning glory was that I was responsible for a single footnote in a summary judgment motion. I probably spent fifty hours on that footnote (a week of my life), researching the law, building the argument, addressing contrary arguments, writing memos and summaries of cases for the senior associates, Shepardizing cases and chasing down alternative arguments that turned out to be dead ends. But in the end it was a damned near perfect statement of the law and was dispositive of the issue in question. A senior associate with whom I worked on the case still uses that footnote every time he needs a cite for that proposition. It was and remains a thing of beauty. I read the motion with pride and almost pinned the thing on my office wall. "See footnote thirty-six," I would tell my family, "that is *mine*." Learning to find the beauty in a well-made thing, however seemingly small or insignificant, is part of what you will need to survive in Biglaw.

You will be infinitely happier if you can take pleasure in the smallest elements of your craft and more efficient if you can learn that that includes the routine employment and reemployment of other people's work and your own. Do not reinvent the wheel every time you are given an assignment. I worked hard on that footnote and I expect it to be immortal (until the law changes). You will actually be poorly evaluated if you try to draft something from scratch, be it summary judgment motion, interrogatory responses, deposition outline, whatever. It wastes too much time. Your firm has been practicing law a lot longer than you. If you need to draft something, chances are someone at the firm has done it before, and done it well. Look through your document database, the library, or wherever the firm keeps its repository of past work product. This kind of repository is the true power of Biglaw. Find stuff in your jurisdiction, or recently done, and use it as a template. If you cannot find anything useful after extensive searching, this might be one of the rare times to use those "all attorney" or "all associates" email lists to see if anyone has worked on something similar. (See chapter seven for an extended discussion of email etiquette.) This is not lazy practice. It is not a cop out. And it is expected. How you adapt the template, the arguments and documents from your case that you include, how you reorganize the document the better to tell your story – all of these are good places to exercise your creativity. Figuring out where the Statement of the Facts goes in a brief is not.

Your main purpose as a young associate is to wade through the vast amount of information in any case – millions of documents from both sides, hundreds of pages of pleadings, depositions and interrogatories, hundreds of relevant cases, whatever is involved – then synthesize and summarize the information – distill, pinpoint the most important facts, the most important legal issues and the cases that support your client's position, identify the relevant issues at play – and present your summary to the senior attorneys in a quick, clear way that is useful to them. This is the main value you add to your team. The senior attorneys do not have time to review all the cases you looked at. They cannot sift through the thousands of documents you have seen to have a deep understanding of what the main issues of the case will be. In fact, they will often not even have time to read the important cases or documents you have found. They rely on you to distill them.

This was one of my biggest surprises in my early days in Biglaw. You will spend a significant amount of time as a young associate feeding the information you have found to senior attorneys – printing cases, organizing them in chronological or subject matter order, highlighting and flagging the important sections, summarizing your conclusions in a memo, even summing up that memo with bullet points in an email and then discussing in person what you already stated in the email and memo. It is frustratingly duplicative for a young associate, but it actually serves an important purpose. As we have said, senior associates and partners simply do not have time to learn everything you have learned. To reach your conclusions, you may have had to read hundreds of cases, chase down several angles that turned out to be dead ends, consider and reject any number of alternative possibilities. They cannot spend that kind of time. They need the bottom line in as clear and concise a form as you are capable of giving and they need to rely on it absolutely. The more successful you can become at presenting only the necessary information without a bunch of junk they have to wade through, the more crucial you will become. The great short story writer and novelist Max Steele used to tell his students, "Information is anything that makes a difference." That is not a bad mantra for a young attorney. Determining what makes a difference is itself an art form.

At my former firm I worked on a trial with one of counsel for a year or so who almost never read cases until right before filing the brief. I did not understand my function or purpose in Biglaw at the time, so I was confounded by what I viewed as her negligent, lazy behavior. How could she just steal my work? She liked me to draw smiley faces next to points that supported our claims and frownie faces next to those that harmed our position and sum up the most important point of the case in a single post-it note on the front page in the upper right hand corner. It made me crazy. I was constantly frustrated that she did not have or seek the same in-depth comprehension of the case law that I had acquired. I would write long summaries of my legal analysis from all of the cases and then she would call me into her office and ask me to tell her what the cases said. She had read not my memos, emails nor even the plagued smiley faces. She would drill me on the holdings, minor points found in dicta and other details. I would get one-line email after one-line email: "Can I make this argument?" or "Can I state this proposition this way?" and "Can I make this claim?" She would write a summary judgment motion based solely on what I told her about the law.

While I have come to believe today that it is wise to read any cases that go into a brief and never rely completely on the work of junior associates, unfortunately, and while I think I can be forgiven for chafing at some of her methods and wanting some form of communication more nuanced than an emoticon, I now understand that what was going on was exactly how things are set up in Biglaw. My early confusion came because I fundamentally misunderstood my place in Biglaw in those early years. I did not comprehend the hierarchy. I did not understand that I would not be thinking strategically about a case for a long time. On the sixth round of edits, being told that I had not found enough, or that I needed to look in another area I had not considered, I would often think, "Well, why don't you just do it yourself?!?!?" Partners and senior associates clearly know exactly what they want and how they want everything done. They are exponentially faster at sifting through information and more adept at searching quickly in large databases to find what they need. Our efforts are usually completely off base initially and they could do what they ask of us in a tenth of the time and perfectly to their satisfaction. Why don't they just do it themselves and be happy?

By now you know the answer to this question and your life will be infinitely easier and less frustrating if you simply take it as a given. They do not have time. And they cannot take the time because their time is too expensive. The single most important job of a junior associate is to get dead-on accurate, comprehensive and focused information – whether legal analysis or factual data – needed for a case up the chain to those who will use it strategically for motions, trial prep or whatever. We have seen why trust is so important. When you say that the state of the law is this, it must be so. When you say you have thoroughly and extensively checked for documents evidencing certain misconduct and have not found *any*, it must be so. The partner needs to sign his name to a document or affirm to a judge that there were no such documents in evidence that his firm was able to find with diligent efforts. It is dead serious. Smiley faces or no, the of counsel had to trust that my information was correct, fully researched and double-checked, and she staked her reputation and career on that trust. In massive cases, the partners and senior associates cannot possibly do all the work on their own. Senior associates must rely on the information they get from those whose billable rate is low enough for the client to tolerate their spending the hours and hours it takes to wade through the documents and case law, ferret out the information, discard the rubbish and focus in on key points.

You must master a vast amount of information and sift, cull, compile, organize, analyze, recognize patterns and holes, find and explain information important to your case in the best, most efficient, most accurate and thorough way possible. And you must get all that you have learned up the chain of hierarchy to the partners. It is – in one way – an incredibly inefficient system. Think about it this way: the person with the least amount of knowledge and experience practicing law has to make some of the most important decisions about which documents are ever even seen by the more senior attorneys. Important, game-changing documents may be lost or overlooked, simply because those reviewing them do not have the same experience in practice and knowledge in a particular area of law to realize what is relevant. It would be much quicker and one would be able to have infinitely more confidence in the accuracy and completeness of the work product if the senior attorneys – or even the partners – reviewed the documents themselves. With their years of experience, they would know in an instant if a certain document were relevant, important or privileged. But that is not the system. Partners cannot possibly slog through documents in a first review – it would be prohibitively expensive for the client. So the responsibility will fall on you.

There is no denying that this process involves a lot of wasted effort. A vast number of your assignments will be frustrating shots in the dark, impossible attempts to prove a negative – "Tell me that there are NO documents whatsoever that say X," which could take years to prove conclusively – and hunts for the never-found needle in the proverbial haystack. Partners have a general sense of the law and facts of a case and a lot of experience, but they often write a brief on what they would *like* to argue and then ask you to hunt through hundreds of cases to find a cite to back up some crazy assertion. You will spend hours looking for something that is not there. Also common is the "I thought I saw a case on this last week, can you go find it" assignment. So you will spend hours digging, reading, skimming and scanning. In the end, you will be frustrated in your searches more often than not but that is not the whole issue. They are not solely concerned about you finding the cite. If you find it, all well and good, but if you do not it will still be important as long as you can confirm beyond all reasonable question that it does not exist. And, as we have seen, you will often not know which answer means what for the case.

A pitfall you will be able to avoid is the knee-jerk reaction of most new associates: "Why am I doing this? What is the point? This will never be used, never be seen, never be needed. Why am I wasting my time?" They are simply feeding their own frustration and missing a major point of the practice of law. Lawyers do innumerable things to prepare for contingencies. Ninety percent of what we do falls into the category of "just in case." We take the meaning of "diligence" to new heights. Clients turn to attorneys to cover what cannot be foreseen and to deal with the unforeseen when it blows up, as, inevitably, it will. We do not spend our time – as young Biglaw associates in particular – drafting stunning appellate briefs or arguing motions to dismiss. Much of the practice of law is focused on being prepared for the worst, on the "what if" scenarios and on making sure that we have diligently and carefully protected our clients' interests to the last dotted "i."

Why does it matter? Why does any of this matter? It is what people rely on lawyers to do. This is why we spend countless hours preparing a privilege log that may never be served; that is why we spend long weeks preparing an anticipated response of three hundred pages to a possible motion for summary judgment that is never filed. Our job is not only to do things that end up being used at trial or to reserve our really brilliant efforts for the tasks that we think matter. We must prepare for *every* eventuality, *every* possible twist and turn and we must devote our best efforts to all of it. We pursue a way of practicing law that strives to take everything into account, to prepare for everything that could possibly happen. It may not be possible but the pursuit of it is our purpose. You will save yourself a painful quantity of existential angst if you find the fascination in the pursuit of perfection and do not allow yourself to become frustrated or to think that all you are engaged in is a futile exercise of anal hyper-preparation. It may be the case, time after time, that it turns out to be such an exercise. But that is what lawyers, Biglaw lawyers most of all, do. If you end up chucking three weeks of your hard work in the trash afterward, no matter.

It is your job to make senior associates' and partners' jobs easier. You will read the documents for them and highlight and extract the key issues, facts, holes, lack of data, possible new witnesses or custodians from whom to seek documents. You will develop questions for further follow-up and weed out superfluous, distracting dead ends. You will sift through mountains of documents to find the small handful that the partners really need to see. Your job will be to read through every one; understand the context, relevance and possible importance to the issues in your case; identify where each relevant document fits into the case and then cull the set down further. Depending on the size of your case and the staffing, you will then pass your fifty or so cherished documents on to a mid-level or senior associate, who will go through them all just the way you did, culling them down even further. At the end of the process, the partner will get a stack of about twenty documents or so of only the most crucial findings.

Because of the sheer amount of time junior associates spend with the documents, they can, if they read with focused attention at all times, end up knowing an impressive amount about a case: the facts out there in the universe of documents, the way the industry in question works, the roles of various key employees, the background and context. If you approach doc review simply as a robotic exercise in coding eight hundred documents a day for months on end for general responsiveness, subject matter and issues relevant to the case and possible privilege, you will gain nothing from those years you languish in the doc review war room and you will contribute very little value to your team, and thus, you will be easily dispensable. It is important to know your place, yes, but that does not mean you turn your brain off.

This kind of synthesis of information will be expected of you, but never clearly explained by more experienced attorneys. I used to stare blankly back at senior associates when they would ask what other issues I might have noticed during my review or whether I saw any information about a different issue that had arisen in the case after the parameters were set for my review. I would mumble in confusion that I had not, thinking to myself that that was outside of what I had been asked to do. I was told to code five thousand documents Responsive, Not Responsive and Potentially Privileged, in order to get them out the door in time for a production deadline the following week. Since I was expected to go through at least eight hundred docs per day, how would I possibly have had time to *think* critically about the documents and read them carefully as well? Some amount of blinder-like focus is necessary to get through that many documents in the time demanded. The key is to learn to balance the time crunch with the very important goal of developing in-depth knowledge and critical skills and adding real value to the team with which you work. This is a part of being proactive about your career and focusing on where you hope to go. It is a huge mistake simply to float along and let Biglaw run over you.

If you stay focused and find ways to steer your career, you will move slowly and incrementally towards substantive work. Junior associates labor in the mines of doc review (always mindful that staff attorneys labor below them and contract or project attorneys labor in obscurity still deeper in the depths). Mid-level and senior associates get to draft the deposition outlines that will be used by more senior attorneys who actually get to do the depositions. Slowly, slowly, you will make your way up the chain of hierarchy. I resented this a great deal in the early years. Why did I have to struggle over issues, work to grasp them, make sense of them, incorporate them in our arguments, search for the important documents, scouring through hundreds to find the best and then waste my time summarizing them for someone else, with flags, highlighting, email bullet notes, written arrows and smiley faces? Why didn't the senior associates read the damn documents themselves and see why I marked them important? Why not digest all those on point cases I found themselves? I wasted a lot of energy in resentment. I hope my wasted energy will fuel your determination to conserve your own. To fight this is to miss the entire point of Biglaw practice: *you* must struggle with the issues, *you* summarize and condense, *you* make a Gestalt formulation of how it all fits together and you make sure the partner wastes no time trying to figure out what you have already learned.

You will sail through Biglaw's many frustrating realities if you firmly grasp this point. You did it so that your superiors would not have to. And every minute they spend questioning why you marked something the way you did, why you thought something was relevant to the issues or what you saw important in a doc, is wasted partner time. The better you get at communicating essential information efficiently, the happier your life will be. The crazier you get with your marked up PDFs or bullet point emails, the more you are able to be clear, concise, exact, comprehensive in explaining what you have gleaned, the more valuable you will be.

Your job at this point may not be to think big picture thoughts or global strategic courses, but you should try to incorporate a big picture understanding into your review and you should settle it in your mind that you are needed to work deep in the forest. You need to make hundreds of individual decisions every day about whether a document is responsive, whether it is potentially privileged, whether it is "hot" (what some call "important" and others call a "document of interest" or "potentially interesting document" (PID)). It is a constant challenge, but if you learn to see the important facts and documents of a case so that you can contribute substantively, if you develop the steely determination and discipline you will need to remain engaged, focused and alert day after day in the fourth slogging month of a near endless document production, if you learn to place the massive wave of documents and information in the bigger picture of the case, analyzing and developing a story and the important issues and themes, you will become invaluable to your team and you will emerge with highly desired and marketable skills. Those who do not will have spent two years of their lives as depressed doc review minions, having gained almost nothing from the time and effort expended. This need not be you.

Chapter Four

Document Production and its Discontents

By this point you may feel that if you have to read another word about doc review you will gouge your eyes out. Consider this feeling carefully as it is only a pale shadow of what you will feel if you enter this world. You may think you get it already and we should move on. Consider this chapter an effortless warm up for the first two years of your life in Biglaw. We will get to some of the health consequences (short of the absolute loss of your eyes) at the end of this chapter and more nuts and bolts of doc review, along with ways to cope with the Biglaw stress and tedium in the rest of the book.

The simple, unavoidable fact of being a Biglaw junior associate is that you will spend much of your billable time (and thus, your life) reviewing documents. Your work will ideally be split between a mix of doc review and other tasks like legal research and analysis, supervising staff attorneys and providing feedback/QC of their work and attending the occasional hearing or deposition, so that you do not have to suffer through eight to twelve hours of straight doc review every day. It will only be in the way of an occasional bone thrown your way that you are permitted to second chair a minor deposition of a witness, or be taken to an evidentiary hearing, and that will only be to keep you from throwing yourself out of a window and to allow the firm to tell new law students it recruits that it will give them a well-rounded and interesting training in the law.

Doc review and legal research are the bread and butter of litigation associates and will be most of your work for the first two or more years. Corporate law associates will also review mountains of documents for due diligence and preparation of corporate filings. You will go for long stretches with nothing but documents on your horizon. There is no escaping doc review. By now you understand clearly how this works: you are the cheapest labor in the chain and it simply would not work to have a $400/hour senior associate plow through thousands of documents for a simple electronic discovery request or subpoena.

When someone is sued or investigated today – especially the massive corporate clients of Biglaw – both sides must release documents that are relevant to the case. Email, Blackberry, voice mail, paper files taken from an employee's desk, entire laptop hard drives, handwritten notes, lab notebooks and journals – every imaginable medium in which any form of data might be stored will be collected in litigation and will need to be reviewed and coded in order to be produced and then usable to you in the case. You may assist in document collections in which you go to corporate offices, take hard drives, download email accounts of key people involved in the case, collect hard copy documents from their files and even take things off their desks. With multi-billion dollar, international companies, the number of persons from whom you will need to collect documents grows exponentially. This results in millions of documents to review for relevance and privilege, to code and produce to the other side. And when you receive the other side's documents, you will need to review those documents and make sense of all the information contained within their vast reaches in order to build your case.

You will review documents for any number of reasons: cursory, first line review in response to a subpoena to produce documents, in which you mark documents "responsive" or "not responsive" and move on; second line review for production, perhaps including marking the documents for key subject matter categories relevant to your case that may be useful as the case goes along as well as determining whether they are "not confidential," "confidential," "highly confidential – attorneys eyes only"; you will review documents for privilege logs and documents to use in preparing witnesses for depositions, interviews and trial. You will review documents in response to fire drills when a new, damaging fact in a case comes to light and a partner wants to understand it ASAP or to rebut allegations in the other side's brief. You will review documents to create a case chronology or set of important documents. You will review documents to get a better understanding of the job responsibilities and functions of key corporate witnesses. You will create binder, after binder, after binder of the documents you have reviewed, compiling and condensing the most important findings. And you will QC those binders, highlight the binders, flag the binders, summarize the contents of binders and have the most intimate relationship in your life with those binders. Life in the fast lane, indeed.

As I have suggested, if you are lucky, your firm will have the practice of hiring contract or staff attorneys for large document productions, which will save you from having to do the worst, most tedious, first line responsiveness reviews for production in a case. Then, your job will be to supervise and manage the attorneys, perform QC of their review, provide feedback and do a little review yourself. With harder economic times, more and more firms are cutting back their staff attorney programs and giving that work to the incoming first years and other junior associates.

CHAPTER 4 · DOCUMENT PRODUCTION AND ITS DISCONTENTS

Depending on the intensity and timing of the case and how humane the partner, you will review documents from eight to twelve hours a day. No one thinks that a person can intelligently review documents for longer than twelve hours a day, although it may be necessary in crunch times. The number of documents you are expected to review in a day will change, depending on the nature of the review. First line responsiveness reviews should be fast. You will look at upwards of eight hundred documents in a day. Specialized subject matter reviews take much longer, because each document needs to be carefully analyzed and coded for any number of subjects, in addition to attorney-client privilege codes. Under such circumstances you might be expected to review no more than about one hundred and fifty.

With the age of electronic discovery, doc review has taken on an entirely new and horrific scope. In a large case, one side can have millions of responsive documents for production. Partners regularly stress the importance of doc review. Young associates will not make partner without having a sophisticated understanding of electronic discovery, of working with vendors, finding efficient and cost effective ways to organize the data and knowing how to master the information in millions of documents.

The important thing you need to understand about doc review is that it is actually a necessary part of your development as an attorney and it is a crucial function in Biglaw practice. Young associates can become the most important members of their teams. They know the documents, the history, the context better than anyone else on the case. You will become an expert on whatever the subject of your case might be and learn about entire industries: promotional and sales activities of big pharmaceutical companies, the electrical components of a popular video game subject to a patent infringement suit, hiring practices of major companies in a race discrimination law suit. The young associates are in the trenches, reading through thousands of documents in order to understand the facts of the case, the important issues to be litigated and possible defenses.

A partner once told me that he always has junior associates coming to him and whining about too much doc review and wanting to get out of doc review. He shook his head and said, "They don't understand. You have to master this before you can move on to better things. This is crucial." He believed that no one would be able to make partner today without having mastered electronic discovery and document production. Corporations are demanding, more than ever, that these productions be efficient without sacrificing accuracy. This is clearly a complex and problematical demand, calling for both the extremes of diligence and close reading and the most innovative and creative problem solving techniques at the supervisory level. These are qualities of mind often found in separate individuals but which must be combined in the successful attorney. Large corporations will spend millions in document production alone, they expect from Biglaw the level of attention, intellectual engagement and efficiency for which we are famous. And that is why you must master it.

The skills you learn slogging through those documents for hours and hours are vital skills. You will learn how to read and understand documents, what is relevant and important, how to sift out the useless information, how to hone in on what is key. How to look at everything through a lens of the facts of your case, procedural and strategic issues and the legal landscape in which you are operating. You also learn how to manage the discovery process, which you will do over and over as a mid-level, senior associate and partner. You will know what works best in an efficient, successful document production, how to staff and train your attorneys to get the results you want, how to achieve your goals of fact development in the quickest and cheapest ways. And you will also discover what does not work, how to avoid duplicative, wasteful reviews. Unfortunately, that partner is right. This knowledge only comes the hard way. As with any valuable experience in the practice of law, you cannot learn this without spending the hours, months and years in the trenches. Don't fret – you will graduate from Binderia and doc review hell, although it feels at times like you will never escape. Remember, you will become too expensive to do it eventually. It cannot go on forever. But you must actually go through it. There is no way around it. So you might as well use the time to get very smart about a lot of industries you now know nothing about and to hone your skills in an ever-changing and expanding universe of the management of vast quantities of potential information.

The key to surviving doc review is to remain engaged and to add real value to your team in whatever way you can. Associates are most valuable when they comprehend the big picture and when they know the documents – the information and relevant facts of a case – cold. If you review docs mechanically or allow your brain to shut off, you will miss new issues you should be catching and drawing to the attention of a partner. You need to read them and understand. Why did this person say that? Is it relevant that she said it in 2004 as opposed to 2003? If a date is not on a document, you have to dig deeper and narrow it down. Does it cite the date of a recent meeting? Does it only list publications up to 2001? Is there an employee on the email list that you know left the company in 2009? You must always be thinking as you go along; always engaging your brain and adding information to the big picture, or you will contribute very little of value. There are computer programs that create "intelligent" searching software in the hopes of making discovery more economical but these can never replace a Biglaw associate.

Before I sit down to plow through a set, I always orient myself. Are these hard copy scanned images from one single custodian? What was her job, and thus, what types of documents will I see a lot of? The relevance of the documents changes depending on whose they are. What are the issues of the case to be alert for? Why have I just seen eighty copies of what look like the exact same document? Is this a vendor error I need to address? Why have I *not* seen anything relating to issue Y? Was there a gap in collection efforts that needs follow up? When

CHAPTER 4 · DOCUMENT PRODUCTION AND ITS DISCONTENTS

I approach a new document, I do the same thing. Is this an email? Who was it sent to? Who was cc'd? What is the relevance of sending this information to the CEO of the company, instead of just a lower level manager? Think, think, think. Always pull yourself up from the weeds to look at the larger picture. You can get buried quickly if you focus on the irrelevant details of the documents you see. Figure out what is important and what you can breeze over. I promise you, if you just code like a robot, you will not be doing your job. If you just glaze over line after line of text, without processing or comprehending what you are seeing, you will not be useful to your team. A contract attorney can do that much, much less expensively than you. They often do not have the analytical abilities or knowledge of the case. If a cheaper labor source can do the job you are doing, you are in trouble.

It is a slog. If you have 1800 docs to review, try not to look at numbers because they will crush you. I go one, by one, by one. Eventually, you get to the end and for about two seconds it feels great. Until you are handed your next batch of 1800. It requires a Zen mind and that only comes with time.

Mastering doc review is not easy or fun. It will take putting together everything in this book. Like a complex final exam in physics, you cannot simply cram the night before and expect to pass. You cannot slack off, daydream or zone out. Really reviewing a set of documents, understanding what they say and how that relates to your case and how it can be used to help or hurt you is hard (and not always exciting). Grasping all of the many facts and events that shape your story takes time. Understanding what facts in a document mean, in real life, to your case, seeing the patterns and what one document means in the context of other documents you have seen, takes focus and intellectual engagement. This long and painful process of honing your analytical abilities is key to your development.

You will develop judgment about which issues are important and which are irrelevant. Most "bad" docs that can make or break a case are not so obvious as an email saying, "I've just embezzled thirty million dollars and hidden it in Long Island." Those kinds of smoking-gun moments are great fun – and they may happen once in your entire career. You have to learn to see patterns, read inferences and piece together circumstantial evidence to build your case and defend your clients. Sexy, it is not. But it is absolutely essential to your success in Biglaw that you develop the precise analytical skills of a top attorney and doc review is the way you will do it.

Here is one quick, real world example. In defending a pharmaceutical client against charges that it illegally paid bribes to hospitals to induce them to buy the company's products, a friend on another firm's review team began to see documents talking about a party some doctors attended along with their client's sales representatives. Boring, no one noticed at first. Then there was one document that mentioned that one of the sales reps would bring wine to a party held around the same date as the one that had been seen referenced in other documents. Still, not very interesting, but it raised a small flag. Pharmaceutical sales reps are very limited in the amounts they are allowed to spend before it starts smelling like a bribe. (Bringing donuts to the doctor's office staff is usually okay, while a luxury trip to Hawaii for a doctor and his spouse for a "conference" starts to look like an illegal kickback.) Then one document contained an invoice from a caterer for a "staff appreciation party" paid for by a sales rep. That invoice alone could have meant nothing at all to a tired reviewer with blinders. There is nothing wrong with a caterer's invoice for staff appreciation. But the invoice also contained an address and a date. An unwary reviewer could easily have assumed it was the address of an off-site event venue commonly used for promotional gatherings and failed to note the importance of the date. Someone who did notice the date and connected it with the other memos about a party and who then investigated the address would have discovered that the party, paid for by company sales reps, took place in the private home of one of the chief hospital administrators. This apparently innocuous receipt, in the context of the other documents that referred to a party attended by both execs and the client's pharmaceutical sales reps, was in fact evidence that there was an event on the same date mentioned in other documents, catered at the home of one of the administrators in question and paid for by employees of the client. Then, hundreds of documents later, there was an expense report from an employee of the client submitting that same invoice, seeking corporate reimbursement for a standard promotional event (totally fine) on that date. Then one single document mentioned a party on the same date at an administrator's house that some employees were planning to attend. A week later a reviewer found an email from a vice president of marketing expressing gratitude to the administrator for helping the company win a coveted contract with the hospital. None of these documents was itself alarming, but all of them together amounted to damning evidence that a handful of pharmaceutical employees paid thousands of dollars to host an extravagant party at a top level administrator's house attended by sales reps and doctors and that the administrator in turn might have expressed his gratitude by making sure the client was awarded a prized hospital contract. That is the stuff of which very bad things are made. From such things you must protect your clients.

A. Witness Prep

Witness preparation is crucial to litigation and it, too, takes up a fair amount of junior associate time but – you guessed it – behind the scenes with – right again – the documents. For depositions, trial testimony, expert testimony, government interviews and interviews associated with corporate internal investigations, attorneys will meet with witnesses (such as employees of companies

CHAPTER 4 · DOCUMENT PRODUCTION AND ITS DISCONTENTS

represented by the law firm) and prepare them for handling questions, help them to frame answers that will do the least amount of damage to their employers' cases and educate them generally on the issues of their case and some documents (often bad, or useful to the other side) with which they may be confronted. It is extremely important to prepare a witness thoroughly. Dumb things blurted out in a moment of surprise from a zinger question can derail a case. Witness preparations can last anywhere from half a day to two or three full days – or more if it is a complicated case or a very important witness. Usually it will be the more senior attorneys who will meet with potential witnesses and discuss how to handle depositions, testifying at trial or interviews in general and clarify strategies for responding to questions. Much of this will be familiar even to the most casual viewer of television shows about lawyers – answer only the question that is asked, never volunteer information, never speculate, pause for a moment after the question is asked to allow time to formulate a careful response and give your attorney an opportunity to object to the question – but it all has to be instilled in the witness until it is second nature. What you know you should do and what you can reliably reproduce under pressure are two different things. Then witnesses need to be made familiar with all of the documents that were thought important for their testimony – these are usually the "bad" documents that turned up with your witnesses' names on them – whether those materials amount to one binder or twenty.

And that binder, that belongs to you. To prepare for the preparation, a witness's documents need to be reviewed, summarized and organized prior to the first meeting with the witness. This document universe can be a couple thousand or hundreds of thousands of documents. Maybe if the volume is too great and the time to prepare is constrained, you will decide to focus only on the most important years, or you will search a witness's documents – those that show up in your productions either including her name in some significant way or sourced to her – for specific key words in your case. For example, you might decide a certain witness is most involved with product development in your patent infringement case. You will focus on the documents in those areas, while always on the alert for any bad or potentially unsettling documents of any kind. The review process will involve all of the common headaches: you QC the contract attorneys' review and realize they are missing some key issues, you provide feedback and more training and send them back through the documents; you re-review; deadlines are moved around and the witness's date is changed and suddenly you have half the time to get everything done. You learn that for some reason, this witness's email files were only produced up until 2008. It turns out after talking with the client that his archived files after that date were located somewhere else and were never turned over when you did the original collection. This means you have to have them reviewed and produced before the deposition while the prep is going on, or the other side will probably be able to argue that it should be allowed to depose the witness a second time, since the docs were not even available at the time of the deposition. Giving the other side a second bite at the apple is never good.

The document review portion of witness preparation may be done by any number of contract attorneys or be handled by junior associates alone, depending on the scope and size of the case. There may be multiple reviews – a first pass with contract attorneys, then junior associates culling down the documents that were selected by contract attorneys and finally a senior associate further narrowing what documents the witness really needs to see.

Along the way, you will be highlighting one copy of a binder set, usually for the partner's use, so he does not need to spend time figuring out why you thought a doc was important. You will highlight the witness's name, to ensure it is immediately obvious why this document is relevant to this witness (she sent the email, she received the email, etc). You will flag and highlight what is important about the doc – why you decided to include it. Then you will have paralegals make several clean copies, for witnesses and other attorneys who should not see your notes and flagging, fretting all the while about what color slip sheets Partner X does or does not want to see delineating the various sections in a binder or separating a document from its attachment or which partner insists on tabbed binders only and no slip sheets at all.

When you can turn your attention from highlighter and slip sheet colors, there are substantive issues to consider as you review, document by document. How inclusive should you be? In general, a witness preparation binder needs to include anything the witness might be asked about – anything that might raise a flag. A common source of pain for junior associates is the important document that is missed by the preparing attorneys – never found at all or possibly weeded out somewhere in the review chain and never shown to a partner – a document a witness then gets blindsided by in a deposition. Imagine what would have happened if the relevance of the party invoice expense report had been missed and the employee who submitted the expense report had been confronted with that out of the blue in a deposition. Partners become very exercised over such surprises. So a good rule is to err on the side of over-inclusiveness. On the other hand, if the materials to be reviewed are too extensive you will never get through everything and you certainly do not want to waste a CEO witness's time going through duplicative documents or less than crucial material. These witnesses are taking time away from their businesses and will not sit through a long march of useless documents.

There are gradations to master in the world of Binderia. For example, the highest level of inclusion is probably appropriate for a typical briefing binder, which is a binder put together to provide in depth coverage of an issue for internal use. Here you include everything that will contribute to capturing all the nuances of an event or issue. But a successful witness preparation binder re-

CHAPTER 4 · DOCUMENT PRODUCTION AND ITS DISCONTENTS   57

quires that a document meet a higher standard for inclusion, because you must take into consideration the time of the client with whom your superiors will review the material. But you should still err on the side of inclusion. Calls are required on every document: does the witness really need to see this? Early on, this tight rope you must walk will require that you bring countless issues and documents to the attention of senior associates so they can make the calls as to whether something is important enough to include.

As you gain experience you will develop the right kind of filters and focus along with the ability to hold onto the big picture. Young associates often seem to have blinders on while reviewing documents, seeing only what is relevant to their specific cases, which leads them to miss other issues that might be important to bring to the client's attention. While it may be true that the email in which an employee made a meaningless quip about his company's competition is not legally relevant to your patent infringement case, the fact that the very same competing company is now your client's adversary in an ongoing case makes remarks like: "I can't believe this – you should send your friends from the Chicago mob down there to kick that guy's ass!!!" worthy of note. It could be disconcerting for a witness to be reminded of such a remark in a deposition and it could have consequences in the press. Or you might learn from the documents that your witness is having an extra-marital affair with a coworker. This has no legal relevance to your case, so you leave it out, right? Wrong. It sure plays powerfully with a jury who cannot possibly follow all the technical subtleties of the wireless local area network device you are fighting about but will remember that your client is "the bad guy." And it can have a life of its own in newspapers and the internet. Many of these kinds of emails are missed by studious, young lawyers – who rightly conclude that these emails would not alter the legal landscape of a case, that the issues are completely irrelevant, but mistakenly forget that there are other arenas in which your clients may need protection: the court of public opinion, the media, etc. It is your job to insulate them from harm there, too.

Another way in which having blinders on while reviewing can compromise a witness preparation is error by misdirection. An associate sees a document during a review of the witness's documents that has a crucial paragraph – something really important to the case – so he highlights, flags and includes it in the witness prep binder, only to be shown later that, yes, that paragraph is extremely interesting, but this particular witness had no involvement with that portion of the document. The witness's name is found much further down the email chain, thus, the witness would never have received that part, and it is completely irrelevant for the preparation of *this* witness. Here, the associate thought deeply about the case and understood the implications of the document but forgot to focus on the relationship of the document to the witness in question.

All of this takes place against the continual pressure of the clock. You need to get through the documents, double check enough to make sure you are confident that a thorough review was achieved and nothing was overlooked, then review and compile the documents (does the partner want them in chronological order, or by various subjects?), then summarize those documents, highlighting for the partner what is important, often in an outline to accompany the partner's binder, and it all needs to be done in less than half the time that might be reasonable if you had twice the experience.

Maintaining motivation is hard: you will not be the one doing the prep until much later on. You may not even get to attend a prep for years as clients will not pay for redundant attorneys and junior associates, whenever possible, are kept far, far away from direct client contact. So you get to slog through thousands of files for weeks on end, spend hours painstakingly reading and summarizing them and then hand them off to a more senior attorney. It is hard to care what docs get included, or that it looks nice and professional under these circumstances, but it must be done.

And why is it so important to find these documents anyway? Why is it worth a month of your life and all the attendant misery? The other side will find that little email sooner or later and get a lot of mileage out of it. You cannot prevent it since the document cannot be kept out of the case. So why should you spend those agonizing months reading product specification manuals and employee evaluation reports in order to highlight one random email in time for one half-day prep? Why is it so important that it be flagged now? Biglaw clients, mostly mega-corporations, are highly risk averse. You always want to be able to apprise them of their liabilities early on in the litigation. They want numbers. How much trouble are they in? How bad is it? How much should they budget for your fees and settlement? If the many thousands (sometimes millions) of dollars they are spending on you every month did not even help them learn about a few bad documents before they were hit with them in a deposition, what the hell are they paying you for? And if you missed that, what else did you miss? Terror of what still lurks out there sets in and clients have zero tolerance for that. And finally, your charming corporate witness – who happens to be called as a 30(b)(6) witness under the Federal Rules of Civil Procedure, which means he speaks not only on his own personal experience and behalf, but represents the company itself and speaks as the company – who had no idea what they were going to throw at him, has just admitted under oath, in front of the court reporter and on video (for those lovely little excerpts played at trial for the jury) that there was nothing wrong with making phony threats about the competition – everyone does it and, of course, there is no company policy against those kinds of statements and what is the problem anyway? Very, very bad. You do not want to be the associate who missed that document.

B. The Priv Log

You will also spend a lot of time doing privilege reviews as a junior associate. It is probably the most hazardous-to-your-health assignment you will get. Consequences for making mistakes are the most intense. If attorney-client privilege is not zealously guarded, it is considered waived, leaving all of your private deliberations, advice, strategies and discussions open for the other side to pry into. That means documents containing attorney-client privileged communications must be held back from production and logged with enough specificity so that the other side can determine if it wants to challenge your withholding of a particular document.

A priv review is similar to a document production review in many ways – you will get a binder of materials before you begin, with guidelines, examples of privileged docs, coding instructions. Every document, save the simple email to an attorney saying, "Can you give me advice about X?" is a potential trap for you. Those are the easy ones, and they are not the norm. The hours you will spend in rooms with other attorneys going back and forth about which docs to assert privilege for and where to draw the redactions and which ones you should produce will astound you. And so will the differing approaches you will find. Never assume that because one partner made privilege calls one way that that is the way things are done. Partners and clients have very different levels of tolerance for risk. Some clients will claim privilege for every document with an attorney on it, no matter how business-like (thus, non-privileged) or how far removed the attorney is from the content. And they are ready to fight those battles in court if they have to, in order to protect the highest level of privilege. Many of their grey-area calls would not hold up if challenged in court, but they are willing to test it. For these clients, you will be over inclusive. Every time a document lists something as "attorney approved" you will redact. The cost for missing any possibly privileged content will be heavy.

Other clients are much more pragmatic. Knowing it is dangerous to push a judge with trivial or heavy-handed and superfluous privilege claims, they expect their privilege calls to be more deliberately made – reflecting calls that they believe would withstand a challenge in court. They are most concerned about those few, highly-sensitive documents they hope to protect, not alarm bells going off every time the word "lawyer" appears in some sales presentation. Your privilege calls will be different for that client. The standard of review for these clients is more like: what claim of privilege would likely win if challenged.

When you face your first privilege review, you should make no judgment calls on your own. Honestly, not one. If there is anything grey, if you pause for a moment to weigh both sides, put it aside and talk with a senior associate about it. Legal practice is not intuitive and, as we have said, your intuitions at first will almost always be wrong.

For priv reviews and doc production reviews alike, you will often find a common room set up with several computers, so associates can review and discuss as they go along. It is best that everyone be on the same page right from the beginning. Say there is a potentially privileged email chain that appears in your document universe twenty times with different custodians, different parts of the email chain, etc. Those twenty emails need to be coded consistently. How could the partner's strategy for how to treat privilege for a particular client be implemented in any meaningful way if a half dozen or so associates were off coding however they pleased? The early phase of priv review requires the most oversight and calls for daily team meetings so no one goes off on a frolic and costs the review serious damage and time.

And with the priv review comes the dreaded privilege log – in which you must list every document you have withheld or redacted and describe the basis of your claim for privilege. Those descriptions will be carefully hashed out and decided upon: "email chain and attachments containing confidential client to counsel and counsel to client communications regarding corporate governance" or "draft memorandum prepared at the direction of counsel in anticipation of litigation containing confidential information provided for the purpose of obtaining legal advice regarding product design and development." Every entry needs to be individually drafted to characterize accurately the document or portion of a document you are withholding. There can be thousands and thousands of entries in a large case. Different partners will have different standards for the amount of detail needed in a privilege description. That is why the thought of priv logs will make any junior associate groan.

This is the typical priv log review. There will be times when it will be very different. Say the other side has produced a priv log that is unbelievably, even sanctionably bad. Every entry is simply: "email in furtherance of legal advice regarding X corporation." There is no detailed description of why a document is privileged. Does it contain privileged communications from an attorney? Does it reflect legal advice given to an employee? But, instead of challenging that log, your partner and the client decide that it is best simply to produce a priv log that is similar in detail to the one the other side produced. This will save the client thousands of dollars and you a lot of headaches. You will produce it in a week, instead of a month and you will do as little as possible. This is the exception, not the rule. But, then, there are always exceptions with this and with everything else in this book – there will always be exceptions to the general rules I am discussing.

In addition to reviewing the docs marked potentially privileged and painstakingly drafting the log one document at a time, you will need to spend a significant amount of time in QC – conducting searches to see whether there were docs in the universe that were missed and not marked priv. You will have a list of all the in-house and outside counsel for your client – a list that can run into the hundreds – that you will run a search on each name to try to isolate direct attorney communications. You might look again at every doc that has the word "legal" or "lawyer" for example; following up with a client to see if a certain document that looks like it might have had attorney involvement actually did. Was there an attorney at that meeting involved in drafting the meeting minutes? If it is not clear from the face of the document, you will need more information to make a privilege call. Or some over zealous senior associate, managing her first priv review, will read an esoteric treatise on attorney-client privilege and conclude, "Ah ha! It says that only the actual communications *from* the client to the attorney are privileged and nothing else." Of course, in practice, this is nonsense but that will not save you from the week you will spend haggling over each document that seems clearly privileged to you but which she will not withhold, until she finally passes some of her crazy priv calls by the partner on the case who then goes through the roof, at which point you have to go back and recode everything you knew was privileged in the first place.

Then you will need to format the log, usually putting an asterisk by every attorney's (or other legal representative's) name on the log. If contract attorneys made a first attempt at drafting entries, you will have to look at a certain percentage of their docs, to feel confident that you agree with how they were characterizing and describing the documents. You cannot look at every document, but you need to make yourself reasonably certain that they were consistent and accurate.

At the end of the day, the priv log process is a nightmare and there are no clear benefits for the junior associate, other than rigor and discipline. It is another of the hideous and tedious Biglaw tasks that you will learn to approach with a Zen mind and a firm resolve to make it through without committing any egregious mistakes.

C. Resistance Is Futile

We already know how difficult it will be to keep motivated and engaged in the face of all the things that will be conspiring to make you crazy – being low man on the totem pole with no life of your own, fighting to get your key information up the chain, the Scylla and Charybdis choice between no feedback and destructive criticism and the ever-present force of the hierarchy. I am urging you to engage with doc review and take ownership of your case and pride in your work product. And then you will work in the trenches for months, review thousands of docs, spend two weeks creating targeted binders for a key witness. You will spend hours highlighting and flagging all of the key portions of every document and creating a memo summarizing in detail each doc. You will create bookmarked PDFs of the most important documents to email to local counsel. The senior associate will then take that binder and summary memo and she will accompany the partner to the interview or deposition or hearing, not you. You will know the documents cold (she may even email you during the deposition to look up something or find a document), you will have lived with the issues far longer than she has and you will be keenly aware of how greatly you would benefit from the experience. But by now you know that is not how it works.

Being a Biglaw associate requires the ability to sit and concentrate for long, long periods of time on dry and detailed things without letting yourself be distracted by things like wondering if you will ever do anything else. Like mastering yoga or transcendental meditation, it is hard at first. You resist and lack the discipline to read through thousands of pages of documents over and over. But skipping the resistance piece of it will save you a lot of energy and after a few years, you will find that it becomes easier to sit with the documents, take in all that they have to say, the context and nuances. It becomes easier. These days I don't resist and rebel internally when I am given a set of 1200 documents. I have learned how to sit and go through each one, carefully. And I have learned to accept that when my work is done it will be taken forward to the next step by someone who knows less about it than I do. But it has taken time. Maybe that time will be shorter for you.

D. Biglaw Side Effects

No matter how diligently I may try to prepare you, no matter how receptively you read this book, no matter the strength of your Zen mind for doc review or your patience for the feudal system, you need to know: Biglaw can be hazardous to your emotional, physical and psychological health. Many young associates live with chronic stress, frustration and anxiety. I have watched marriages and friendships strain and fail. I have seen Biglaw bring out the worst in dear friends. If you do not understand that this is the reality before you enter it, you will be battered about with each new indignity, each insult, each injustice until you become jaded and bitter. If you are too sensitive, every criticism and edit to your hard work, every time you are discounted or put down, will cut and wound you. But if you remain clear on the reality of Biglaw as it is and that you cannot change it, if you keep a focus on what you want and why you want Biglaw, you will survive.

In the first two years of Biglaw, I went through two new eye prescriptions. My eyesight is still deteriorating with abnormal rapidity. My hair thinned alarmingly. I pop analgesics more often than I take vitamins. My caffeine tolerance would stun a lumberjack. I have gained too much weight at times, and lost too much weight at others. Although I jealously guard the time I have with my family, I know always that it is not enough and probably never will be. I leave my husband alone too often to work in the evenings instead of enjoying a glass of wine together. I have frequent existential crises, wondering what I want to do with my life and what the meaning of it all might be. I had one young associate friend who would get nosebleeds with no warning every time he got stressed out and, unfortunately for him, Biglaw can be very stressful. Another friend aged fifteen years in his first two years of practice. He started out a good looking, fit young man, former president of his fraternity, and two years later had gained forty pounds, had salt and pepper, thinning hair and hadn't had a date in a year. I have had enough people crying in my office or on the phone to populate a soap opera. I have heard these words more times and from more colleagues than anyone in any career should hear in a lifetime: "I can't take this anymore. I have to get out of here."

I did not read a single non-law book during my first two years in Biglaw. After reviewing documents all day for months on end, doing lightning quick scanning for keywords and names, speed reading for general context and the occasional careful scrutinizing of the most relevant documents, I had lost my ability to be comfortable "reading." When I tried to read for pleasure, my eyes would wildly stream down a page, searching for and grabbing important words that were relevant to my cases – names and dates and key word topics. I began to notice my eyes frantically grabbing these words all the time. After ten hours of doc review I could not drive down the road without noticing "key" words in the road signs. I was a doc review machine constantly searching for responsive themes. And I could not read a novel.

My time became so valuable, so constrained, that I had to give up all but the most crucially important things. There was simply no time for pastimes or hobbies or anything as ubiquitously ordinary as going to a movie. For many months my life encompassed work and time for my family, with nothing else left at the end of the day.

They need little discussion, but common side effects of Biglaw are:

1. Frequent tension headaches
2. Bouts of crying and moodiness
3. Gaining/losing weight
4. No exercise (except for walking up three flights of stairs to a senior associate's office for a meeting)
5. Sore shoulders and back from sitting at your desk for long hours
6. A confused stare when someone you meet for the first time asks what your hobbies are or what books you have been reading or what you thought of the latest Academy Award winning film
7. Thinning hair
8. Teeth clenching/grinding
9. Extreme caffeine tolerance
10. Crankiness, impatience (possibly increased by the terror that if you stick around Biglaw long enough, you will watch yourself turn into the dreaded, micromanaging, über-anal, obnoxious and obsessing senior associate who is currently making your life hell and who is so incredibly cranky and impatient . . .)

11. Depression/anxiety
12. Hopelessness
13. Exhaustion
14. Insomnia
15. Marital and family problems
16. No time to date/marry/pursue a lasting relationship
17. Alcohol/drug problems
18. Burnout

E. Biglaw Benefits

So, why would you do it?

1. Money
2. Money
3. Money
4. Quickly paying down student loan debt (see 1–3 above)
5. Résumé gold
6. Work with some of the smartest lawyers in the world, who are also unique, passionate and creative on the most sophisticated, challenging and high stakes legal matters
7. Flexibility and control over work hours: part-time/flex time options, generous family leave arrangements
8. Skills/training
9. *Pro bono* opportunities

All of which we will discuss in the next chapter and throughout the rest of this book.

Chapter Five

Compensation, or, Why Would You Do This to Yourself?

There must be some reason to subject yourself to Biglaw. I have briefly alluded in the previous chapter to what you are going to be in for in terms of the travails of endless doc review, some of the health costs and some of the most compelling and widely sought benefits. Money is clearly one of the biggest reasons to go into Biglaw. For students graduating with enormous student loans, it is often difficult to see any other option. While many top law schools offer loan forgiveness programs to a small number of students who choose to work in public interest, that loan forgiveness may not be forthcoming if the graduate has a spouse who makes even a marginal amount of money. So many, if not most, law school graduates will be waking up to a hefty monthly student loan payment.

We have already talked a little bit about money as a motivation for going into Biglaw but I think we need to pause to consider what that means. And it is not just money for student loans. Biglaw is awash in money. I remember the impact on me as a summer associate when I was taken out to dinner by my firm at one of the most expensive restaurants in the city. All of us ordered our fill of twenty-dollar drinks and then went on to amass an embarrassing pile of appetizers before dinner and dessert and no one ever blinked at the cost. As a hungry grad student, that was a life-changing moment for me and it became a regular occurrence. I was a single mother at the time and Biglaw allowed me to choose where I wanted to send my daughter to school, provide for all of her needs and wants and my own and to feel secure and independent on our own. Not to have to think about money, to have more than enough to buy whatever indulgences you desire for yourself and those you love, is priceless. It is probably the main reason Biglaw is able to do what it does. With so much to put up with in the early years, with very little reward other than money, the money has to be life-changing. And it is. But be careful: even those who only plan to be in Biglaw for a couple years often find it impossible to let all of that money go.

The amount of money we make is staggering. You can Google the current standard Biglaw lockstep salary and have a good idea what associates are earning in most firms in major markets. There are countless blogs and message boards in which these issues are discussed by law students and job seekers ad nauseum. (Above the Law is my favorite.) Basically, everyone knows what the salaries are in the major markets and everyone knows what the raises will be. If, for example, in a given year in New York City Biglaw first-year associates are making $160,000, they know that the lockstep raise will bring their salary to $170,000 in the second year, $185,000 in the third year, $210,000 in the fourth year or something close. When the market changes, it changes for everyone. Everyone watches what the leading firms, like Skadden, Arps, Slate, Meagher & Flom or Cravath, Swaine & Moore, will do and then they set their salary structures accordingly. I received two raises before I even started working after graduation simply because the market had jumped up. Early on, I probably made $100,000 a year more than my friends in the government. A good friend started at my firm as a lateral hire on the same day that I started. She came from a public interest job where she had been making $35,000 a year and started in Biglaw making over $200,000. Very few people can take in stride an amount of money that increases by a factor of six overnight.

Lockstep compensation is the predominant way associates are paid in Biglaw. It is often criticized and articles show up all the time announcing the end of lockstep, but it has not happened yet. Our starting salaries are usually based strictly on our date of graduation and they increase each year in the same amount as every other associate in Biglaw, thus the raises are in lockstep. There are some anomalies, of course, and some differences in the pay structures for New York City, Washington, D.C. and the west coast, but in any case compensation remains comparable and set by the market. Those firms that fail to keep up with the market are seen as less prestigious and not playing in the same field.

A very few highly prestigious firms try to retain some privacy about their compensation structure, Wachtell Lipton Rosen & Katz and Williams & Connolly among them, but, for the most part, associates' salaries and bonuses are public information and track with what other similarly-ranked firms are doing in the same cities. Even if the information is not public, it is often leaked to law blogs, like Above the Law, so it becomes public. Many firms are trying to be more transparent, perhaps as a result of those blogs or the evident frustration of associates.

In horrible economies, like the conditions that prevailed in 2008 and 2009, firms begin to talk about doing away with lockstep and moving to a so-called merit-based pay structure, mainly in order to institute pay freezes or cancel bonuses, but in good economies, they all pretty much fall in line. Most of the firms that established merit-based pay during the recession had dropped it by 2011 or, if they had not officially made the change, it turned out that their pay structure still ended up pretty closely tracking the market. Since merit-based pay tends to be tied to billable hours (what else does one measure?), this system in a great or even decent economy would give us way too much money for most law firms to tolerate, so it tends to be considered only during down times.

In strong economic times, end of the year bonuses, clerkship bonuses and other signing bonuses are common. Everyone knows the highest bonuses with the fewest strings are always in the New York firms. But, under most circumstances, you know going in that if you are thinking in terms of a year-end bonus you will need to bill some targeted number of hours, like two thousand or two thousand two hundred, and that if you meet that benchmark, you will receive X amount of money when the year-end bonuses are distributed. There are certainly differences among firms as to how that bonus is calculated, e.g., how many hours of *pro bono* work they will accept. In some firms there is no *pro bono* maximum, while others will only count one hundred to one hundred fifty hours toward qualifying hours for the bonus. But, in any case, it is rarely very secret, which does not mean that the process is perfectly open and transparent.

Just as with starting salaries, a small handful of the highest ranked firms in New York City usually set what is considered the market rate for bonuses every year, think Cravath. So, say, one year they give bonuses of fifteen thousand dollars to all qualifying first years, twenty to all second years, thirty to all third years, forty for fourth years, forty-five for fifth years, fifty thousand dollars for sixth years. Top tier firms will then match that. In 2010 one firm surpassed Cravath but that was big news. Other firms will match only if their stated billable requirement is met, which may be higher than that required elsewhere, or match only in New York City and Washington, D.C. or impose some other requirement. Firms do tend to feel free to change their requirements for a bonus, based on the economy, without telling associates in advance. So, you will be working along, thinking you are on track for a bonus based on what was used last year as the benchmark, and bonus announcements will come out with new requirements, more billable hours required or fewer *pro bono* hours accepted.

Some firms, mine among them and lots of "lifestyle" firms, do not attempt to match the market and purport to have more merit-based bonuses, taking less definable things into account like contributions to client development or mentoring. There are instances in my firm of associates' receiving five thousand dollar bonuses or other smaller amounts in circumstances where no bonus would have been paid at another firm. This does not mean, however, that billable hours are not always key. They are. It can be frustratingly difficult to figure out whether you will receive a bonus and what it will be. I think first-year associates are rarely told in clear terms what they need to do to qualify for a bonus. They are left to figure it out. One thing that remains consistent across the board is that the firms that pay the highest bonuses, in New York City and elsewhere, are also the ones known for being the worst meat grinders in terms of billable hours.

However transparent or opaque a firm may be, bonus numbers always get around eventually. I am quite aware when I bill the same number of hours as a colleague in another firm and get a bonus that is half of hers but talking about such things is simply not done. It is not polite to talk publicly about who got a bonus and who did not or who got how much. Some associates decide it is better for their sanity not to try for a bonus, as narrowly missing the hours requirement can be excruciatingly painful.

In my first year two thousand hours was the threshold for a bonus at my first firm, I billed over two thousand four hundred hours and thus, qualified for the "bigger" bonus. In addition to my salary that year, I was given a $35,000 bonus. That was my entire year's salary before law school. There is a reason people talk of Biglaw's "golden handcuffs." The money is all too easy to enjoy and quickly becomes difficult to forgo. If you hate Biglaw and want to do something else, how easily can you leave when the high compensation has landed you with a high mortgage, luxury car payments, your child's private school bills, a taste for Prada and good champagne? You may not ever have time to enjoy the money, but it is still incredibly seductive.

If money is your sole motivation, if you want to make a ton of money and that is your goal in life, you should go into investment banking. You will have a generous salary in Biglaw, but it will not make you rich. If your main reason for entering Biglaw is to become filthy rich, you need to go somewhere else (or make partner, I assume). In Biglaw you will make a great salary, have financial independence, but it is no longer, if it ever was, the true vehicle for multi-millionairedom that it may have been reported to have been in the heyday of Biglaw storied extravagance.

And the years of your life you give up for the salary you earn will not seem worth it in the end. You will never make enough to make it all worthwhile if you truly hate it. If you add up the hours we work and factor that in, you will see that we do not make all that much for the amount of time we spend in rooms without windows doing work we can come to loathe.

Despite how large your salary may feel, you should never feel sorry for your firm for the amount of money you make. Believe me, it is doing just fine. By the time you are a fifth-year associate you could be billing in the vicinity of $455 per hour. The recent average profit a firm made for each of its attorneys is in the ballpark of $895,000. This figure includes partners, who may be billing upwards of $600 per hour, but, still, we are talking about a profit of $895,000 *per attorney*. So while it is paying between $160,000 and $250,000 and up to its associates, it is raking in money hand over fist from their billable hours, in amounts far larger than the salaries and bonuses it pays.

Flexibility

Aside from the money, there are several other incredibly valuable benefits to practicing in Biglaw. Believe it or not, one of the chief benefits is flexibility. Compared to my friends in the government and other practices, I have a lot of flexibility about when and where I work. Yes, I often work far more hours in any given week or month or year than they do, but I do not always have to be at my desk all day, every day during business hours. Face time (having to be at your office and be seen much of the day even if you have no work) is less and less important in many Biglaw firms. And Biglaw is becoming more and more tolerant of alternative work arrangements: working four days a week; leaving work early and working from home after spending the evening with the family; working "part-time" (which, in Biglaw-speak, means working from nine a.m. to four thirty p.m.); working from home some mornings; taking a three-month "sabbatical" from the firm to become a certified Bikram yoga instructor, or a sabbatical to take an economics class for graduate school or living in a different city and telecommuting altogether.

As long as you get your work done, are available when needed, and it is not one of those absolute get-the-motion-electronically-filed-by-midnight crunch times, associates are usually very free to determine when and how they get their work done. This is a huge side benefit. I do not have to miss all of my daughter's school concerts or sick days. If I want to take an afternoon to go shopping, and I can fully communicate with my team and forestall the typical senior associate micromanaging panic attacks if I should chance to be needed, I do it. If I want to meet an old friend for a three-hour lunch, I can. If I feel slightly under the weather, or need to get repairs done at home, I simply work from home for the day. You must learn how to manage your professional life wisely and you cannot abuse the flexibility. If you can learn how to take advantage of down times, how to recognize when you are not needed, you can be more flexible with your work schedule. All the usual caveats, of crunch time, all-hands-on-deck calls that take over your entire life no matter what, always apply, of course. But overall, I have found that Biglaw is much more flexible and I have more control over my work schedule than many other career paths.

You will need to develop judgment about your own schedule and when you can take some breathing time and when you cannot. There will always be partners who insist on coming by your office at any hour and finding you there so when you are working with them you will be in your office at all hours. And it will take judgment to know when the crisis times require you to be at the firm constantly. You must learn to manage your time wisely. It simply makes sense for your health, sanity and productivity that you take advantage of the slow times. In the slower weeks and months that are inevitable in the cycle of Biglaw practice, there is no expectation that you will or reason that you should sit at the office all day. When I have no possible expectation of work to do, I leave. It is insanity to stay at the office for "normal" work hours during the month or so of down time that will inevitably come. You know you will surely make it up in droves during the crazy periods, so the smartest thing young associates can do when things finally do slow down in their cases is to get out of the office. Not to worry, you will be back to billing two hundred and fifty hours a month and wondering if you will ever have a life again soon enough. Get out and relax when you can. If you are professional, do your job well and are around when people need you, no one will think you are a slacker for taking time away when you can afford to.

Training

One day after two years at a Vault top-seventy-five Biglaw firm I was trying to update my résumé. I had no idea what to write and joked to my then-fiancé that I was a master at making binders and reviewing thousands of documents but had nothing else to write about. That is not a very impressive set of skills to show after three years at an elite law school, $150,000 of student loan debt and two years in the trenches. I had to learn how to understand what I had learned, grasp what I had absorbed and feel confident in my ability to apply it in new situations and, especially, how to increase my opportunities for learning. In later chapters I will discuss in greater detail the valuable, highly marketable skills you can develop at a Biglaw firm but you will be in a much better position than I was if you understand going in all the ways Biglaw work experience can be résumé gold. Along the way, as by now you know, you will make an endless stream of binders and other assorted preparation materials and review an uncountable number of documents. But the skills you will acquire, the lawyer you will become, will last a lifetime if you understand what you are doing and consciously choose your path and manage your career. The level of professionalism demanded, the crazy focus on information mastery and preparation, stratospheric levels of perfection to which we aspire, the ability to troubleshoot and manage huge cases, coupled with the basic legal skills we develop, are what make Biglaw training and experience second to none.

One of the reasons Biglaw is said to be résumé gold is the top training you will supposedly receive. There is, however, a catch, one that should come as no surprise to you by now: yes, you will get top training, but it will not be the training you would expect or choose as a young attorney. In my second year, one former classmate of mine at the Department of Justice was flying around the country deposing witnesses and taking her own cases to trial. You know what I was doing: slogging through millions of documents and putting together unending waves of witness preparation and deposition materials. Another friend in public interest had several of her own clients, was doing the work that she chose to do and was passionate about and was in court every other day. I was scouring Westlaw for some obscure, needle in a haystack, "hail Mary" point of law for a footnote in a summary judgment motion, a footnote that may or may not have made it into the brief after devouring twenty-six hours of my life. My friends at smaller firms had real client contact, were taking on important assignments like arguing motions and drafting briefs, while I had gone ten months without even seeing the main partner with whom I worked. I was asking myself endlessly what the value was – to me – in all this endless doc review and binder making?

I was years into my Biglaw career before I realized what kind of training I was receiving in Biglaw and it was some time after that before I understood why it was valuable, why we are some of the best lawyers in the world and, yes, why we make the big bucks. The determination and discipline we must develop; the tolerance for and ability to meet stratospheric standards of perfection; the concentration and drive; the level of detail we demand of our work and the critical attention we are able to bring to bear; the characteristically exhaustive, full-throttled approach to a case; the way of thinking through and exploring to its maximum every possibility, every angle, every strategy – all of these things are enormously valuable. This approach to the practice of law, which is developed only at Biglaw firms, will, I believe, guide and shape how I practice for the rest of my career.

No other kind of legal practice has the time or money to approach a case with such intensity. You have known this since chapter one: in Biglaw, anything can be done any time, at any cost. We learn to harness the enormous resources available only to Biglaw firms and balance that with the ever-tightening demands of the client for efficiency and cost-reduction. We master the art of getting it done as perfectly as humanly possible in the smallest, most constrained amount of time, under enormous pressure in a state of exhaustion. The professionalism, judgment, dedication, discipline, commitment and communication skills that have been developed in the refiner's fire of crushing demands, extreme stress, crazy deadlines and the highest stakes cases are precious indeed. This training does not come without significant cost but it is irreplaceable and that is why Biglaw is rightly considered résumé gold.

Government and public interest lawyers do not have the time or money to spend on the kind of practice at which Biglaw excels. Public interest attorneys may only meet their clients the day they are going to represent them in court. They cannot possibly prepare the way Biglaw can. Government attorneys have similar time, money and staffing constraints. My friend in the Justice Department gets thrown into cases with no preparation or training whatsoever. She is simply told to go and conduct an evidentiary hearing in Colorado or do a round of depositions in San Diego. She must prepare her cases alone, from the ground up – everything from reviewing documents, writing briefs and even creating Tables of Authorities to arguing motions and handling every aspect of a full trial. In such positions, attorneys do not have thirty first-year associates on call to review a million documents or develop the record for a case, nor reliable paralegals to assist with minor filings and record management. They do everything alone.

And they are not as likely, in my opinion, to develop the drive, the competitive spirit or, perhaps, the dread of defeat that characterize Biglaw attorneys. They are the government; if they lose, they will just move on to the next project. Biglaw attorneys offer discipline, thorough exhaustion of all possibilities in pursuit of the best outcome, thinking strategically and creatively with the full support of a large firm behind your plans, immense resources and brilliant colleagues from which to draw, a competitive drive that is fueled by billion-dollar corporations and interests, highly-honed focus, strength under the pressure of high stakes cases and impossible deadlines, highly-developed efficiency and all the advantages of working in fully-staffed teams. Through these advantages Biglaw attorneys are able to deliver the very best quality work product. You may not take a deposition until your fourth year of practice in Biglaw, but when you do, you will have prepared documents, outlines, procedural rules and summaries for so many that you will have vastly more preparation to do so than many a government attorney who has had to stumble his way through dozens.

There is no advocate more zealous than a Biglaw attorney. No one else has the time, money, pressure and drive to exhaust every option, chase down every possibility and fight every battle. I worked on an antitrust/patent infringement case as a junior associate in which I learned the crushing resources available to Biglaw. We had dozens of young attorneys in three U.S. offices in addition to a full complement of senior associates and a handful of partners. Each one of us focused on one specific issue almost full-time. We did more work simply in anticipation of what we might be faced with than I could have imagined before I did it. Once, we were expecting to receive a summary judgment motion and spent a month preparing for it. The judge's rules would limit our response to the length of the other side's motion. The page limit for each motion was thirty pages, but a party could file as many individual summary judgment motions dealing with specific individual issues as it wanted. The partners expected a massive onslaught and so we prepared a three-hundred-page monster, with possible responses to every possible claim we could dream they might conceivably make. It turned out that the other side filed a single, twenty-page motion. That rush, that frantic preparation, that glorious, three-hundred-page work product and all those hours of sustained effort, all were forgotten as we honed all that preparation into a single, twenty-page bullet. Only Biglaw can prepare and anticipate to such a maniacal degree. It may seem crazy, but it is the best protection money can buy.

The contrast of the experience of the government attorney friend to whom I have been referring and my own experience as a young associate is a perfect example of what I am trying to make clear to you here. In my first years, I must have prepared for a dozen depositions. This meant reviewing key docs of the witness and any docs with her name on them, determining what to include in the binder of materials to be used at the deposition, drafting deposition outlines and document summaries for each witness. I would occasionally attend the deposition, or at least the prep of the witness. I took notes and submitted summaries of key issues that came up. I went back after the fact and read through the transcripts, looking for information to use later in the case. But I never took a deposition. Not one. Not for years. But when I finally did, I knew all about them and how to prepare. I had gone through the motions to help others prepare dozens of times. I had prepared witness binders hundreds of times.

My friend at the government, however, was, as we have discussed, doing depositions her first week on the job. This sounded great and I was envious. It is not as if that path does not have its advantages. Who wouldn't rather jump in to the exciting stuff, the actual practice of law as we think of it, instead of slaving over witness binders for two years, obsessing about highlighter colors and slip sheets and metadata information? (Don't worry; we will talk about the inclusion or exclusion of metadata information in chapter nine.) And there are definite plusses in working in government. But in talking with her, I began to understand the down sides. No one learns well when off balance. She was repeatedly thrown into new situations with no help, no training and no preparation. She was not going in with a team of paralegals helping her get materials ready. In fact she often bemoaned her lack of support and her inability to depend on paralegals for anything. There were no legions preparing outlines and witness binders and analyzing key documents for her and thinking up new issues or possible lines of questions. She had no idea how a deposition was run, what objections to make, how to respond to the issues that came up since she had never taken a deposition, read a transcript of one or even sat in on one.

Constantly learning on the fly, she had regular nightmares of making massive mistakes. Once, she was sent with an hour's notice to handle an evidentiary hearing. Everything seemed to go well. It is only after she returned to her office that her boss asked her why she had not actually moved to enter into evidence *any* of the government's exhibits. She had no idea she was responsible procedurally for moving all evidence into the record. She still has nightmares about getting to trial only to discover that she missed some trivial procedural step she knew nothing about and now has blown the case. She tells me that lateral hires who come into her office from Biglaw are much more prepared than she was. They know how to approach a case, how to prepare, how to get the information that is needed. They have done it hundreds of times, while she has been thrown in to the practice of law without a net and has had to learn everything in a trial by fire, which has often meant education by error. And at the end of the day, litigation is litigation, which means she was regularly spending Biglaw hours at her government job, but getting $100K less and that is not a fun realization.

Which way is better? I have no way of knowing. I would love to spend my time on things that are actually relevant to my case, avoiding stupid eye-gouging exercises in futility and endless tedious tasks, and I remain envious of the experience she is getting. After three years I had not done a single deposition, and my friend had run trials. Huge. And I have no argument with any claim that, on balance, the government is a better career choice, with the opportunity to throw yourself immediately into a practice that is important, that makes a difference in the world and gives you unbelievable boots on the ground experience. I am not trying to convince anyone to choose Biglaw as a career. What I am trying to do is to help you understand Biglaw and to get the most out of it if you find yourself toiling in its depths.

Much of what you learn in Biglaw you will learn through osmosis, by doing it endlessly every day. There are ways to get other kinds of training in Biglaw, but they can be difficult to find. If the core purpose of Biglaw were to train the best attorneys in the world, it would excel at training beyond all imagination. It would throw all of its focus, energy and might into achieving that end and it would be stunning at training. Unfortunately, that is not the purpose of Biglaw. The purpose of Biglaw is to provide its clients with the best legal representation that is humanly achievable. So to get the great training, it will be up to you to build your practice proactively by seeking out the practice groups that interest you, by making sure you work for different partners, by expanding your horizons as much as you can. As you go on doing things you think you have already mastered you are building your professionalism and confidence and gaining the skills, knowledge and expertise you will need to take on more responsibility with fewer consequences to clients. Three years of Biglaw practice on a résumé tells an employer at least two things immediately: you are very smart and went to the best schools and performed well; and you developed at least some of the attributes I describe in this book. You cannot be at a Biglaw firm for three years and not come away with many of these skills and all of your potential employers will know it.

Pro Bono

The other source of training and soul-satisfying compensation to which we have alluded is the pursuit of the elusive grail of meaningful and varied *pro bono* work within the confines of Biglaw. I have been consciously propagandizing my daughter since I was in law school. Since she was three-years-old I have told her repeatedly that lawyers fight injustice and help the poor. She used to think I was some kind of superhero with a hidden cape when I went to work. While most of my time is actually spent representing the wealthiest corporations fighting for still larger slices of the money pie, *pro bono* work is my chance to keep a little part of the reason I originally went to law school alive: to fight injustice and help the poor. It also provides superb opportunities for expanding your skills and experience as a lawyer. Choose wisely and you can save your soul, your sanity and at the same time greatly expand your skill set.

Most Biglaw firms strongly encourage their associates to take on *pro bono* cases and allow them to treat some or all of the *pro bono* hours as billable hours for the purposes of bonuses and evaluations. As we have said, some firms set a limit on how many *pro bono* hours will be counted towards a bonus – usually around one hundred fifty – but the better firms have no limit. Perhaps their motives are not completely angelic. They enjoy, no doubt, the lucrative tax write offs available for all *pro bono* expenses. And ranking systems like Vault and AmLaw take *pro bono* hours strongly into account in their law firm rankings. But, whatever the reasons may be, Biglaw offers more freedom and support to its associates for *pro bono* opportunities than is offered anywhere else and they often have long-standing, deep relationships with every major public interest foundation out there. You can tell your public service coordinator what kinds of things you are interested in doing and he will pick up the phone and get it for you. Of course, if you are positive you are only interested in public service and your student loans are not too crippling, you should probably go immediately into a public interest job and pursue your ideals full-time. But I am convinced that Biglaw offers the best opportunities for *pro bono* work. Some of the best assignments I have had in Biglaw have been *pro bono*.

Keep in mind there are always at least two compelling reasons to do *pro bono* work: one, you are passionate about a certain cause and want to dedicate a chunk of your highly paid time to remembering you have a soul in Biglaw and, two, you want to develop real skills that you will come nowhere close to developing to the same degree as a junior Biglaw associate.

Because Biglaw is awash in money, it has incredible resources at your disposal when you take on a *pro bono* case. I once represented a refugee seeking asylum in the United States. Not only did the firm support me in spending over 170 hours of my time, which amounted to a sacrifice of more than $45,000 in billable hours, but the firm paid thousands of dollars to get the necessary psychological and medical evaluations, transportation costs, etc. All of the firm's vast resources were at my disposal: paralegal and administrative support in compiling evidence and preparing evidence to submit, the help of firm librarians in tracking down articles for country conditions to submit with our application. I do not see smaller firms or the government expending this kind of time and money for *pro bono*. And if you actually work in public interest, you may not have the opportunity to branch out and pursue other areas of interest you might want to focus on. In fact, your time may be so limited, because of the sheer number of clients who need help, that you may not be able to do *pro bono* work at all.

Because of the time and resources available to me, I was able to prepare the best case this asylum-seeker could have had. And we were able to take care of her in ways both large and small. Each time she missed her train because we had to sit at the government asylum office the firm paid for a sedan to drive her home to the homeless shelter at which she was staying. No one thought twice about it. She was our client and no difference was made between her case and those of the biggest corporations in the world, whose retainers filled our coffers. She received the same consideration and focus that a multi-billion dollar corporation would have expected as its due. And in the end we had the satisfaction of seeing a good person with a hard lot in life successful in her quest for asylum, settled in Maryland, working on her GED and raising her child. You cannot put a price on that.

Being in Biglaw also allows me the freedom to decide what kinds of projects I am passionate about and I often have a wide variety of choice among any number of interesting and cutting edge *pro bono* cases. My firm, as do many others, has full-time *pro bono* attorneys who coordinate *pro bono* opportunities and have connections in all of the major non-profit organizations. I can choose any kinds of cases I want: an arts foundation, a private school, petty criminal defendants, death row inmates, a double murder trial, a local indie rock band just starting out, an orphaned child needing a guardian *ad litem* to represent his interests in court, a homeless shelter, a New York documentary filmmaker, Holocaust survivors petitioning the German government for remuneration, the Humane Society, a local church organization or anything I find that I believe in. There are endless numbers of worthy people who need legal services beyond the reach of their economic circumstances. My firm will allow me to choose my clients, spend my valuable billable time in their defense and will provide endless resources and assistance. The rich satisfactions inherent in that simple fact can make up for a good deal of doc review restlessness.

Another great thing about *pro bono* work is that it allows very junior attorneys opportunities to take on and manage their own cases, stand up in court, argue at trial, take depositions, write briefs and do any number of things that they will not come anywhere near doing in their billable cases for a very long time. I am in charge of my *pro bono* cases. Although I am supervised by a partner, I manage the case, determine the strategy and take on the responsibilities. This is huge for a Biglaw associate, who may not argue a motion at trial for eight years or more. And it is vital if you want to develop the skills you will be expected to have. This is what I mean about consciously managing your career. Around years three to five, partners will start asking you why you have never taken a deposition. You may not have had any chance in the world on your regular billable cases. It is often the case that they are so heavily staffed that, while you may be asked to sit in on a deposition occasionally, you have never actually had that responsibility yourself. And yet, you will still be expected to have found a way to develop the skill. Partners will expect a positive response to the question as to whether you have taken a deposition, argued at trial, etc., before they will allow you to do that on their cases. So it is a vicious cycle. You cannot do it because you have never done it and no one is going to let you do it until you have.

This is where *pro bono* comes in. In Biglaw there will be tremendous variety available to you in the *pro bono* cases you take on. If you know you need to argue a motion in court, choose a case that ignites your passion, feeds your soul – and is headed for litigation. If you know you need to handle a deposition, look for a class action, you will handle dozens. Yes, you would get that experience earlier on in your career as a trial attorney for the government, or in a smaller firm or public interest career. But if you decide that the path of Biglaw is the one for you, for the sky-high salaries or whatever reason you have come to, *pro bono* cases offer you incredible opportunities to choose the clients and causes you want to represent and have the full backing, abundant resources and support of a Biglaw firm behind you.

This may be for some the greatest argument for a life in Biglaw and everyone should take full advantage of it. Do not try to wait until you are not busy on your billable cases at the firm, those days are too unpredictable. I suggest that you decide what it is that you want: trial experience, appellate brief-writing skills or helping a specific cause about which you are passionate and then go after it. Partners are more and more coming to accept that if you have a *pro bono* case it has the same priority for your time as their case. And if they do not accept that, the managing partners of the firm will and you will certainly find support. There are always ways to juggle your workload and this is one of the most important ways a Biglaw associate can feel human and gain real skills early on.

We have talked in this chapter about the benefits and compensations of Biglaw, the money, the flexibility, the training, the opportunities for *pro bono* work. But as we have stressed throughout, the key to surviving Biglaw is knowing why you want to work in Biglaw. It is not likely that you will have come to Biglaw because of a passion for making binders. Take the time to figure out what is important to you in your life and your career and go after it. Be proactive about your career from the very start. By now you should clearly understand that Biglaw is engineered to make full use of you, and it will, so you should feel free to use it.

A sane person might wonder – if my description of Biglaw is accurate and it is, to the extent of my information, knowledge and belief – why anyone would put up with it. Young associates are easily cowed, anxious, wondering if they are the only ones in the world to screw up. They are drawn forward on their narrow path by glimpses of great work here and there and the memory of their on-campus interviews, in which the partners assured them that, of course, they would work hard, but they would be given great opportunities to develop and grow, with real responsibility and that they had real chances to make partner. Unfortunately, in practice, these opportunities are often few and far between, unless you can figure out how to make them happen and even then you will still be putting in your time in doc review hell. But they have you in the door, you are cashing the big paychecks, holding on with both fists to the dimming hope that the next assignment will really be the one in which you can do something substantive and show your brilliance.

Someone should tell the poor hapless law students the entire cold truth so they can make good decisions. This is why I am writing this book. There is a need for candor. Partners in on-campus interviews talk up the great opportunities at their firm for mentoring, training, increased responsibilities, professional development, exciting *pro bono* and "real" substantive work. Associates brought in to help out at the interviews vigorously agree. Of course, you are not getting the whole picture. Maybe the associates chosen to participate in interviews talk in half-truths about their firms because they do not want to believe the truth themselves. Who would want to expose to anyone – especially to oneself when one is in the thick of it – the central fraud, the miserable truth: that Biglaw is a meat grinder for most young associates. It is not pleasant for me to write these words but, while no one can go back in time and remove pain, one can learn to avoid it and one can send up a flare for those who may be following into the dark. In the pages ahead we will talk about the survival skills I have accumulated and some nuts and bolts about the work ahead.

Chapter Six

Judgment, Prudence, Precision, Diligence, or, Professionalism and the Billable Hour (The Devil You Don't Know)

So now you have a little picture of what Biglaw is like – not the fantasy version of the on-campus interview, but what it is really like for junior associates, most of the time. The rest of this book is devoted to showing you how to get through it, and even, I hope, get something valuable out of it. A lot of my advice is very specific, but it is not unimportant: the devil is, indeed, in the details. But first I want to introduce some overarching principles that will, if you allow them to guide all of your work in Biglaw, see you through. These qualities are implicit in much of what we have been talking about so far but there is a unifying principle here that perhaps bears some elaboration.

When I was in law school, former Attorney General, Janet Reno, came to talk to the students. She shared a story that I carry with me, one that has had a role in shaping my professional and personal life. The truth and wisdom of it has deepened for me over the years. She talked about building a family home with her mother in Florida when she was young. I may not remember all of the details or have the story exactly right, but here is the point that stayed with me. She and her mother built their house, with complete care and diligence, together. They knew it was built as it should be, down to each brick and each nail. It was strong, and they knew it would not fail, because they had done it themselves and they had neither cut corners nor skimped in any way. They had built their house right. Then came a powerful hurricane that shook Florida and was destroying everything in its path. While the young Ms. Reno cowered in terror inside the home she and her mother had so painstakingly constructed, she looked at her mother and found her serene throughout the horrendous storm. Her mother knew that she had built her home to withstand hurricane force and she had no fear.

Ms. Reno then talked about her experiences as a young lawyer. About the importance of taking ownership and pride in every element of her work, about spending her time, diligence, intellect and effort on a case – about building her cases and her professional life with the meticulous attention of the finest and most accomplished craftsperson. Even when she did not win or things did not go her way and the inevitable problems arose, she had no need to fear. She encouraged us all to build our lives so that we would have no need for fear when the hurricanes of legal practice came. Today, I understand much more than I could when I first heard her speak what Ms. Reno meant. There is a deep sense of pride and security that comes from diligence, care and a thorough exhaustion of effort. If you develop that in Biglaw, if you build your cases, your career and your life in this way, you will not win every case, but you will develop a serenity and a stability that will define your career and keep anxieties and fears at bay. So, build it right.

If you are going to spend your time in Biglaw, you should make the most of it, and the way to do that is to embrace Biglaw's professionalism from the moment you walk in the door. Being an attorney in Biglaw is a huge responsibility and you need to develop the professionalism that is expected of you. You must guard well the confidences of your clients and never treat lightly their interests or concerns. Guard your own secrets as well. Don't blab to other associates on your floor about how you hate working for Partner X and how loony he is. Don't share in half jest that on some drunken midnight in the office you almost deleted two entire compilations of "hot" documents from the server. You must be aware of where you are and what you are saying at all times. Never chat about your clients in an elevator or a crowded café or on the Acela train from D.C. to New York. Never leave confidential documents lying around face up on a desk. These things sound basic and self-evident but you would be surprised how often such obvious and elementary rules are broken, just this once, or just for a moment. Becoming a conscientious attorney is a way of life. We *practice* law. It is something we *do* and it shapes who we become. It takes constant practice to create the habits that will protect our work and our clients' interests in the midst of the chaos that so frequently descends on our working lives. Our habits, professionalism, prudence, careful deliberation, attention to detail, thorough and exhaustive preparation – the way we practice – becomes so second nature that it changes who we are and how we behave both inside and outside of the practice of law. For all the bad lawyer jokes (and bad lawyers) in the world, at the end of the day, a phalanx of lawyers is the only thing standing between the crushing oppression and force of the powerful and the rights, interests and lives of the people who call on our expertise. You must treat that as a sacred trust. Being an attorney is a burden and a responsibility.

If you take nothing else from Biglaw, you should develop the judgment, precision and prudence of a Biglaw lawyer. You must exercise good judgment in everything you do. Of course you will not always be right, you will not always succeed in your endeavors, but the right starting place is to set the bar high and expect the best from yourself at all times. You cannot wait until your big moment, when you finally have an important and exciting role to play, to pull everything together and put all of your efforts into your work product. You must do that from day one, on every single, silly assignment you are given. From steeling yourself to read the six hundredth document of the day with a clear focus, to realizing when not to send that satisfying "zinger" email to someone on your team who has irritated you. From writing up your billing each day to deciding when to take on a *pro bono* case that will mean more work but give you the chance to learn valuable skills. Whether you decide to approach the senior associate on your case for the fifth time that day with yet another seemingly useless question or press on and perhaps make a monumental mistake for which you will be seriously sorry.

The good news is that a focus on professionalism actually helps you to develop many of the particular – and even mechanical – skills you need to do your job well. As you progress through the ranks, you will develop precision in honing and focusing your efforts. You will notice every typo; you will find mistakes in a draft that has already been proofed by three junior associates. You will learn to anticipate the questions senior associates will ask upon reading your draft and you will address those in the first round before you submit your assignment. You will realize they will want more detail here or a fuller explanation there, in order to create perfect clarity for the reader. You will automatically include more cites for support, or add summarizing sentences to each new paragraph. Your first draft will be worlds better than in your junior years for this reason, and yet, you will understand that there will always be edits.

Prudence comes from successfully learning to balance the many demands of Biglaw we have already discussed: perfection, timeliness and cost efficiency. You know that everything you do should be as perfect as you can possibly make it, within the demands of its deadline and at a reasonable cost. But sometimes cost will be the most important factor in your case, due to client demands or other factors, and you will shift your work strategy to accomplish the task in a reasonable way at a lesser cost. Sometimes the immovable deadline will rule your work. It must be done by five p.m. today and that means it must be done – by whatever means necessary – so other factors will take a back seat. The quality, professional polish and dead-on accuracy of the work will suffer, but it will be done – and done with all reasonable efforts to achieve a high quality work product. Some projects require utter perfection and then that will be your focus, regardless of the time and cost. You need to be able to recognize the demands of your project, prioritize and balance the various requirements, and do the best job you can possibly do, with the priorities of the particular circumstance firmly in mind and directing your efforts.

We talked a little bit in chapter three about making good use of good work that has been done before, not reinventing the wheel every time you are given an assignment that is new to you. Part of doing your best work, part of your professionalism as an attorney, is knowing when and how to incorporate the work of others efficiently. We have talked a lot throughout this book about the importance of the junior associate as a processor of information. Your value increases as your ability to isolate the required information from the universes of information available increases. For any assignment, whether looking for a case or finding documents that support a given proposition or drafting a memo, you will learn to go first for the low-hanging fruit. It is often the best way to balance the competing demands of perfection and speed. Never eschew the easiest, most direct route to gathering information.

If you receive, say, an assignment to "find all financial documents" and you begin to construct complicated searches to hunt them down in a million-document database, chances are you will be wasting tremendous amounts of valuable time. No matter how sophisticated and impressive your thinking may be, there are probably easier ways of getting to some core documents right away. If there have been discovery documents that you have already prepared that list a handful of financial documents, check there first. Those are documents that you can identify immediately and they may well be the most important. Interrogatory responses, responses to requests for admissions and responses to requests for production of documents often identify at least a start at what you have been sent to find. Perhaps there is a recent white paper to the client with examples of key documents. Use that information to help you formulate better searches. Your ability to use what has already been done to provide an immediate response while you continue to process wider searches in the background will serve the case better. This is good judgment. Diligence will keep you working and widening your searches but your good judgment will guide you to an earlier result. Low hanging fruit allows an associate to be productive right away (thus keeping the senior associate at bay), while hunting down the harder to find stuff that takes time.

Think about this in the context of witness preparation. If you get an assignment relative to a new witness to prepare, why would you not immediately employ an earlier witness binder to look for key documents that also relate to the new witness – especially documents actually used in a deposition or interview? Junior associates very often do things the hardest, most inefficient way, sometimes through panic and sometimes through inexperience and sometimes through a misguided effort to demonstrate abilities they do not really have yet. It is important to learn how to use what is already out there and available and avoid duplication of effort.

For legal research, dig out that memo written by another associate a year ago which focused on the issue and grab those cases, make sure they are up to date and go from there. Or start with a treatise, which will list the key cases for whatever topic you are researching. The object is precision: always to get to the right information as quickly as possible. Often, a partner will give you an assignment simply as, "I need to find documents that show that the company engaged in tax fraud using off shore shell companies from 2009–2011," with no guidance on the best way to find those documents. Beginning a search from scratch with "tax or taxes" and sorting chronologically will not be the best use of your time. Have the staff attorneys coded for tax fraud issues in the document review database (likely, if it is key) so you can quickly isolate those documents? Were documents cited in any pleadings or discovery responses? Was there a whistleblower who described the nature of his evidence in a complaint? Did a witness from that company mention or describe types of documents that addressed this issue and were produced to help you hunt them down in the vast universe? All of these possibilities should be considered before you move forward on the assignment. In a big case you will be gathering the same kind of information over and over: a zillion witness interviews, presentations/mock trial exercises for the client, discovery and summary judgment motions, deposition and trial exhibits, expert reports, etc. Low hanging fruit will get you half the way there almost every time and help you demonstrate that you are worth every penny of your billable rate.

In the normal course of your work, you will always seek to achieve the perfect balance among the competing demands of cost, efficiency and the quest for perfection. Here is a better way to think of it: you should strive for excellence, not perfection. You could spend your life making absolutely certain your 800,000 documents were coded with total accuracy and consistency, and go back multiple times to re-review in order to ensure everything was double and triple checked, with all relevant issues flagged in each document and with a nice little summary in the Attorney Comments field of the review platform. But that would cost the client an obscene number of billable hours for wasted and duplicative work far beyond the point of diminishing returns. And there would still be a mistake in it somewhere. You can make a pristine privilege log that costs a client $100,000 (yes, I have seen $100,000 priv logs), but not every client is going to be willing to pay for that level of perfection. You must always strive to get the best job done in the most efficient, cost-effective and timely manner and your efforts to succeed at this balance in everything you do will build judgment and prudence.

Lawyers are not smarter than everyone else in the world, but we are trained to be precise and exacting in our thinking. Exercising and building the judgment, prudence and diligence of a Biglaw associate comes through learning how to thoroughly and carefully exhaust all possibilities in your daily practice. You must apply steely determination to press on hour after hour and still do your best work. You must consider all the angles and critically analyze your work. These are all professional attributes you must develop if you want to survive Biglaw and leave with anything of lasting value. You will have the chance to develop these qualities every single day, through every assignment you complete, every email you write and everything you contribute to your team. Every day you must struggle to balance between the demand to get it done perfectly and the other competing demand to get it done now. You will constantly seek to balance how to give your client the best possible work product, with how to get it done in a reasonable amount of time and for a reasonable cost. You will fight to keep your intellect engaged through boredom and exhaustion. There are no easy answers and each partner or senior associate for whom you work will have different priorities. But if you develop these skills, you will succeed and you will be honoring the sacred trust of your profession.

The Billable Hour

Although its faults are much debated and its demise often heralded, until a sea change occurs in Biglaw, your time as a young associate will be broken down into tiny segments in order to bill the client for your legal work. Every five or six minutes or so (depending on your firm or client demands) that you spend for a client will need to be tracked and entered into your firm's timekeeping and billing system. You will begin to think, live and breathe in small six-minute chunks, dividing everything you do into billable or non-billable time. If you run to the bathroom and stop by your friend's office to hear about a movie he just saw, that is twelve minutes of non-billable time. If you are asked to help a partner edit an article she plans to publish, that is usually non-billable time. If you have to attend a firm-wide associates meeting or training, that is non-billable. If you help out on a firm committee or agree to assist in on-campus interviews, this, too, while a valuable contribution to the firm, is non-billable. New associate integration, client development efforts, practice group meetings. All non-billable. If you zone out in a doc review stupor: non-billable. If you email friends, update your Facebook profile or stop working to browse for new shoes online: non-billable. You can bill for the amount of time you are actively engaged in work for your client. If you thought about strategies for a deposition outline on the way home in the car, that is billable. But do not let yourself be seduced into the lazy and unethical practice of making up time, stretching time or exorbitantly rounding up.

All firms have their differences, of course, but most Biglaw firms expect, suggest or require their associates to bill somewhere between 1,850 and 2,000 hours a year in order to be in minimally good standing and perhaps to qualify for a bonus or salary increases. That is over thirty-eight hours a week, fifty-two weeks out of the year. As you can see from the discussion above, you will be in the office many, many more hours than you are actually able to bill. It is all but impossible to bill eight to ten straight hours every day, unless you are on some kind of automated doc review and you are a machine. Even if you determine to get into the office before most of the firm, work through lunch every day, and avoid chatting or internet surfing, it is often hard to bill your time efficiently. You will find that many of your assignments come in waves. You submit an assignment and spend the rest of the afternoon with nothing to do, waiting for the senior attorney to review it and get back to you with follow up questions or further direction. You sit and wait, and wait. Unless you have another matter to which you can turn your attention, there is nothing billable about this time. Then, after sitting for much of the afternoon, you are heading out the door when the phone rings and the senior associate wants to know if you have time to discuss your work. It is very common to be kept waiting for feedback for hours and days and then get slammed with several urgent fire drills all at once. It is just the way it is – you almost never have a smooth, continuous stream of assignments. It is feast or famine, crazy rush or long wait.

Unless you are reading this book out of order you already know why. Many partners do not have time to look at your work during normal business hours. They are busy rushing around dealing with clients and going to meetings, so they finally sit down and read through your work at six in the morning, a week after they insisted it was urgently needed. And you also know that when they do finally get around to the work they made you jump through hoops to produce they will then need eighty other concerns addressed immediately. Your workload is never consistent and you are always seesawing between the struggle to manage a crushing amount of work under inhuman deadline pressure, or dead silence with nothing to do. I will talk more about time management in the next chapters but it is first of all essential to learn how to bill your time.

Like so many things in Biglaw, the process of entering your time scales unbelievable heights of anal absurdity, but making it a habit to bill your time in a professional, clean and accurate way will help you avoid pitfalls and angry partners for years to come. First, as with everything else you do in Biglaw, you must spend the time to do it right, meaning consistently and with painstaking accuracy and insight. Yes, it is stupid, but you simply cannot turn in your time for three months of ten- to twelve-hour days with only this same one-line descriptor: doc review. That may very well be precisely what you have done, but that is not what the client (or billing partner, who is, after all, your direct client) wants to see. Despite your glazed eyes and aching head at the end of the day, as ready as you are to sell your soul to see your cat again, you have to take the time to do a professional job of entering your time.

The work you have done needs to be described in complete sentences, usually starting with a verb in the present tense, and you should separate each assignment for that client with a semi-colon:

- Analyze email and hardcopy documents of J. Doe regarding employment discrimination claims; supervise staff attorney review for finalization of production number N +1; strategic discussion with Partner X regarding case status and priorities.

The way you describe your time needs to show movement over time and demonstrate progress in a case. In a perfect world it would create a kind of narrative for the client, one that makes the client happy that you are working on his or her case; one that makes the client content to pay the billable rate that is being charged for your time. Each day you should show some kind of progression, goal or purpose to your work that is visible over a week or a month.

- Examine hardcopy documents regarding sales and promotional practices of drug X for deposition of J. Doe.

Then throughout the week:

- Analyze and compile documents for deposition; draft deposition outline.

Then later:

- Finalize documents and supporting materials for deposition exhibits and preparation materials.

Then:

- Attend and assist in witness deposition of X.

It does not matter that your work will, in reality, mostly be reviewing documents, researching case law and the like. You need to make your time tell a more meaningful story. In the process you will be reminding yourself what your work means. You need to understand that the billing partner may have to defend what you have written to an angry client who does not want to pay a bill for eighty hours for a two-page memo. I am not saying to make up your time entries out of whole cloth! But you must characterize your work in a way that reflects the professional value you have provided as a Biglaw associate. You are not a staff or contract attorney and your work descriptions need to show that. It will not hurt your commitment to your work or the case at hand to think a bit more deeply about what your work and your contribution to the larger work really means. It takes a little more time but it simply cannot be done sloppily or long after the fact. In Biglaw everything you do – everything – must be done carefully, precisely and with good judgment. Your entries need to be crafted in a way that will not put the partner on the defensive with the client and will reflect your significant, professional contributions to the case. That is another reason why senior associates cannot do standard, first-line doc review and it will fall to you to make clear the value you are adding. A client will go through the roof if it is billed $450 an hour for a review that would have cost $250 an hour with a more junior associate. Your time entries must show the value that you, as an associate at a prestigious Biglaw firm, have added. Take pride in your work, however slogging, and make it show in the time entries you submit.

This story falls into the category of "when in doubt: ask." A friend once worked on an estate that came to a small litigation firm that rarely handled them. The case was thrown to the firm somewhat casually by the executor, himself a high-powered attorney who did not realize how much work, or money, would be involved. The man who died had been a solo practitioner with a busy office. The administrative staff of the office had been let go immediately so it fell to my friend to wind up his office. The closest code her law firm had in their billing system was "office business," which, of course, is normally non-billable time. She billed that code for all the time it took to dismantle the office and the time was considerable. The client had apoplexy and my friend had to go before him to defend her time. The executor truly believed that her firm had been billing the estate for work being done to keep the little firm afloat and nothing could have been further from the truth. She made a boneheaded mistake in coding her time and it almost cost her firm a client.

You must develop an understanding of the bigger picture of the world around you. You will certainly work at times for mega-corporations where no one cares what you write on your billing entries as long as it does not describe a felony in action. Some partners I have worked with have never mentioned time entries, while others focus on them each month with a microscope. But many clients these days are hypersensitive about what they are paying for and are hoping to point to some poorly written entry and piously refuse to pay for such a waste of time and talent. For example, some clients hate seeing massive team meetings on a bill. Who enjoys seeing eight partners, sixteen associates and three paralegals all billing for the same forty-five minutes? All they see are the billable rates of each attorney racking up by the second. I almost never write: team meeting with X, Y, Z (listing all attorneys in attendance). A $7,000 bill for a meeting with twenty lawyers in one room to discuss case deadlines is a recipe for a pissed-off client. I will instead list the main attorney or two, and I characterize it as a strategic or tactical discussion, rather than a "meeting."

You want to give exactly enough information to make clear what your contribution has been and no more; you do not want to include every mundane detail. Your entries should be concise and accurate, but general enough not to describe actual legal strategy or give away more than you should about case decisions. And, as we have discussed, you need to be eternally vigilant as to word choice. Those twelve straight hours a day for three months straight you have put in on doc review? No one wants to see that many entries of "doc review" with nothing more, any more than you wanted to do just that and nothing more for those long three months. I am not being cynical, and, again, I am not advising you to write anything untrue. The reverse is really the case. If you are doing your job well, you are contributing an enormous amount to the work of the firm. But it is easy, and tempting, to fall into sloppy habits in describing your hours in uninformative ways, both because entering your time is intrinsically boring and because trying to be more particular in your wording can feel trivial or even deceptive. It is not. We are talking about communicating the value of your work and that is worth doing. It serves the firm in billing the client, it serves you in getting the firm to recognize and reward your work and it can help you maintain your focus and motivation in the midst of repetitive assignments. And it serves the main objective of this book: to keep you out of trouble.

Here is a list of helpful verbs I use every single day. Memorize them, write them on your hand, say them in your sleep, whatever you need to do so that you use them. Some of them have been passed down to me by senior associates over the years, as if from on High and they will make your life easier from the beginning. They are tried and true action verbs, and if you use them, you will not have to deal with angry partners wondering what kind of idiot you are.

- Examine
- Analyze
- Compile
- Draft
- Edit
- Supervise
- Manage
- Oversee
- Assemble (exhibits for witness interview of . . .)
- Address and resolve (technical issues in document review platform with vendor)
- Track (status of ongoing review projects or discovery work streams)
- Strategic discussion
- Tactical discussion
- Assist (with the deposition/interview/preparation of . . .)
- Prepare
- Provide (feedback for staff attorneys for quality control)
- Finalize
- Build (list of key employees)
- Create (case chronology timeline; tracking spreadsheet of ongoing work flow and research assignments, etc.)

- Summarize
- Submit
- Assess (litigation strategy for client presentation)
- File (motion to dismiss . . .)
- Participate (in client conference)
- Update
- Confer

Notice two verbs that I did not include in the list: Review and Code. I *never* use these words. Biglaw associates do not review and code documents. That is an appropriate entry for a staff or contract attorney, but you are presumed by clients to bring more to the table – your analytic ability, your attention and focus, your impressive intellectual contribution and legal expertise. It is all too easy to fall into days and days of "doc review" descriptions. And I never simply say "documents." Whose documents are they? What are they about? Are they electronic documents from a hard drive? Email documents? Scanned hard copy images? What issue or subject are they generally addressing? Fill in these details when you can.

It can feel like a complete waste of time, another futile exercise in overkill, but this is Biglaw and it is expected. As we have discussed, there are reasons for all of this and your life will be easier if you master these things right up front. Don't fight it – it will just make you miserable. The more exact and descriptive you can learn to be in everything you do, the more the billing partner will leave you alone. Many partners and senior associates often seem geared solely to pick you apart. If they have reason to be unhappy with your performance, they may even go fishing for other complaints and dig deeper into your work habits and professionalism. Do not leave yourself unnecessarily vulnerable to attack and further criticism. Make your entries clean, concise and descriptive of the full value you are bringing to the table and it will be one less thing they can pick apart.

It bears repeating: it is always essential to make your description of your billable time reflect the value and expertise you add. There will be times when you will have to do more menial tasks than your billing rate would support. Maybe you are shorthanded that day and something needs to get done. Maybe the paralegal is out sick and no other help can be found. You will certainly one day or another find yourself inserting indexes into twenty-nine witness preparation binders before they can be shipped out on a day when they must go out. You will sit in a room piled high with exhibits and thumb through the pages, one by one, to ensure that the blue slip-sheets have been inserted everywhere they belong in between sections and the green slip-sheets have been inserted between documents and their attachments. This might be a good place to use that "finalize" verb. You cannot simply make up your time entries but in all of your entries – in fact, in *all* that you do in Biglaw – ask yourself: does this raise *any* red flags (for anyone looking at my work from the outside)? If so, rethink it and redo it. Make it a habit to characterize your work in a way that reflects your professional contribution – or at least does not cause the client to go through the roof. You may feel that all you are doing is something entirely mechanical but the truth is that, if you are truly engaged in the kind of practice we have been talking about, your eye on that stack of binders *does* add value. There is always the possibility that there could be something amiss that no one else has caught. Your being there increases exponentially the likelihood that it could be detected and corrected.

A related issue is how much time to bill. You should never inflate your time. Partners and senior associates understand in general the amount of time required to accomplish a given task, although they often forget that junior associates need much more time than their superiors tend to expect. But even if you are a junior associate and, thus, expected to be slower and less efficient, they will know if your time does not add up. Do not try to bill eighty hours of work for a two-page memo. Do not claim to have taken four full days to review one hundred documents (talk about red flags!). It won't wash and it will destroy your reputation – not to mention being a violation of your professional ethical responsibilities. You should understand that a partner has the ability to "write off" your time. This means what it says: your time is written off as a loss and is not billed to the client. Having your time written off more than is reasonable will become a bad mark in your file and cause people to refuse to work with you.

I saw this happen to one associate. He billed enormous amounts of time for every assignment and got away with it for a long time. He would review documents with an online chat window always open, constantly checking football scores, shopping and surfing online. He frequently left the office for long lunches. And yet senior associates would comment that he actually seemed to write down billable time for almost every moment he was physically in the office – which is impossible. He turned in time entries for eighty-hour two-page memos and the like. Eventually this got around and everyone at the firm knew that he was a waste of money. Whether he was just a horribly slow worker or was writing fraudulent entries did not matter. He suddenly found himself with very little work and in a precarious position at the firm, not to mention having to vigorously defend all of his work all of the time.

If you have sufficiently small regard for your professional reputation – or the state of your soul – you may find you can get away with such actions for quite a while. Perpetually swamped partners and senior associates may not have the time to notice. Mega-corporations with billion dollar legal budgets may not ever pick up on one single associate's follies. But you will not get away with it forever. You may often feel as if no one would notice if you jumped out a window, much less object to your time entries in the rush of Biglaw, the crush of documents, the unending stream of fire drills and the frantic hours you put in, but do not tempt fate. Eventually, you will run into a persnickety partner who will make you redo a full month of entries, which will, by the way, result in two hours of non-billable time spent by you, or you will be working on a case for a client who has a fit after receiving your bill, and then you will have to learn the hard way. Choose to be a professional in all that you do from day one and your Biglaw experience will be much happier – and longer. Understand that, like everything else you do in Biglaw, the relationship between your work product and your billing record can at any time be scrutinized, poured over, held up to the light, and if what you write in your time entries raises red flags for a partner or senior attorney or, God forbid, a client, one day or another, it will not be pleasant for you.

If it really did take you eighty hours to write that memo, you better be able to write a lot more than a simple one-line entry. The longer the period of time you are billing for, the more extensive and informative your entries should be. You should include the specific research inquiries you exhausted, consultations with senior associates on the case, drafting and editing multiple revisions, incorporating feedback, etc. You should make it clear that you were worth every tenth of every hour for those eighty hours, that unforeseen issues arose repeatedly, that there were nuances and changes in the scope of the task, that the lead partner added to the assignment halfway through, whatever it was that made the amount of time required feel out of proportion to the eventual work product presented. Always make your entries reflect value commensurate with a Biglaw associate's billing rate.

On the other hand, if a simple memo really did take you eighty hours and there is really no good reason, the best course would probably be not to bill for all of that time. Your firm will encourage you to bill all of your time, even if you were careless or less efficient. But if you do this in every case, you permit the firm to gather negative information about your performance, which it might decide to use against you one day. Make every effort to make up the time somewhere else and keep your billable hours at expected levels and the amount of time you bill per assignment reasonable. If you get the reputation for being inefficient, uninterested, slow or dishonest, it will hurt you at the firm in any number of ways. If you really did screw up that assignment and it took double the time that it should have, take a long look at what you can do better the next time. How can you be more efficient, more accurate, less wasteful of your time in the future? Talk with a trusted senior associate or partner and see whether they suggest that you write that time off.

Over time you will develop the ability to turn in top work product in a cost-efficient way. At first, you will be incredibly inefficient and will usually take double the amount of time actually needed to do an assignment well. You will get some leeway at first, because everyone understands that you will be this way. But be careful not to let it go too far. As we discussed in chapter two, your reputation is everything in Biglaw, and if people begin to think that you are inefficient, it will hurt you. In the very beginning of my career, if I felt that my work was less efficient than it should have been, I would occasionally under bill my time. While it is important to get credit for the work you have done and to report your time correctly, it is also important to project a competent and efficient work image and sometimes that means you might look back and think it better not to bill eighty hours for that one memo.

Always approach billing from the perspective of what the client might think after a careful reading of all of your entries. Or image what a managing partner of the firm who might have a problem with your work might think. We have established this ad nauseum: clients do not want to pay $300 an hour for "doc review." A $20 an hour contract attorney can do that. There are even sophisticated computer programs that can run complex searches on key words. You, as a Biglaw associate, must add value to all that you do. And many clients do not actually like to see that you worked Christmas Eve, Mother's Day, or whatever. You will certainly work on Mother's Day at some point, but use the judgment you are developing and move that time to another day in your entries. It may sound silly but you are going to have to trust me on this one. Clients, and thus, partners, bless their hearts, do not want to see that you spent Thanksgiving Day in a doc review war room plowing through fifty boxes of documents in a mad rush to code them "responsive" or "not responsive" for production before the subpoena deadline. That may be how you spent your Thanksgiving, but they do not want to see it.[1] Some clients may not want to see you bill hours in excess of twelve hours a day. Seeing evidence of long hours and holiday work makes them uncomfortable, probably not out of concern for your welfare but more likely, if you really examined the matter deeply, because the likelihood of error increases exponentially with long hours, especially long hours on the same task. If you worked more than twelve billable hours in a given day, you might consider consulting a senior associate on your team on the advisability of moving some of that time to another day or to the weekend. The important point is to develop – in all that you do – precision, accuracy and a constant focus on how a client, or someone else with interests adverse to your own, will evaluate what you have written.

Always be conscious of avoiding duplicative tasks. For example, if you just reviewed a large number of documents for one issue and need to run more searches on the same issue on a larger pool of documents, be sure to run your

---

1. An important caveat here: if your firm awards bonuses or salary increases on a supposed "merit-based" system instead of the strict lockstep system, you will likely want to go ahead and enter your time worked over the holidays. In these cases, firms look to contributions you have made such as vacations you have voluntarily given up and other substantial personal sacrifices you have made for the firm, in calculating your compensation.

searches to *exclude* the previously reviewed documents from your new searches. You cannot waste your time and your client's money re-reviewing documents you have already examined for the same issue.

Use all of the vast resources of the firm. If you are supposed to draft an appellate brief, check to see who at the firm has done that recently and use their format, styles, etc. At first, it was very difficult to know how to use my administrative assistant and paralegals efficiently. When I knew exactly what I wanted and it felt like it was taking longer to explain everything to him or her and make sure the task was done correctly than it would have taken me to do it myself, that was frustrating. In the long run, time was saved, if not on the first task, then certainly on its next iteration. And you should never find yourself filing, making copies, proof reading, composing a cover letter, making labels for exhibits, reformatting a document, arranging your own travel plans or running quick errands. Never type out applications or forms on your own – handwrite a draft and have your assistant type the official document. All of these tasks are way below your billable rate. Imagine the reaction of a client being charged $300 an hour for collating and stapling documents and just don't do it. Develop the ability to use your assistants as often and for as many things as you can trust them with. You will need to take the time to check their work for quality control, but this will be a lot more efficient than you doing everything yourself. It means becoming a good supervisor and working through the inevitable communication lapses and mistakes, but that is part of developing the judgment and efficiency of a Biglaw attorney. Never waste your time – it is too expensive.

As we have said from the beginning, you must proactively manage your Biglaw career in all that you do. In any decision you face, there will be a number of workable choices. Make them deliberately and with care. In the background of all that you do, you should always be aware of your professional image, your reputation and you should seek to manage those carefully. Remember to ask yourself, "Will what I have written raise any flags for the partner or the client who reviews the bills?"

If the partner on your case feels that you spent an absurd amount of time on a project, billed for work that was below your pay grade, or that she cannot easily defend your entries, she will either have you re-write them, or she will just write them off. Although a partner can write off time for any number of reasons, not all of which are your fault, the firm will track your percentage of time that is written off and that will become part of your file and be a factor in your evaluations. If you have an unreasonably high percentage of time that has been written off, that is a huge negative for you in the long run. This is all about the kind of lawyer you are, and much of that, at least in the beginning, boils down to the kind of lawyer you successfully show yourself to be.

So how much time *should* you bill? It depends. I can tell you that as long as I keep my average billings at around 160 hours a month, I feel okay. I am doing my part, earning my keep, and I do not need to feel stressed about my place at the firm. Billing 160 a month is not killing yourself or winning any sweatshop prizes, but it is respectable. The amount of time you are able to bill will not, however, be consistent, month after month. As we have discussed, Biglaw practice is often cyclical. You will have crazy months during which you bill 310 hours and others in which you bill almost nothing. But if you manage to average about 160, you are going to be all right and you will be able to ride out a month in which your billable hours are very low, or even a couple months.

If things are slow for a few weeks in a row, you should proactively begin seeking billable work. Contact senior associates and partners with whom you have worked in the past and see if they need any assistance. Let them know you "have some time available." Email partners who are doing the kinds of cases you are interested in and let them know you have some time and have always wanted to work with them. Contact the partners at the firm who are primarily responsible for distributing work and tell them you need a new assignment. Contacting these partners does not usually result in anything useful because the bulk of firm assignments seem to be obtained in a "free-market" manner, by senior associates and partners seeking out those whom they already trust and junior associates directly approaching those for whom they want to work. But it will at least establish a paper trail that you routinely sought work when you needed to, in case your workload is ever challenged.

If a month goes by and you are not getting enough work, you need to begin to evaluate your situation. It is not time to panic, but you do need to begin to think defensively and to take steps to correct the situation. Why are you not getting any new assignments? Is the economy in a freefall? If so, are the senior associates on your teams hoarding more junior-level work for themselves? Are others in the firm having trouble, too, or are most other associates around you slammed? Have you been working with only one insular group for too long, so that other partners are not familiar with your work and you have become stuck in a small niche where other partners do not seek you out? There is a real danger in working with only one or two partners for most of your assignments. Has your all-consuming case just come to an end, during which you were too busy to take on new work when others sought your assistance on new cases then being staffed? Are the partners and senior associates with whom you have recently worked unhappy with your work and, thus, giving available assignments to other associates instead of you? Are you actually being slowly or even abruptly kicked off a team for some reason?

Depending on your answers to these questions, you will have a number of things you can and should do immediately. If the economy is slow and everyone at the firm is dragging, stop worrying. In fact, take advantage of it. You know what to do: get out of the office and take care of the many things you left undone when you were busy, leave early, at four or five p.m., take a vacation, do whatever you need to do to take full advantage of a rare opportunity to recharge.

If, on the other hand, you suspect that the partners and associates with whom you work do not like your work and have decided for whatever reason that they are better off without you, you need to act very quickly to stave off potential disaster. You have no time to waste on hurt feelings or anger – getting sidelined can happen to anyone, and often, for no rational reason. Be aware of the warning signs: if your group remains busy but you are receiving fewer and fewer assignments overall or you are assigned more limited or menial tasks, while others get increasing responsibilities, you should be concerned. If other new associates are being brought onto a case while your workload is diminishing, that is another sign. In my first year, I handed in a research memo and never heard another word about it. Two days later the mid-level associate in the office next to mine was directed to write the same memo all over again. Apparently the partner had not been happy with my work and had quickly gone to an associate with whom he had previously worked whom he trusted to get the job done. Would I have benefited greatly from learning what he was looking for and how I could have improved my work? Of course. But you know that does not happen very often in Biglaw. You should be armed by now with enough information to be able to resist paranoia if these warning signs should come up for you. But be aware. Nothing happens in a vacuum, there are always multiple signs of impending disaster before the eventual blowout and there are always multiple opportunities to act to mitigate, correct or make up for your mistakes.

So what should you do? If you find yourself in trouble, go to your superiors and ask what you can do better. Then do it. Demonstrate that you are concerned and that you feel a sense of ownership in your work and commitment to your team. Seek out other work immediately and from anywhere. Even if you feel that you have been doing all you could before, do more, and make sure that your work is superlative. Do all you can to get work from partners with whom you have not yet worked, in order to at least provide a counter to the negative evaluations you might receive for past failings or perceived failings. This is what I mean when I say you should always be proactive about your career. Learn to read the Biglaw writing on the wall and understand the warning signs so that you can have some control over what happens and where you end up. If you do all of these things, you will probably be able to avert disaster, mend bridges and continue at the firm. My recurring message throughout this book is the same: be strategic and proactive about your Biglaw career in all that you do.

If two and a half to three months go by and you are still not getting work while others at the firm have enough to do, it is time to reevaluate completely. There is no clearer warning sign that your performance is not acceptable and your days are numbered. For all the reasons outlined in earlier chapters, partners simply do not have the time to take you by the hand and guide you into becoming the attorney who will be capable of turning in the work product they expect and require. If after several attempts you are still turning in work that has to be redone – at great cost to the firm and the client – or work that is inconsistent, unreliable or subpar, they will move on. It may not be your fault. With no feedback and crazy demands, you may be doing all you can. But it doesn't matter. If this happens, do whatever you can to protect yourself, including protecting your self-respect. Find work, whether it is work you want or not. This is a time to forget overarching career-building strategy and take on anything you can do well. Take on *pro bono* assignments, become active in firm committees or mentoring programs, do whatever you can to demonstrate the value you have been adding. Do all you can to establish a record that shows that you have been actively seeking work and that your work quality is acceptable. If none of this results in a resumption of work flowing your way, you should probably polish up your résumé and begin to look for another job because it is only a matter of time before the ax will fall.

So how much time *can* you bill? How much time can you bill and maintain some grasp on health and sanity and how much is (inhumanly) possible? Even in busy times, I am perfectly comfortable (read: I still feel human and can manage the details of my life and grab time for my family and cat) with billing up to about 210 to 240 hours. Between 240 and 286 hours, I become strained, exhausted and generally not happy, but I can manage it. Dishes are late getting done, but I am still holding everything together. After 286 hours a month, it is every man for himself. I work and sleep. I don't feel human and am clawing to get through. I am cranky and everyone wants to avoid me. I have done it, and you will, too, but it is hell and you will be sleeping in your office and washing out your underwear in the sink. But it will always pass. And suddenly you will have a month of billing only 110 hours, when you become so afraid you will never work again that you would willingly take almost any assignment just to have something to bill. Remember, this is Biglaw, and you know the way it is: it will come around again.

These guidelines are few, some seemingly picayune and some quite general, but I have seen them keep many others on track, and they will do the same for you. If you build your Biglaw career with good judgment, prudence, precision and diligence; and if you build a wall with your professionalism and superior work as impenetrable and impervious to challenge as you can, then you need have no fear.

Chapter Seven

Email Etiquette, or, How Not to Flame Out on Your First Friday

Email is a dangerous thing in Biglaw. Careers have been destroyed in the seconds after a rash digit hit a "send" button and millions of dollars have been paid in malpractice lawsuits on the basis of one foolish email from a first-year associate. An entire book could be written on this subject and I make no claim to be covering everything here, but I will draw some bright lines around some major pitfalls to avoid and provide a few tips that should increase your chances for survival in Biglaw.

A. Think Before You Email

We have just spent an entire chapter stressing that survival in Biglaw requires developing care, judgment and deliberation in all that you do. Never is the lack of judgment more volatile and obvious than in the use of email. We have all read the horror stories on Above the Law and other legal news/gossip blogs.[1] We all know what happens when someone gets too stressed out or upset and sends off an irate email to the entire firm, one that lives on in infamy indefinitely. By now you know I have no problem stating the obvious: never burn bridges. Think and

---

1. Above the Law, at abovethelaw.com, is by far the best legal blog out there. I read it every day. Part of surviving Biglaw means staying informed about the legal world. You will learn about how other firms are setting salaries, which firms are conducting stealth layoffs and which ones are moving to "merit-based" compensation. This is vital information for a junior associate – and will also help you see that you are not alone in all of this. The legal world is smaller and more closely-knit than you think and it is important to stay informed in order to make the best choices.

then think a little longer before sending off any email in anger or frustration; if in doubt – at all – do not hit "send."

Avoid sarcasm. It does not communicate well over email and can be easily misunderstood. In fact, be careful using humor of any kind. Make sure your audience is small and composed solely of friends on your own level. It will not serve you to be cute with a bunch of partners copied on the email. Remember that email is much less formal in nature than a letter or hand-written note. Err on the side of being rather more formal than less. Do not permit informalities to affect how you address partners or clients. These points should be obvious, but there are an infinite number of other ways that junior associates make email mistakes every day, mistakes that can irritate and offend, or that make them look unprofessional or foolish and you should at least make yourself aware of the potential pitfalls in the list below. The bottom line comes back to the same thing we stressed throughout the last chapter: just be professional.

1. Do not reply to all

People in every profession rail against this every day and yet it continues to happen. Every other day I get emails needlessly clogging up my inbox from people throughout the firm wrongly hitting the "reply to all" option. Think very carefully before replying to all. Do you need to send your "Thanks!" email to the entire team/office/firm? Do you need to let every one of the forty-seven attorneys and staff members on your case know your availability for a meeting? Would it not be better to limit your response to the person who is responsible for scheduling the meeting? Most of the time – not always – but most of the time the answer is that it is better to avoid replying to all. It is very rarely appropriate. You might even consider, if you must send an email to a long list of people, whether it might not be helpful to send it to yourself, with all addressees reached via bcc addresses. You would then be preventing someone else from hitting the "reply to all" button and irritating the entire list. I do also offer some thoughts about the hazards of cc and bcc below. There are no hard and fast rules, with the possible exception of "think!" There are no black and white lines in Biglaw email etiquette. But in this, as in everything, use some judgment and think about what you are doing. We are all drowning in emails every day. Think for a moment, do we really need to get yours?

2. The copy conundrum

Be careful with cc and bcc. Bcc can be especially tricky. Including someone on your email correspondence without the other party or parties knowing about it can backfire if the person you bcc'd decides to respond to everyone. In the above example, where we were talking about avoiding the annoyance of "reply to all" clutter in the inbox, the assumption was that there were no visible addressees other than the sender, sending to herself, and no cc addressees. So, in that case, a reply-to-all response from an individual who received a blind copy would land harmlessly on the original sender and no one else. No one can see the addresses to which you sent bcc copies except the individual bcc recipient. The bcc recipients, if plural, cannot see each other. If, however, you send an email to open addressees, either in the "to" or "cc" fields, and you bcc someone else, you are at great risk. If a person you bcc'd replies to all, his message will go to you, the open addressees and anyone you may have cc'd on the message, thereby revealing to those you addressed or copied openly that there was another recipient you attempted to conceal. If you had a good reason for not disclosing that recipient, then whatever consequence you wished to avoid is now upon you, and worse as it becomes obvious that you attempted concealment. And of course you would never want to do that to anyone who sent *you* a blind copy, but email can be a blunt instrument with a deceptive control panel. It makes you think you have control when you do not. You should always use email in ways that give you the greatest degree of control over the conversation.

With cc, a common mistake is to email one person, Jim, about something, while cc'ing Robert without making a reference to that fact in the text of the email. Equally dangerous would be suddenly to include Robert at the end of a long string between just you and Jim. If Jim is in a hurry or on Blackberry, he may not notice that someone else is on the email. He may respond in a way that would embarrass both of you. The professional thing to do when a new party is introduced into an email conversation is to announce it in the text of the email. "Jim, I'm going to send you the documents regarding X. When you are finished looking them over, please send them to Robert (cc'd here)." It is simple, but it avoids embarrassment and confusion. Partners will be grateful that you let them know clearly that there is another party on the email.

3. Listserves that do not serve

As with all email etiquette, this is a matter of courtesy. Beware using all-firm email lists and think five times before sending the ISO email ("In Search of a Physician near the Firm who Accepts the Firm Insurance"). You are not on facebook. Does your office in Hong Kong want to hear that you are looking for a good chiropractor near your office in New York City? No. Neither do your colleagues in D.C. or San Francisco, I bet. Nor do the vast majority of the seven hundred people at your firm. Do not be so lazy or self-involved as to send emails to "All Firm" or "All Attorneys" unless it is really necessary. If you must use an email list, use the narrowest list available to you. Do the corporate attorneys or the tax group in your office want to help you with a Motion to Dismiss sample (with bonus points for the Southern District of New York)? No.

4. Ridiculously abbreviated language

This last point is really just my own pet peeve and not of cosmic consequence, but for heaven's sake, take the extra millisecond it requires to spell out entire words. An email that reads: "perf, thx!" can be received as terse and even unbelievably rude when the only communication that you have with a senior associate for weeks on end consists of "tks!" or: "no prob" or: "pls snd draft by COB."[2] Does it really take that long to type: "thanks!"? No. Lawyers are some of the fastest typists in the world in my experience. In my opinion, it is unprofessional, too informal and irritating to get these emails day in and day out. It comes back to learning to manage your professional image. Be more formal than you might think necessary with senior associates and partners until it is clear that formality is not expected. Never assume intimacy. Never address an email to a partner on a new case: "Hey, Fred." Take the extra two seconds it requires to spell out: P-e-r-f-e-c-t. T-h-a-n-k-s!!

B. Don't Put Anything Bad in an Email, Ever

There are plentiful reasons never to put anything bad in an email, ever, and most of them have to do with covering your own ass. It is often the case that it will be a single bad email of your client that will cost it millions of dollars in a litigation or investigation. If you have found an unbelievably bad document in your client's files, never, ever, send it to a senior associate in an email with the subject: "OH NO!!!! BAD DOC!!!!! WE'RE SCREWED! CHECK THIS OUT!!" You do not ever want to highlight and flag the crucial document for your adversary – or a future, as-yet-unknown adversary, if you should be forced to produce your communications for any reason. You never know what will happen and you must always act in a way that does not expose your clients – or you – to risk. Always. In fact, some attorneys prefer that you never use the common term "hot doc" when describing a document. If you are sued for any reason, a "hot doc" will certainly be given a lot of attention. A safer term is "document of interest." Simply email the document with a brief: "Here is a document of interest that I will call you to discuss," or even better, print it out and run it up to the partner's office in person. You can see how this might be preferable to writing: "Wow, this is going to kill us. This is horrible!!!!"

---

2. A brief aside: COB, close of business, in Biglaw does NOT mean 5:30 p.m. or some other civilized closing time. When a partner or senior associate says she needs something by COB, she means: "before *you* leave the office tonight, *whenever* that may be."

Do not memorialize problems, ever. We have talked at length about all the ways the deck may be stacked against you as a new associate and how much harsh criticism you may have to swallow despite its unfairness. If you internalize those descriptions of how it is in Biglaw, you should be able to resist reacting angrily against harsh criticism. You will know you should not memorialize in an email to the team all of the ways the doc review has been poorly managed in an effort to prove that a mistake for which you are being held responsible was therefore not your fault. Do not write: "I screwed up on the doc review because: 1) there were no adequate training materials distributed to the staff attorneys; 2) there were not enough attorneys staffed on the case to meet the deadline; 3) the senior associate gave conflicting instructions."

You can imagine the potential consequences of an email like: "Dear Partner X: We really screwed up and chose a bad vendor who is costing us $30,000 more than we should have paid in data processing fees. Then we didn't catch that one important issue until halfway through the review, so we had to go back and pay ten attorneys to re-review all of those documents." Pick up the phone and talk about it, do not create a record. You may someday have a client who refuses to pay or who sues you for malpractice so that it does not have to pay its bills. In the litigation that follows, all of those emails will come to light and they will cost you. Is such a scenario unlikely? Of course. But being a Biglaw attorney means preparing for and guarding against every possible eventuality. No matter how unlikely. You protect your clients and you protect your own firm, and, thereby, your job.

And, on the subject of preserving your job, do not admit to your own errors, oversights or screw-ups in writing, no matter how trivial. You do not want to give anyone any ammunition that could later be used against you – and this includes your friends and those seemingly laid back, sympathetic senior associates with whom you might work. This awareness should always be present and should govern all of your actions. Do not give in to the impulse to write the sheepish, but seemingly harmless, "I'm so sorry I was so exhausted and missed that important document!" Or: "#@$!! I have the worst hangover EVER and I have forgotten to code for privilege for the last hour!" It may feel like you are just being a good team player, or adding a little humor or levity, a little witty banter to lighten the mood, but in the cold light of some miserable review months or even years later, it can hurt you. Or when the senior associate is in trouble of her own for the review being too expensive or too slow, you will not want to have provided her with an easy scapegoat. Do not make yourself vulnerable. Lawyers, especially in Biglaw, are paid to be paranoid and you should begin to develop that early – and on your own behalf as well. Again, in all that you do, you must learn to protect your clients' interests, your firm's interests and your own. So you would never do anything to open yourself, your firm or your client to liability. Similar advice: be careful what you use your professional email account for. If you should get into trouble at the firm, you will have no guarantee of privacy.

A very good maxim that I have heard repeatedly is: imagine that everything you write will end up on the front page of the *New York Times* (or Above the Law) the next morning. Would that be a problem for you? If it raises any flags whatsoever or causes you even a moment's hesitation, you should rewrite, rethink or refrain from sending at all. The advice not to be rash, foolish, hotheaded or imprudent goes far beyond email, and is something that should guide everything you do.

C. Save Emails With Positive Feedback in a Permanent File

It is important to be able to defend yourself if you need to. I do not mean bristling defensively at criticism, but methodically acting in a way that shields you from future problems, whatever they may be. Hopefully, you will never need to and this will be another waste of time, but, as we have established, lawyers must prepare for any eventuality. This is what we do. I have a separate file for all of the emails I receive that are positive. No matter how trivial. If a senior associate writes in response to input I provide, "Great idea!" – I keep it. If a partner says, "Thanks for the quick turn around," – I keep it.

Similarly, if things are slow and I am trying to get more work by approaching various partners, as we discussed in the last chapter, I keep all of those emails I send asking for work. I want to be able to show instantly that I have not been sitting around or enjoying three-hour shopping lunches when I could have been profitably employed. If I am trying to get more work in a certain area, in order to develop specific skills that were found lacking in a performance evaluation (e.g., more depositions, more writing opportunities, work with experts, etc.), I keep the emails I write to partners asking about those kinds of opportunities. I may not get the work that will help me strengthen the skills that have been identified as needing development, especially if the economy is slow, but it is important to be able to demonstrate that I tried. I have never needed any documentation of this kind, but it comforts me to have it available. As we have said again and again, you want to build an impenetrable wall in Biglaw against any possible problem in your practice. Make it a habit now. You must actively build and manage your professional life from day one and this is an important part of doing that.

D. Put Down Your Blackberry

The great thing about having a Blackberry is that, in a way, it frees you. You do not actually have to be at the office all the time. You can go home at a decent hour, maybe seven p.m.?, secure in the knowledge that if some horrible catastrophe were to descend, you would hear of it and be able to take care of it. I am sure in the olden days junior associates had to be in the office at all hours – just in case. So there are clearly great, liberating aspects of the Blackberry. However, there are also real downsides to this twenty-four-hour access. Partners and senior associates, perhaps now more than ever, know that they can reach you at all times, and they expect to be able to do so. I have been on vacation, at the beach, and gotten the dreaded "I need a response/action right away" email. I have gotten emails that demanded responses at six in the morning. At 4 a.m. Whenever. I can get so compulsive about checking my Blackberry, that I will unconsciously check it while driving, right after a shower, or – in an action as unconscious on my part as it is rude and irritating to others – at a restaurant with friends.

If you don't want your Blackberry to control and take over every aspect of your life, you will have to set limits. It matters less what those limits are than that you set them. Spend a moment thinking about what you want in a given situation. Do you want to stay later at the office, and then, after you leave at eight p.m., not check in again until you return to the office the following morning so you can have an uninterrupted evening with family? Would you prefer to leave earlier, and check in more often during the earlier hours of the evening? When you go on vacation, do you expect to leave your Blackberry at home? If so, you need to communicate that unequivocally and well in advance of your departure: "I will be out of the office from XXX-XXX. During that time I will have little or no internet access." Depending on the kinds of people for whom you are working at the time, this may meet with varying degrees of success. I know of one associate whose team would completely ignore any such message and expect her to continue working whenever they needed something done. She would choose vacation spots where she knew she would find no internet access just to get away from them.

You may say that everything in this chapter is obvious. And it is (or should be!). I may have reiterated beyond endurance things that should be common sense. But I see new associates suffer from these mistakes every day. I am not making this stuff up. Almost every day someone sends around a team email, hits "reply-to-all" unnecessarily, or sends a firm-wide email that makes him or her look like a complete jackass. You know this going in: everyone is under enormous pressure and is insanely busy. Be respectful. Do not waste others' time or fill up their mailboxes with narcissistic spam. If you want to prevent needless irritation of others and the resultant caustic ire directed at you, take the time to be deliberate in your communications. I read emails like those I am cautioning you not to write every day and I see promising careers turn in to car wrecks, suddenly or in slow motion by accumulation of stupid moves. And these are smart people. As we have acknowledged, you do not find your way into Biglaw without impeccable credentials, proven intellect and superb education. And yet. Foolish mistakes that could easily be avoided happen over and over again because someone failed to approach a task with deliberation and prudence. Don't let this happen to you.

Chapter Eight

Making Your Way — It Really is Who You Know

Eighty percent of success is showing up.

Woody Allen

Early on, a partner told me, "The most important key to success in Biglaw is just sticking around long enough." It seems too simple to be so powerful but it looks like Einstein had a point: that solutions should be as simple as possible, and no simpler. Amazing things do happen if you stick around long enough. Some things will change in your experience as a result of all you do or learn, but other things will simply come to you because you have stuck it out long enough to earn some respect. After a few years even your knowledge of Biglaw and how it operates will itself become valuable. If Woody Allen is right, though, that still leaves the other twenty percent.

A. Early On: Figuring Out Who Is Who

There are not a lot of things under your direct control early on in Biglaw. You are assigned to cases according to needs and requirements you may never even glimpse; you are given odious tasks to perform under great pressure; you have no control over a lot of what you do, especially in the first two years. But, as we have seen and as we will discuss in a bit more detail here, there are small ways you can help determine where you go, who you work with, what areas you focus on, things that can have a huge impact on your happiness at the firm and your development as an attorney. At one point or another you will come to the realization – and this happens to every associate with a pulse – that you have had enough of simply going with the flow. You want to be proactive about what you do or with whom you work. I have already shared a couple of my own experiences and those of friends and colleagues: being "given" to the international trade group, being staffed on cases with horrible partners. If you take nothing else from our experiences, you should take with you an awareness of the necessity for nuance in knowing when – and when not – to assert yourself, along with the absolute certainty that at some point it will be necessary for you to be proactive about your career if you want to have the option of continuing to show up.

You will learn about partners at your firm who are impossible, irrational, flaming narcissists if not certifiably insane. Everyone hates working for them. You will want to avoid working with them at all costs. You will find yourself getting sucked deeper and deeper onto one partner's cases, and worrying about getting stuck. You already know the dangers of that. If you are thrilled with the group with whom you are working, the level of responsibility, the possibilities for development and advancement – then great but there is still work to do to maintain your position. You will want to maneuver to avoid being pulled onto other cases away from the areas you are most interested in pursuing and the team on which you are most comfortable. Biglaw may have any number of ideas about where it needs you most and what you should be doing. You will feel enormous pressure to cave in and go where you are told, but there are ways to have more control over your overall course in Biglaw. The individuals with whom you work constitute the single biggest impact on your experience and happiness in Biglaw. It is of utmost importance to be proactive about where you end up.

In the very beginning you know you will not have any choice about the cases on which you are staffed, but within months you will begin to get a sense of those partners who are doing the kinds of things you are interested in, or those partners who are more humane, reasonable, willing to give junior associates real responsibility or whatever. Perhaps you will be most interested in those partners who staff their cases very leanly, giving you regular contact with the partner and not just mid-level and senior associates, thus increasing your chances for more substantive experiences and responsibilities earlier on. Or perhaps you are fascinated with First Amendment law and would love to get more experience in that area. As we have briefly discussed in chapters one and six and will discuss in more detail below, whatever it is that you want you will have to find a way to go after it and that means marketing yourself to the partners and the practice areas in which you are most interested. You will want to stay close to those with whom you love working, successfully avoid those who will make your life miserable and position yourself to get the experience and assignments that you want. None of this will be given to you. Unfortunately, it is rare for the managing partners to hand you all that you want. As we have said repeatedly, Biglaw is a combination of a meritocracy and a free market environment and you must take the actions necessary to get the attention of the people with whom you want to work who can get you assigned to the cases that you would like.

So, how do you do this? At first, you will be overwhelmed by how little you know of any practical value to your day-to-day experience. Many things that are profoundly important to the practice of law are never covered in law school and you are left to pick them up as you can: case management skills; human resources management and supervisory skills; spreadsheet mastery; case organization and workflow management tactics; technology in the electronic discovery era. We only scratch the surface of these things in the course of this short book but at least you will know which skills you will need to sharpen. What you should not forget is that, if you get in the door at all, you will be coming in to Biglaw already equipped with a set of skills that you will need from minute one. If you survived high school with the intelligence to get into law school, you probably also learned how to avoid the crazies in the lunchroom and how to get closer to the movers and shakers. It isn't all that different in Biglaw – or any other job for that matter. In law school, let us hope, you were trained to be a careful reader and to pay attention. If you had the intellect and ambition to get yourself hired you probably come with some experience in reading people and getting what you want. What I am urging you to do is to bring all of those skills to the table. You will need them all. I am hoping that with a little forewarning you will not be so paralyzed by the pressures of what you do not know that you forget that you have them.

B. Beginning to Make Choices: Evaluating Partners and Teams

When you first start at your firm, you will not know whom to avoid, what practice areas you might enjoy or who will give you great opportunities or real mentoring. But that knowledge will come to you quickly if you pay attention, talk with other associates and use what you glean to understand the ins and outs of your firm. Use your mentor or other more senior associates you meet. They can have invaluable information about your firm and how to navigate. You must also make time for the thinking and self-reflection required to figure out what you want. Do you want to work with the partners who are the most respectful of work/life balance? The partner who is well organized, never streams into your office on a Friday evening with a horrible assignment, but has planned his cases and organized the work to give you the most manageable deadlines and assignment flow? Do you want to do the sexiest, biggest name, highest stakes cases, regardless of the jackass attorneys you will work with and the hell your life will become? Do you have a passion for an area of law and want to seek out the partners who are active in that area? These are the things we have been talking about from the very beginning: think about what you want from your time in Biglaw. If you want to make partner, you will make one set of choices, the choices that lead to a high profile in the firm and client contact. If you want to do your time, save money, get some résumé gold and get out after a few years, you will make another, allowing you to find the assignments and partners that will permit you to do that with the least stress and difficulty. It all depends on what you want. If you do not at all know what you want out of Biglaw or in your career you will be bandied about from case to case, partner to partner, without the necessary focus to marshal all of your skills toward increasing the likelihood of having the experiences you want.

There are upsides and downsides to whatever you decide. One of the benefits of working on large teams as opposed to lean ones is that you can get away. Your life does not have to revolve around the case because others on the team can step in and carry your load if you go on vacation. The downside here, of course, is that you have less responsibility. If you want to be fungible, you cannot expect to be solely responsible. On a large team there will be plenty of senior associates to conduct the interviews, depositions, witness preps, etc. You will find yourself doing the same mundane tasks for months on end. You will have nice, easy, regular billing, but you certainly will not be developing many new skills.

On a lean team, there are also pluses and minuses. You will get to do more interesting things earlier on, but you may have trouble leaving the case for a week to go on vacation. Your team will not be so easily able to replace you and the pace of litigation and deal-making, etc. is usually demanding. And it is not so easy to sneak out of the office on a slow day at 4 p.m. when you have daily partner contact. Another downside: more responsibility brings more chance of making serious mistakes without a safety net. When something goes horribly wrong, you are the only one around to blame. So, do you want as little hassle as possible and the ability to leave for family responsibilities or do you want to go after more responsibility, more advanced skills? Whatever route you choose, the key is to choose it and pursue it.

C. Mobility and Stability Within the Firm: Learning How to Get Where You Want to Go, Hold On Where You're Happy and Still Diversify

You can make your own opportunities. Because Biglaw is both a great meritocracy and a free-market environment, if you do good work, you will get more opportunities, and if you are interested in something, you can find new assignments on your own. If you are interested in a certain partner's practice, approach her. Let her know you would love to work with her if she has any new matters or needs assistance. And do not let it go at that. Contact her once a month or so, lightly in passing or by email, to let her know you are still interested. It is the squeaky wheel that gets the grease. Don't be obnoxious – and, no, she does not have time to go to lunch with you to discuss your future – but show regular and steady enthusiasm. If your touch is light but steady, when something comes up, she will think of you and give you the opportunity first. If you have worked with a partner with whom you had a great experience, when the project is over, let him know you would love to work on more of his cases. If you do this sincerely, simply and straightforwardly it will be received as a compliment, and may lead to the opportunities you seek.

If you are happy where you are at the moment and satisfied with those with whom you work, protect your position. One common impulse in the effort to survive Biglaw is to try to maintain as low a billable work load as possible for as long as possible. This seems intuitively right – you want to try to work less so you can have a life. Exhausted associates dream of having more manageable hours and less work to do. But having low billable hours for an extended period can leave you vulnerable. There are several reasons that having a full workload will protect you. For one thing, if you are sufficiently busy, you will not have to show up at firm training sessions, charity events or assist with various, random, non-billable partner pet projects as often because the firm will give you wide berth if you are making it money. You can easily bow out of even those events it has been made clear that you are "expected" to attend. More importantly, if you have a sufficient work load at all times you can justifiably turn down work from others for whom you do not want to work. If your billable hours are light, you cannot turn down assignments, no matter how horrible (and those random calls for emergency associate help to spend a weekend reviewing documents can be frequent). You will get staffed on the next pressing matter to come in the door and have no choice. Then, when there is work available where you were previously happy, you may not be able to take it on. You probably should not ever refuse work when you are not billing full time. Guard your position by asking the senior associates on the teams on which you hope to remain for more assignments, showing an interest in other matters they are currently staffed on and doing your best to volunteer to help out whenever you can. Then, when lunatic partner X (or the managing partner in charge of legal staffing) calls you up out of the blue and says he needs some help with some awful project, you can rightly and convincingly apologize and decline.

You can also leverage the demands of lunatic Partner X to secure more work from the team where you are content. You simply go to the senior associate and inform her of the new request for your time and your desire to be certain of remaining available on her case. She will make sure you get a new assignment on her case instantly and will pick up the phone before you leave her office, to lunatic Partner X, or to the managing partners, and demand that you be allowed to fulfill your obligations on the case to which you were first assigned, calling you "essential" to the case. They have dibs on you and will work to keep you. I have never seen it fail. I have done this repeatedly throughout my career and it does increase the likelihood of getting to do more of what you like doing and less of what you don't. Little by little, you can take more of the kinds of assignments you desire and move away from those that you want to avoid. The quicker you find out what you are interested in, and what you are not, the quicker you can begin to try to steer your course and fill your days with the kinds of matters you want.

Another very common problem for junior associates is getting stuck working for people for whom they do not want to work. Say Partner A always tends to staff massive cases on which you will have no hope of doing anything but first line doc review for the next four years because there are too many senior associates already at the top of the chain. Say Team Y is intolerant about associates having a personal life of any kind and will expect you to sit in your office until nine every night, even with no work to do, in order to be instantly available in the event of a last minute fire drill. Say Partner B is habitually so poorly organized that every day is a different fire drill because she has failed to plan ahead, communicate upcoming deadlines and balance workloads. Say Team Z does not view *pro bono* assignments as a legitimate use of your time and will still expect 100% from you even if you are assisting the Public Defender's Office with a murder trial. Say Partner C is just a complete asshole. There are dozens of possibilities and scenarios for the partners, associates, practice groups, areas of law or types of cases you may find yourself desperate to avoid.

But sooner or later you will find yourself working for Partner A, B or C or Team Y or Z and – beyond your simple human need for better working conditions – you will also know from our previous discussions the dangers to your career of working exclusively for the same team for too long a time – that others will not know your work. The more senior you get, the less likely that a partner will want to begin working with someone with whom she has had no previous experience. And we also touched earlier on the risks of working for one partner who might decide you are a complete screw-up and impulsively shred you in your evaluations – leaving you in a perilous position with no work and no way to get work at the firm with no other evaluators to counterbalance his assault.

This is a dangerous position to be in as a junior associate, whether you love the team you are working with or loathe it. An associate will work exclusively for a single team for a year and a half – leaving other big cases to be staffed without him. No other partners are familiar with his work nor have gotten to know him – he is off their radar. Then the partner with whom the associate works will become unhappy with the associate. Or the senior associate with whom the partner always works will become unhappy or hostile. Or the associate will make a tremendous, horrible mistake. Or the partner and his core team will pick up and leave for another firm. For whatever reason, the partner will decide he does not want the associate on his team anymore and that will be it. There is no forgiveness or making up. He is gone. He will get no more work from that group and if he fails to find other work quickly, he will find himself in deep trouble.

But this will not happen to you. You will have built the means of getting other work by diversifying your work sources even in the midst of frantic work on that one overwhelming matter. You would never give any one group the power over your Biglaw life and death by failing to maintain other "eggs in your basket" at all times since you know partners and senior associates can be unforgiving, petty or completely irrational. Or they might be that tight-knit group who came over from another big firm and who always work together, as we discussed in chapter one. You are forearmed knowing they will hang you out to dry before anyone else on the team. If something goes wrong on one case, you can seamlessly transition to accepting more work on other cases and leave your old team behind without suffering many consequences.

D. The Flip Side of Finding Access to Work: Setting Boundaries on the Work You Find

You have to set boundaries in all of your assignments if you want to be strategic in your career – and I hope I have convinced you that must be if you want to survive. If, for example, you originally accepted a case after being told it would require ten hours of work a week, be prepared to hold them to that, whether it starts to demand more of your time or less. When a case is on fire and heating up for litigation and you are seeing assignments flying at you faster than you can manage, remind the senior associate often that you have responsibilities on other cases, that for his case you originally committed to a hundred hours a month and have no more to give. If you do not, they will assume that your time is theirs and bury you in work. If you have been sitting around for a month on their case with nothing to do, point that out. No one can expect you not to take other matters while he is not keeping you busy. If another case you were on long ago has recently come back to life and your old team has begun demanding your time again, you decide how much of your time you want to devote to returning to it. If they want more time than you are willing to give, let them know you have other commitments. If you do not, they will expect one hundred and ten percent of you, all the time, as if you had been placed in suspended animation all that time until they chose to return to pluck you off the shelf. They have a strong claim for priority over your time since you have the valuable case knowledge, history and experience that they cannot quickly give to a new associate, but you need to at least push back. You should try to maintain your boundaries and never give an inch. Of course this may not always work, but if you do not at least try to maintain your boundaries, no one else will either.

When keeping firm to your boundaries can say,

- I will do what I can on the assignment you've given me, but you said this case would take only ten hours a week and that is what I allowed in my schedule.
- I am so sorry. I know this case is coming to trial but we said a hundred hours a month and I have been on this for twice that. I have other urgent matters with pressing court dates and I must give my attention to them as well.
- I have not been fully occupied on your matter for $N+1$ weeks so, naturally, other cases have come in to fill up my time.

No one will be respectful of your time if you do not set boundaries. There are costs to every choice in Biglaw. People may decide they do not want to work with you if you are not at their beck and call, one hundred percent committed to their matters regardless of what other cases you are on. There are plenty of associates who try to please everyone all the time and never go home. These are also the associates who tend to burn out or flame out in some massive mistake brought on by exhaustion and trying to keep too many balls in the air at once. If you don't want to be like those associates, stake out your territory and hold firm. You want to establish boundaries to protect yourself and get away from groups you need to leave behind.

Maintaining boundaries will greatly aid you in diversifying and keeping multiple matters going at all times. Another side benefit of having multiple matters and groups with whom you work: your whereabouts are less closely scrutinized. If you work with only one group all of the time they will know whether you have a reason to be out of your office on a given afternoon when you may want to disappear. If you have other matters, then anyone is free to suppose that you are doing something important on someone else's case. You really do not want people thinking that you are just a slacker. Most of the time you will be working very hard. And those slipping out of the office moments are sweet, restorative and well deserved. So do what you can to protect your ability to disappear without raising eyebrows.

E. Access to Work as the Key to Survival: How to Escape the "Toxic Team"

I know it feels like I am repeating myself beyond permission but I cannot tell you how many times I have seen careers destroyed when associates became trapped on toxic teams and I cannot overemphasize the importance of protecting yourself. If there is only one partner at the firm who is evaluating your work and you piss him off, you are in danger. If you have been working only for one group for a long time and they decide to dump you, you are in danger. But if you know this going in, you can take the steps necessary to diversify. Never leave one partner or one team in sole command of your assignments. Access to work is key to survival.

I would be remiss if I did not acknowledge that there will be some strong countervailing winds. This does not mean you cannot navigate, it simply means you need to be aware of all the forces arrayed against you. Say you are working on a team for whom you do not want to be working exclusively for whatever reason and you find yourself getting sucked further and further into this matter, having it take up more and more of your time and leaving you with little or no time for anything else. Biglaw partners and senior associates can be very territorial. They want to staff cases with people they trust. Or perhaps they just want to ensure enough warm bodies are always available to get the crush of projects and deadlines completed. But once they have you on a case, as long as you are performing adequately, they will do whatever they can to monopolize your time, even to "warehouse" you at times, to prevent you from getting on other cases that might draw you away and generally ensure that you will be around for whatever they need, for as long as they need it.

To balance this force, and especially if you are in a group you are already trying your damnedest to get away from, you will always act to try to prevent them from fully monopolizing you. You will take on assignments from other partners any way that you can. Go to the managing partners, approach individual partners about whom you have heard good things or who seem to be busy, ask friends and other senior associates if they know of any work on other cases. Read the regular (usually daily) "new matter" memoranda the firm sends out detailing all of the new matters at the firm. If you see something interesting, approach the partner in charge and let her know you would love to work on her case.

If you are trying to get on a new case, the partner will probably ask you if the group for whom you are currently working will be surprised or unhappy if you are suddenly busy on other matters. They will want to know if other groups have a claim on your time. If you are desperate to break out of your current group, your answer must be no and you can make the claim that you are available for twenty-five percent of your time, or more if you can tolerate the consequences. Understand what this means: at least in the short term, until you can whittle away enough time from your current group, you will have to keep both happy and that will mean working twenty-five percent more if that is what you claim you have available. It will not do to announce your current group that you are suddenly slammed on a new project. You know how that works: they will object, go to your new group and demand more (or all) of your time. And they will get it.

For the short term, you will have to continue to work as much as your current group expects, while taking on the new assignment, working much longer hours and doing your best to become important to the new group. You must keep your first group happy at all costs. If you are going to make a big change – groups, practice areas, individuals – you have to understand that for a few hard months, you will need to work one hundred percent in the old group and as much as fifty percent in the new, so that you can build connections strong enough to support your finally making the leap. Only slowly over time will you be able to turn down an assignment with your old group here and there and gently become engrossed in other projects.

It is always best if you can get onto a new matter while your current group is experiencing a slow down. Jump at this opportunity if you get it. If they do not have work for you they cannot really complain that you sought out other work and that now that new work is monopolizing your time. But it must be done with care and you want to accomplish this without giving your current group a hint of your intentions. Remember that your first group will have the power to protest and reel you back as long as they have the oldest dependence on your time. You become valuable as you become increasingly well trained in the procedures, context and history of a given case. You know the facts and relevant issues. Every time a team has to train a new associate it takes a month or more to get her up to speed. Of course, if your new assignment is with the "rainmakers" of the firm, those partners will have more pull and may be able to retain you even over a team on which you have significant experience. In any event, you will have to tread carefully, but you can act to ensure you do not get hopelessly enmeshed with a single team. Eventually, you will play such a small role in the first team that when they approach you for something, you can easily say that you are too busy at the moment on another matter that has recently flared up. Until then, you will need to work even more than you might regularly. But it is worth it if you want to be somewhere else at the firm.

F. When the Empire Strikes Back: How to Avoid Getting Sucked Back by Your "Toxic Team"

You will have to steel yourself for the pressure, not just of the long hours and the silent juggling of demands, but of the personal appeals. When you are trying to get control over your workload, with whom you work, with whom you do not work, there will always be push back. You need to steel yourself and be prepared to handle it. When you get a call from the group you want to leave, have ready these statements so you will be able to slowly whittle down one case while building up others:

CHAPTER 8 · MAKING YOUR WAY – IT REALLY IS WHO YOU KNOW

- I'm sorry, because of activity of other matters, while I am confident that I'll be able to meet my responsibilities in the cases I am currently staffed on for you, I will not be able to take on any new projects/cases/assignments at this time.
- I'm sorry, I am slammed on a fire drill for another matter for the next couple of days and will not be able to help with your recent request for a small/urgent project until X time (next week/three days from now, etc).

Make it clear that your time is taken up with other pressing matters. Fight the urge to cave in, agree, people-please, back down. You will feel it – there will be pressure from the team that needs a warm body – but you have to resist if you are going to break free. They will not be happy that they cannot count on you to be there. But if you have made the decision that they are not where you want to be, or you need to diversify, you need to be firm. You can do that without burning too many bridges if you have charted your course deliberately and have your answers ready.

Build up the weeks, one by one, that you have billed very little on their matters. Then, one day, perhaps months and months down the line, you will find you have severed your ties completely, without anyone the wiser. There are quicker ways to do this, but if you want to burn as few bridges as possible, and avoid the risk of being compelled to remain and continue to take on new commitments and responsibilities in an area you want to leave, I believe this course is wisest.

There are, of course, other possible ways to help ease out of the groups you want to leave. Make plans long in advance for a vacation and try to time it for a downtime in the case you wish to leave. When you get back, it will be a natural time to seek out new work. Or take advantage of your firm's *pro bono* options. Some have six-month full-time *pro bono* rotations with local public interest offices like Legal Aid. I have known several associates who pursued those opportunities with the express thought of divorcing themselves from their practice groups, changing areas of law entirely or getting away from a certain team. I even knew one associate who accepted a six-month project in a Third World country, just to make a break from his team. Another used her maternity leave as the perfect way to sever ties to her group.

When I have been trying to get out of a group and am taking responsibility elsewhere, there is always push back from the senior associates who want my time. They are not happy when they perceive that I have obligations somewhere else and have less time for them. They will always ask, after I have not been available a couple times in a row, or have not been at their beck and call, "So, how is your work balance? How are *you* managing *your* work?" This is directly implying that I am not holding up my end of the deal with them – that I owe them more time or have not been meeting their needs. You have to push back. They will always try to make it look like you are not managing your time wisely, or you are not committing enough of your time – which clearly they deserve and to which they feel completely entitled – to their cases. Don't let them win. You need to be able to push back and say something to demonstrate that you have boundaries and are not obligated to be at their beck and call. Be ready with your responses and do not give an inch.

G. Identifying the Toxic Team: How to Know When Getting Out is Essential

How to know when it is right to push back and when it is unwise is an open question. There are legions of reasons you may wish to leave your current group and I list a few of them below. But there are some things that are not judgment calls; some things that you should know are not okay. There are all kinds of actions and behaviors in Biglaw that, while obnoxious and rude, are still within the norms of accepted behavior and you will simply have to get used to them. We talked about a lot of this in the early chapters. Partners giving you last minute assignments that they have had sitting on their desks for a month? Fine. Partners having you cancel family vacations or other plans? Fine. Partners treating you like an incompetent idiot, or screaming from time to time? Fine. Senior Associates who schedule daily litigation team meetings at 7 o'clock in the evening for months at a time? Probably fine. Partners walking the halls in their socks while editing a brief? Fine. A partner making you help him with his ultra-left or right wing wacko *pro bono* pet cause when you have time available? Fine. Erratic behavior, hellish management styles, poor communication skills, anger management problems, passive-aggressive behavior? All fine, and might I add, shamefully commonplace.

Obviously, you should never be pressured to do anything illegal or unethical or that places you at risk of physical harm. And we will leave sexual harassment out of the discussion. But there are other things, short of something actionable but unacceptable all the same. Here is a list of things that are not fine. All of these are things I have seen, heard about or experienced over the years in major firms. You should not put up with any of this and if it happens to you, you should push back and if you need to, seek back up.

- Partners making you get ice cream from that place down the street at midnight. This could in some cases fall into the category of risking personal harm and in any case is not your job. Feign deafness.
- A partner asking you to answer the phone when his girlfriend calls and demanding that you provide an alibi for where he was last night.

CHAPTER 8 · MAKING YOUR WAY – IT REALLY IS WHO YOU KNOW

- Partners behaving like abusive spouses: routinely cursing, demeaning you, insulting you, berating you, demanding to know your whereabouts even late at night, attempting to control and dominate emotionally or psychologically in unhealthy ways.

One partner used to become enraged if she could not walk into an associate's office at any time of the day or night and have him or her be there. She would insist the team show up for some urgent fire drill over the weekend. They would show up at nine o'clock on a Saturday morning and she would not show up herself until six o'clock that evening. Outraged that no one had chosen to spend the day waiting for her there, she would call them all to come back into the office. Another would call one associate at home, after nine p.m., and yell at her for mistakes in a brief. He would insist other associates sit in his office for five hours straight while he edited their briefs – just so they were within reach if he needed anything – berating them all the while and insulting anything the associates did. One partner would ride in a taxi with an associate, throw a tantrum about the fare, jump out of the cab, walk off and leave the frantic associate to decide between leaving the taxi unpaid and flying to catch up with the partner, or paying the fare on her own at the risk of losing the partner in the city.

Nothing like this is okay and you should not have to put up with it. Go talk to your mentor, talk to an ombudsman at the firm, a partner you trust or someone. It is abusive behavior and you do not have to put up with it. You can always frame it as concern for the mental health of the partner in question. There are famous stories of high-level partners in the highest-level firms having psychotic breaks in the office, or bloodying themselves with paper clips prior to some grisly end in a Bronx motel. Surely there were warning signs there? Send up a flare. Associates' lives are hard enough.

The following is a summary recap of some of the more routine reasons you might wish to leave a working group behind. These are things that can happen to anyone and cannot usually be completely avoided in Biglaw. When you feel yourself mired in these kinds of situations, remember that you have options and that it is up to you to make a change. We have talked in this chapter about some of the techniques you can use to increase both your mobility and your stability, both of which you will need to survive Biglaw.

- Micro-managing/controlling/obsessive senior associates and partners make you miserable. Nothing you do is ever good enough. Every little thing is picked apart (even for Biglaw norms). You are given no real responsibility and you are not trusted with making even the smallest decisions on your own. It makes you miserable and gives you no real opportunity for development of skills. It chips away at what is left of your self-esteem and you begin to feel incapable of drafting so much as a cover letter on your own. Beaten down under the assault of constant criticism, your self-esteem begins to crumble. Maybe you really *can't* do anything at all on your own. Maybe you really *are* an idiot.

- You feel you are stuck doing the same things: supervising staff attorneys, second line doc review; QC of priv logs forever and ever and ever, with no chance at getting more advanced skills or opportunities.
- You routinely find yourself with tasks well below your level of seniority. If you are mostly slogging through first line review as a third year, there is a problem. If you are stuck QC'ing binders, supervising legal staff, and not much else as a fifth year, you will not have developed the skills a fifth year is presumed to have.
- Your case is so over-staffed that you are doing things way below your abilities – first line review and other menial tasks, with no hope of advancement – because there are already eight senior associates above you to do all the depositions, argue motions and other more complex tasks. Unless they all make partner or leave the firm, they are not leaving you a lot of room to grow. You haven't even seen a partner in a year, much less gotten to learn anything useful about your practice area.
- The group is intolerant of family life balance, your desire to train for a marathon or doing any *pro bono* whatsoever if it takes time from billing.
- You realize you hate with a passion the practice area in which you are working and want to get experience with something else.
- Your group travels constantly – from Beijing to Brussels to Mississippi – and you want to have more time with your family. Or, you want to travel more and see the world and the group you are with never needs to.
- The partner on your endless case is a complete jerk, unbalanced or a disturbing combination of both.
- You simply cannot bear to be around the people with whom you work for one more second, for whatever reason.

Although any one of the above is a perfectly good reason to seek work from other groups, remember that everything really depends on what you want out of Biglaw and which tack you want to take. If you want to keep your head low, have steady and ample billable work, guarantee a bonus, have more flexibility in when you want to be out of the office or work from home, then working for a huge team on a massive antitrust/Big Pharma/IP/high tech case with millions of documents will be good for you. But you will still need to diversify. If you want to develop skills, have actual partner contact, avoid the more eye-gougingly tedious and repetitive assignments, get increasingly complicated and advanced work, then you really do not want that Big Pharma case. You have to give yourself the time and breathing room to develop a clear view of what you want and then you need to be methodical about going after it. The keys are simple: know what you want, protect your position when it is good, always seek to diversify and make sure you know the people who can get you closer to where you want to be going and make sure that they have reason to know you.

Chapter Nine

Information Mastery and Preparation, or, What Is Doc Review Anyway?

So what is the *practice* of law? It can be many different things: complex and sophisticated legal arguments crafted by appellate litigators; down and dirty procedural tactics and trial strategies for trial attorneys; a laser focus on facts and telling a story for public defenders or others whose cases often depend more on facts than complex legal arguments. In Biglaw, the practice of law for a junior associate – and for most associates not at the most senior levels – is information management and mastery and constant preparation. Your practice, and your life, will be dominated by the effort to master massive volumes of information, enormous quantities of raw data. You already know this is another way of saying doc review. You know what is required of you: to extract from all that raw data the key facts of your case, to have relevant facts and big picture scenarios at your fingertips, to synthesize and combine the facts to tell the story of your case in whatever way you may be asked to present it – from worst case to best scenario for your clients. You will be consumed with various quests for information, for deeper insight into minute issues that arise, for broader pictures of the facts or relevant law. You will have to compile and organize databases for the relevant personae in your cases, chart chronologies of events; boil down the documents to the most important, most useful for your cases, most harmful for your adversaries and summarize them so concisely that the most important points are always easily and immediately accessible to other associates and partners.

The dormant commerce clause doctrine from first-year constitutional law class is probably going to be pretty useless to you for your first couple of years in Biglaw, but you better know how to create a spreadsheet that tracks and updates any and all workflow information a partner might demand at a moment's notice. How many docs have been reviewed? How many are left to be reviewed? What is the rate of review and how many days will it be before the review is complete? How many productions have gone out the door to date and what is the volume of each? How many privileged documents remain to be logged. How many are logged already? You will quickly become adept at negotiating with vendors; managing massive volumes of data; mastering unlimited numbers of document review platforms; understanding how to craft killer searches in a database to locate documents that are privileged, have not been put on the log yet, have been reviewed for certain issues and were from certain custodians and time periods – or you will drown. These are all things you must quickly learn on the fly in Biglaw and it is sink or swim.

All this book can do is prepare you mentally for the experience and attempt to inoculate you by dint of repetition against some of the common diseases of the doc review recruit. I want to do two things here: one, make sure you understand that what will be asked of you is a tall order; and, two, remind you over and over again that many people who knew less than you have managed it, starting from nothing, left to sink or swim with no help in sight. In this chapter we will address a few of the nuts and bolts of document review so that you will at least have some warning and some signposts to cling to when you feel you are about to go under and we will outline some common pitfalls and the strategies most likely to help you steer clear of them.

Always remember all that we have discussed up to now: if you choose Biglaw, there will be career-long benefits, and preparation – thorough and complete training in how to approach a case, how to organize and fully prepare, from the ground up – is one of them. Biglaw associates gain vast experience in document management platforms. It might help you going in if you did a little reading about some of the more common ones: Concordance, Ringtail, iConect, Relativity. You will learn case organization and management, becoming adept at supervising and managing massive, document-heavy cases and mastering the many precise skills (which, as we have seen, are not as trivial in their wider application as they may first appear) and the rigorous qualities of mind that are required to (someday) run a case. You will learn to troubleshoot. You will learn to master resources and information. Every task you take on you will approach methodically and with care. What at first is a slow, clumsy approach of endlessly weighing pros and cons, looking at one alternative and then rejecting it, going back and forth between several options will become something you do with ease and expertise. You are learning how to manage and run the most complex, large scale cases that are out there. Sexy? No. You should no longer have any illusions about that. Biglaw is not sexy for the junior associate. But knowing how to manage the most complex cases is an undeniably valuable skill in the legal market and despite the drudgery, not something one can just pick up on the fly. You are learning skills that only the very top legal professionals have mastered. And it will give you an approach to the practice of law that is solid and will benefit you for the rest of your career.

A. Nuts and Bolts

A friend of mine in a large New York firm once made the mistake of producing to his adversary a batch of documents he had never looked at and the consequences eventually cost him his job. There are a number of things that went wrong in this choice. He understood that in litigation you are required to produce all documents and things that are responsive after a *reasonable* search and that going through, say, nine million hard drive files one by one is not reasonable. Fair enough. Under that understanding he had many times excluded from production files or documents he had not seen. A file name indicated that the content of an entire folder was not relevant to the subject of the litigation. That is often a reasonable decision when faced with more files and data than could possibly be reviewed. Then he made the dangerous and way, way, way above his pay grade (see discussion of "Mistakes" in chapter ten) assumption that the reverse would be true for documents his firm was producing and that documents could be included that he had not seen, thus, providing documents to the other side that no one had laid eyes on. I cannot know what he was thinking but it was a serious error in judgment. Who knows what could have been in those documents so carelessly handed over to the opposing party?

Dealing with documents that will be produced is completely different than dealing with the universe of documents that are not being produced. Vast quantities of those documents will need to be reviewed as well but you may decide to go by search terms to weed out certain categories of documents you are not going to consider for production and will mark non-responsive. You can rule some things out by date or by file name. You document the choice; you make sure your superiors are on board with the methodology. Here, when deciding to exclude documents from production, it may be that you do not have eyes on every page, as long as some senior attorney on your team knows that is how a clearly defined set of documents is being treated and why. It is better to include everything that is responsive in the first go, better to err on the side of over inclusiveness, yes, but if something that has not gone anywhere is later reconsidered it is not as horrific as having entire productions recalled after mountains of privileged documents were found to have slipped through to the other side. A sheepish letter is written and the disks, DVDs, hard drives or whatever the documents were produced on are requested to be returned and then they are re-reviewed. You do not want to be that associate.

For any document produced to your adversary, the default position is that there will be at least associate attorney eyes on every page of that document.

There will be times when this is not possible, but these would be exceptions. In such cases a clear methodology will be carefully designed to isolate from production any potentially privileged documents. This methodology, both for isolation of documents and for further review of remaining documents, will be approved all the way up the chain to the client. To meet an emergency deadline, you might isolate a batch of documents through key word searches that contain absolutely no potentially privileged terms or attorneys' names. You then spot check a number of the batch to confirm that your methodology is sound and this batch has no potentially privileged docs. Those docs can be produced immediately, in an emergency, with a fair degree of security, while the documents that did have potentially privileged terms (law, lawyer, legal, illegal, attorney, Esq., privileged, — whatever you and the client decide are appropriate terms for the case) will be withheld until each one can be carefully reviewed for privilege. Most of those will not be privileged but it is a safe way to make sure no privileged documents slip through.

There are many ways to ensure you are producing and withholding the right documents. You might, for example, have first line review and coding done by contract attorneys, a QC review of their work by a senior staff attorney and you, as a junior associate, might settle with your team on some percentage, say, twenty percent (which is fairly high, but needed in the beginning of a review to ensure things are going the way they should), of those documents that you will personally review and some methodology, also approved by your superiors, by which you will test the rest of the documents to make sure nothing has been missed. Perhaps you will review the first fifty pages and then ten percent of everything that follows. The choice of methodology will depend on your level of experience and the trustworthiness of the first line reviewers and how well you feel you have trained them. The point is that you will have some transparent methodology someone superior to you has signed off on and you will never make assumptions.

Your main doc review task will often be to put documents into various "buckets" devised by a senior associate or partner on your case (which are usually electronic tags or markers in a database to allow for quick isolation of types of documents). As tedious as it is, this work must be done by an attorney because it requires judgment and analysis. You look at a document and see where it fits amongst the many buckets in your case. There can be buckets for almost anything. What, you may ask, is a **bucket?** Some examples may help.

Subject matter buckets are categories for all docs dealing with a given issue, claim or defense in a case. For example, in a patent infringement suit you bring against a rival company, they may claim your patent is invalid as a defense. To prove patent validity you might have to demonstrate, for example, that the invention or product was non-obvious. As a legal matter this might be shown by evidence of commercial success; long-felt need; failure by others to fix the problem your inventor fixed; unexpected results; copying or praise from people in the industry; licensing, etc. Your task is to find documents that demonstrate the legal point you need to prove. The documents will not be neatly labeled "evidence of long-felt need" in your production. You will have to read with that filter and find that evidence and code the document for that subject matter bucket, say, evidence of non-obviousness. As you can guess, in typical Biglaw cases involving complex issues and multi-billion dollar companies, the number of possible claims and defenses and thus complex web of overlapping buckets, can be mind boggling.

Sometimes the bucket will be defined by the **type of document** and not the substance of the document. You might be asked to fill buckets for: business plans; reports; clinical publications; presentations; performance evaluations; training materials; communications with a given federal agency, say, the FDA. A "type of document" bucket might also call for all docs relating to a specific numbered request in a subpoena, e.g., "Subpoena Request No. 14. Please produce all documents and things relating to communications between CEO X and disgruntled employee Y" so no matter what that memo, email or letter was about, if it passed between those two people in the time period of the subpoena request, it would be categorized in the same bucket.

The bucket might also be limited to a particular **custodian or witness** so that absolutely all documents produced from one source would be segregated and examined from that perspective. No matter how carefully documents are tracked as they come in there can be issues about this that require analysis.

And, of course, most cases will be establishing buckets for **privileged** and **not privileged** documents, **hot** documents, **need further review** documents (that need a senior associate's eyes) and documents that **do not warrant further review**.

All of this requires judgment because none of it is obvious. You would think putting all performance evaluation documents in the "performance evaluations" bucket would be a no brainer and most of the time it would be. But what if the documents contained inappropriate comments or evaluated an employee on an illegal basis or contained some statement less obviously incriminating but equally important to some aspect of your case? Sometimes a doc will fit into several subject matter buckets. It might be a business plan dealing with communications with FDA that covers matters treated in a couple of different requests for production of documents or subpoena requests. Which bucket does it go into then? The senior associate or the partner on the case will usually have defined a hierarchical structure for subject matter buckets. The first is the most important, so if a doc fits there, you put it there. The second is important, but not as important as the first. So if a doc fits into several subject categories, you go with the highest priority bucket. Sometimes it is more important to tag every possible issue in a document than using a hierarchy. If a document deals with six issues, you will tag all six. But in this, as in everything, you must communicate with your team and make sure you understand how they want it done. Imagine the consequences if you guess and get the priority wrong and your error goes undiscovered for weeks.

You must always make sure that you understand the parameters of your production in every detail. What agreements have been made between the parties prior to commencement of discovery? Agreements are made about nearly every aspect of discovery. What about **metadata**? Metadata is all the information that documents carry with them digitally but which may or may not appear in a printed hard copy of the document. At the very beginning of litigation the parties come to agreements about how much metadata will be produced. Metadata can include information like who the custodian was, the date the doc was created, whether an email has attachments and how many, the file name of a document. Some of that is visible – as in an email the author and recipients can be seen in the "to" and "from" fields on the face of the doc – but some is not – like the custodian of a Word doc, creation date, modified dates, file name, etc. If you have a Word document that was produced with no names on it, you need the date, who created it and other custodial information in order to give context to whatever the doc says. You sacrifice the maximum utility of a doc in a deposition if you cannot determine who was responsible for creating it. Metadata information can be extremely useful in such contexts. But the more you divulge, the more expensive and time consuming and, of course, you do not ever want to give free information to your adversary. I have worked on investigations with the government where we turned over all metadata in an effort to be fully forthcoming. In litigation, it is too expensive and you do not want to give up any more than you have to, so often we agree to limit metadata information, for example, to custodial info and creation date.

Aside from metadata, parties often agree on how to treat privileged documents that are inadvertently produced, usually with "clawback" provisions. These usually provide that a party may clawback a privileged document by simply notifying the opposing party that a privileged document was inadvertently produced, requesting the other party to destroy all copies of it, and logging the document on a privilege log. You might wonder if clawback provisions are the norm what is the big deal about accidentally producing privileged documents. You would be unwise. Once the other side has gotten to examine a privileged document before it is clawed back and has determined that it is extremely helpful to their case, they will much better be able to challenge your withholding of the document in court. You want to avoid this at all costs because those documents are usually the most damaging and contain the most sensitive information of the company.

In doc review every document requires judgment. What is relevant to your claim? Is the document "hot" and something that would definitely require the atten-

CHAPTER 9 · INFORMATION MASTERY AND PREPARATION

tion of a partner? How do you know which documents are responsive to a given request for production of documents or subpoena request? What does "responsive" mean? It depends on the specific language of the request. If the language is broad, and no argument or objection has been successful in narrowing the request, any document relating to the subject matter is responsive. The document need not be earth-shattering or something that makes or breaks a case to be responsive. If it involves the product or claim or defense at issue and "moves the ball" in any conceivable way, it is responsive. In a product liability case, for example, an email ordering hotel reservations for a business trip might not be responsive, but an email ordering hotel reservations for a conference involving the product at issue would likely be. As long as it is relevant to any possible, imaginable claim or defense, it should be produced. However, there is a fine line. Parties get in trouble all the time for trying to obscure a case by producing more documents than an adversary can possibly review efficiently – a "document dump" production containing thousands of useless documents that obscures the document universe, making it hard to get anything useful. Sometimes this is deliberately obscurantist; sometimes it comes from sloppiness, sometimes from trying to save money. But on the other end of the spectrum, you cannot be too rigid in withholding what might be considered responsive. You do usually need to err on the side of being over-inclusive. Who knows what will turn out to be highly relevant a year down the line in a case? It is better in the long run to have produced it the first time around.

Not all the buckets are equally important. Who knows if document number 13,457 is more a promotional document or a training one? If the legal issues in your case do not turn on that distinction, no one is going to get up in arms if you put that doc in the wrong place. Okay, that's not true. Senior associates will still become enraged if you miscode *any* docs, or, rather, if they disagree with your coding, but that rage will be nothing to what will break over your head if you mark a doc privileged that is not, or let a privileged doc go out the door, or fail to find a very, very bad document or a very, very good one. The consequences of these mistakes can cost an entire case and your life will be miserable if you commit one of these errors. Your eternal vigilance is all that stands between you and a grievous error. Do all that you can to avoid missing these kinds of documents.

Before talking with a senior associate/partner about a problem think: how can this be blamed on me? You know it will, so you should try to be prepared. Perhaps the coding system you came up with is confusing reviewers – they are marking false positives as something else or you are missing a bunch of some type of document. Even though you will have made sure your superiors signed off on the coding before you set it in motion in your document review, you know it will be on you if something systemic is going wrong.

All coding systems come complete with *innumerable* headaches. How do you get people to categorize documents in a way that is useful in litigation, categorize them so that you can search for them later if you need them, and not get too many superfluous or irrelevant docs? How do you locate that one document or fact in a sea of case documents and information? I keep telling you this will be your quest for years in Biglaw and you may still think it all sounds quite elementary. What is complicated about reading a document (or one hundred thousand) and coding it for various issues? On a simple review, maybe it would not be complicated. But they are never simple. And you will find headaches even when the only thing you want is a doc marked for five substantive categories. Let's look at how complicated it can be.

You have a database tracking various documents that report the results of sales calls made by representatives of your client, a pharmaceutical company. Every time a sales person in your pharmaceuticals case goes on a sales call at a hospital or doctor's office, they make a quick report of what they discussed, to whom they talked, the various drugs that were promoted and anything memorable for their next visit. In your review you have 800,000 such documents going back many years. Some of them contain very damaging statements for the company – proof that a sales rep promoted off-label use of a drug approved for other purposes, or offered "kickbacks," inducements to prescribe in the form of expensive dinners, ski trips, etc. – but most are just fine. You have a meeting with the government and want to put those few "bad" docs in context. You want to demonstrate that, overall, the sales practices were aboveboard and that the questionable practices were not rampant in the company. How do you do it? You decide to run searches on the 800,000 documents using several key search terms – search terms that may, but may not, mean there was off-label promotion or other questionable behavior. Let's say from those searches, you boil it down to a universe of 190,000 docs. You want to quantify them and categorize them: which docs are problematic, which represent false positives entirely and have nothing to do with anything relevant, which do contain a search term but do not document an illegal promotion. But you want to break it down further. For every sales call in which off label use was discussed, was it your company's representative who initiated the discussion? If he did, that is very bad for your client. But what if the doctor initiated an off-label discussion? That is perfectly legitimate. You want to weed those out, quantify them, tell a story that accurately represents your client's practices. How do you do this – in two weeks?

Forty contract attorneys read through every single document and code them for all the issues; then junior associates QC ten percent to make sure they are making the right calls; then senior associates look at the data, make pretty charts, and send them to damage experts and help prepare for a presentation to the government. The contract attorneys have to code for who initiated the conversation, if known, or, if not known, that it was unclear who initiated it. You have to make sure you have a tag for docs that are exculpatory, i.e., in which the existence of the search term is not an indicator of a bad action on the part of your client's sales rep.

At the end of the day – thousands of dollars, weeks and maybe months later if things go awry – you will have a nice, pretty PowerPoint presentation, showing the government how many problematic search terms there were total, which percentage of them were false positives, which were correct but not problematic, and which were actually problematic – bad and initiated by the sales rep. It may only be a handful of slides by the time you are done. But before you get there, everything that can go wrong will.

This is doc review at its most hazardous to your health. There are innumerable ways that this can get confused and all of them will occur before it is all over. What if the document contains no problematic use of a search term, but something else completely problematic is said? Do you create a new category? Ignore it on the grounds that no review can be exhaustive and things are bound to fall through the cracks? If a certain problem is common, do you run a whole new search and include the new term, setting the review back a week? If you do that, you may find yourself continually adding new fields until the review becomes unmanageable. There will always be something you missed. What if there are misspellings in a document and, as a result, it is not captured in a search but it does contain relevant information? What if there are two problematic terms in the same discussion – which do you count? Is it considered rep-initiated if the note just says the parties "discussed" a given drug in unapproved applications? Do the staff attorneys understand that seemingly innocuous statements like "Told doc to use Drug X for all his osteoarthritic patients," is actually an off-label promotion for this particular drug, since it is limited to only extreme cases of osteoarthritis because of harsh side effects? These are all judgment calls – for a senior associate. If you make any of them on your own, you only increase your peril. Does it begin to become clear how much can go wrong and how easily you may be blamed for it?

The whole intellectual exercise of looking at a document – wrestling with its nuances, weighing in your mind if this or that aspect of the document tilts in favor of its being responsive, not responsive or privileged, or how it colors your case – discussing it with others, going back and forth, is the exercise that strengthens and seasons the junior associate. I do not think this is taught in law school and that is probably why first-year associates are not very valuable. By the time you get to be a senior associate you will be able to grasp the salient qualities of a given document in a flash because you will have wrestled with the difficult questions of applying facts and the law to different case issues or put up the prism of your own experience to countless previous problematic documents numberless times. There is a place in your brain for the information to go, patterns you will instantly recognize, the confidence that comes only with time in the trenches.

B. Pitfalls to Avoid

Overconfidence. There is an old newspaper editing term for what sometimes happens on deadline: railroading the copy, meaning that the editor takes a look at the lead, skims a few paragraphs and lets the story go to press. Of course, you would never do that in your review of documents. You know you have to develop a critical and thorough eye and you know you cannot do a lazy or lackadaisical job. You remember the story of my friend who allowed documents to go out he had not seen and who lost his job. You know all this. And yet, I promise you this will happen. You will be rushing through a stack of docs to produce to your adversary, coding for responsiveness and privilege. You will have thousands of docs to review and you will be under an enormous time crunch. You are being hounded by the mid-level associate to finish up your batch. You will look through the first three pages of one thirty-page doc, see that it looks like a hundred others you have already painstakingly reviewed and decide to move on to the next doc, marking that one responsive, not priv. Days or weeks later, the senior associate will storm into your office and throw that document in your face (yes, she knew you reviewed it because once everything hit the fan she took the time to look back over which batches of docs were assigned to which associate and found that this document came from yours). On the third to the last page, buried in the back, is a highly privileged document that got forwarded along with the other pages you had seen a hundred times over – a document with attorneys all over it, a document that could have been and needed to have been withheld from production. You missed it. No excuse possible, you just did not look or read closely enough. You failed to put your eyes on every page and you missed it. You will only go through this once, believe me. Or surprise me, be the one associate who does not learn this the hard way. Read through every doc. If you do not read every word, and no one could, then at least have your eyes on every page of every document that is going to be produced. There is no excuse for just not bothering to look.

You should look at every page of every document as if your eyes were the only ones ever to be on it before it goes out the door. It does not usually happen that way, of course. As we have discussed, there are often multiple levels of QC and review, but not always and you never know, so you should approach every review as if your eyes were the only attorney review a document were ever going to have.

In the very beginning of your practice, focus on information mastery and communication, rather than brilliant legal or factual analysis. That will come. But first you need to be good at communicating what you have found, where you have searched, what you have seen. At the very beginning, as we have seen, you are not going to know what is relevant and what is not, much less what is key to a case. That will be your job more as you move up in experience. You will not always have the case knowledge or legal background to know a good fact from a bad one. Senior associates will not have the time to give you the full background on a case. It takes too much time and the job you are being asked to do does not require it. At first you need to report to those who do know and be as accurate and thorough as possible so they can make good calls. You are not the one making those calls early on.

As I said in chapter two, I cannot count the number of times I showed a document to a senior attorney, saying, "Look, I found this great document!" Or ran to someone with something I thought was horrible. I do not want to tell you how many times they would look at it and come to the opposite conclusion about its value – or how often they chucked it aside as useless. No junior associate is going to be brilliant right out of the box at picking up on subtle factual and legal nuances, they simply do not know enough. To be truly valuable and needed on a case, you need to be vigilant and you need to become good at synthesizing and summarizing, including all relevant, needed pieces of information in your summaries. You do not make assumptions or skip steps and you leave the conclusions to others.

Sloppiness. Young attorneys tend to be sloppy – sloppy thinkers, sloppy workers, sloppy writers, sloppy researchers. Part of this is the fault of the impossible demands and deadlines in high-pressure environments, part of it is inexperience. It takes time to develop a concise, clear, focused way of thinking like an attorney. But there are things you can do to counteract this. One simple, simple methodology will help: always leave a trail. If you send a summary of key documents you reviewed to a partner, you must include the dates, who was included in the communication – be it email, memo, report or letter – the Bates numbers and custodial information necessary so that your docs can actually be found again by someone else. It is easy to think all that information is not a big deal as you are going along. It is. Anything could be important and you must leave a trail. If partners see an interesting document, they want to know when it was sent, whose files it was in, everything about the context of that document so that they can know what other things they may want to follow up on. You will not have the background to recognize the relevance of half of what you do until much later, so you must be meticulous in your recordkeeping and document everything. You cannot afford to be sloppy. You need to develop the ability to sum up information in a concise, tight, but thorough and useful way. Include, or have available, every piece of data that might be important.

Fragile ego. We talked in the first part of the book about the hierarchy. So you already know where you stand and that you need to check your ego at the door. That is much easier said than done. And oversensitivity is a major pitfall to avoid. It is painstaking work to trudge through a hundred documents, noting their custodians and dates, summarizing what they say instead of letting the partner read them on her own. It feels like drudgery. But we have already seen why it works this way and why this is the job of junior associates. And even though the senior associate does not really care what you think about the document, and even though you will often be wrong, it is good to share your opinion. But your job is to give them all the information *they* need to do the important analysis.

They cannot re-read all the documents themselves, go searching through all of the databases, scan the thousands of hits in a search. They often do not even have time to read the documents you might send them and figure out why you thought they were important. So it is your job is to do that for them. If they find they need to go back to the document and look at it to understand its importance, you have not done your job and what you did do was a waste of time. Everything you do should be to save time for your superiors. Give them the information they need to do the analytical thinking for the case. You cannot waste your own time being offended that they will not read the thirty or so key, key documents you painstakingly compiled. They won't even read the bullet point summary you provided of the key parts in each key document. You will always have to work to get the important stuff to their attention.

When I talk about preparation, I mean that your job will most often involve preparing partners, senior associates or mid-level associates for something. You compile and master all that information so that you can prepare someone above you to go and do whatever he or she needs to do. The fact that you do not get to go and do any of it yourself in the early years is simply not about you. It is the way it is. You prepare. You will draft deposition outlines for a partner to use (or hopefully take a couple points from) in his deposition outline. You will write small sections of briefs, not to be included in the final brief usually, but to give senior associates the cases and citations they need to plug into their drafts. You will create mountains of document summaries, interview and deposition materials, background information that will be used by other attorneys who actually take the depositions, etc.

Impatience. The most common complaint of junior associates is that they are sick to death of doc review. They have had enough of the drudgery, the seemingly useless, endless reviewing and coding of documents, the months and months of sifting through page after page after page of emails, handwritten notes, calendar entries, lab notebooks, promotional materials, draft insurance contracts, CEO briefing materials, "impactful" marketing schlock, and on and on. Day after day is consumed by the search for information. A partner asks, "What was Vice President X's understanding of this corporate event?" And the next ten hours are swallowed up in the effort find out. Impatient young associates want to move quickly past the hours and hours of scrutinizing emails and documents and get on to the "real" stuff. Depositions. Motions practice. Brief writing. Arbitration. Oral argument. Anything that resembles law! It is understandable. Reviewing documents is what makes junior associates want to throw in the towel

CHAPTER 9 · INFORMATION MASTERY AND PREPARATION   133

and walk away. But the fact is, the information of a case is key. Mastering the facts is essential. And, unfortunately, you will not move up in Biglaw until you have mastered how to master information. You will only understand how to succeed as a senior associate or partner and move on to other things when you know what it takes to master the facts in a case. If you embrace these facts of life now, you will save yourself years of frustration, resentment and hopelessness.

Instead of chafing at the repetition, you can determine to be great, not only at mastering the facts, but also at keeping your mind on the overall picture of how document production works. How long does it take to review a thousand documents? How many staff attorneys will be required to complete a review within the allowed timeframe? What do you need to do to train those attorneys to catch successfully and reliably the kinds of documents you are looking for? What is the best way to handle quality control and efficiently check their work to ensure they are not missing obvious calls and important information? How much will the vendor charge per gigabyte of information? What is the best way to run searches in a massive database in order most quickly to isolate the documents you need? How can you use your databases to ensure you are not reviewing documents you have already seen, or duplicating your work somehow? How can you use review platforms to find the documents you need instantly? Every time you look at each one of the thousands and thousands of documents you will review in your quest to understand what might raise flags or issues in cases of every imaginable kind, you will be, or can be if you approach it in the right spirit, adding to the stock of information that will answer these questions and many more. And you will greatly be increasing your value to the firm. That is the simple truth. Visualize your work in the trenches as the training montages in the Rocky movies, if that helps. But whatever you do, embrace this fate now and learn to be great at information mastery, and then be prepared to continue to do it patiently for a while after you have mastered it. If you understand what the practice of law is for junior Biglaw attorneys, and do not waste your energy fighting it, you have a chance at developing the skills that will make you efficient, useful and eventually valuable enough to move on.

When a Biglaw partner walks into a courtroom or negotiation or meeting, he or she has had the benefit of any number of other highly intelligent and driven lawyers who have spent the last portion of their lives frantically trying to make sure everything – everything – has been done to prepare for that event. Numbers have been run, re-run, checked and double checked. Exhibits have been compiled, ordered, re-ordered and evaluated. Legions of outlines, summaries, analyses, legal and factual, have been drafted and edited and then re-edited at three in the morning by several different attorneys. Arguments have been bolstered. Counter-arguments have been exhausted. Weaknesses and holes have been identified and addressed. Every possible strategy has been considered. The drudgery and monotony of preparation and information mastery is what can make your life feel like a frustrating run on a hamster wheel. But preparation and information mastery is the key to Biglaw practice. This training is useful anywhere, in anything you choose to do if you leave Biglaw, but Biglaw is the only place you will get it.

Biglaw is a master of information. Compiling, synthesizing, charting, tracking, understanding and mastering the enormous amount of information in the most complex cases is what Biglaw does best. No other legal entity comes close, I would venture. The government can take years to weed through document productions at its own cumbersome pace, smaller firms simply do not have the manpower to do the in-depth analyses. It is the almost full-time job of junior associates to understand, explain, ferret out, boil down and crystalize the important information and crucial facts of a case. And the better you become at distilling, summarizing, explaining and organizing, the more invaluable you will become.

I have heard scores of partners say that they do not have any idea about the details of the facts of a given case. They have not sat mired in documents up to their ears for months on end. You have. They are shown a handful of the most problematic or interesting documents and that is it. But you have the context, you understand the relevant corporate practices, you have the key events in your mind, because you have been reading about them for ten hours a day for months on end. Like your own twisted soap opera version of Mega Corporation Days of Our Lives, you will have learned about all the key employees in the case, followed them (in emails) through divorce and a string of workplace spats, you will have seen their progression and evolution over a span of years. Entertaining, sadly it is not, but highly useful. If you know the docs well, you will have made yourself an invaluable resource. Only you, sitting in on a deposition or interview can say, "Hey, that question you just asked that the witness denied knowing anything about, I saw a document that proves her wrong."

Remember the story in chapter four, about the process of triangulation on that invoice for reimbursement for a party? What would you do if you noticed it? What would you do if you were alert enough to make the necessary connections and figured out that your hospital client had paid all those thousands of dollars to set up a lavish environment for sales reps and doctors to socialize in the home of a doctor. You are doing the document review; you added two and two and got four ways to improper. What do you do? The moments when a young associate has the opportunity to bring something to the attention of an equity participant are few and far between and you will never be able to get anyone's attention if you get a reputation for requiring too much of it but if something like this happens to you, you cannot leave it buried in a memo, however bold your bullet points. I have said you should concentrate early on on information mastery and communication over legal analysis but that does not mean turn off your brain. And you should, and must, be as relentless as any crusading cub reporter

CHAPTER 9 · INFORMATION MASTERY AND PREPARATION

when you find your way to something you know will hurt the firm if it goes unnoticed.

Write the memo. Make sure you have made the situation crystal clear. Read other summaries. Make sure you understand what the firm's overall understanding is of the client's exposure. If what you have discovered opens up a new area of risk you must make sure someone from inside your firm (*never* you, of course) is the one to make that known to your client. Clients are not forgiving. No matter how much pressure they have put on the firm to get a production done in a certain amount of time for a certain amount of money they will expect it to be foolproof. If something goes undetected and comes back to haunt them and their attorneys are not the ones to bring it to their attention that can mean anything from some seriously unpleasant conversations at the highest level of the firm to the loss of a lucrative client. If your senior associate does not give any sign of action on your memo, follow up. If he still does not understand the danger, make it clearer. If you have to, and only if you have failed in several attempts, make your way around the blockage. Start with someone you trust, seek advice, ask how she would deal with the problem. Start with another senior associate or trusted mentor. Do not go running to the partner immediately superior to your thickheaded senior associate. Seek confirmation from another superior that what you have learned requires action. Then do whatever you have to do to make sure that someone with direct client contact understands.

I have said that running to one's superiors with your own interpretations of things is risky and that you should concentrate on clear representations and summaries of the facts in the documents and on being able to track the work you do in document review. All true, especially early on in your tenure. This example is meant to be illustrative of an unusual situation, one that we are hypothesizing takes place a bit later in your document review career than day one and a situation about which you would seek redundant confirmation before taking it to the next level. And it is still risky. But so is doing nothing.

Chapter Ten

Mistakes

In my life before Biglaw I performed as a professional opera singer for a number of years. While I often worked with people with intense artistic temperaments and massive egos, I once had a voice teacher who was a memorably insufferable diva. In the fifties she had been a huge star on the world stage and she still treated those around her like playthings and servants. She would bring her little, blithely-un-house-trained dogs into the music school, let them have the run of the place and expect her voice students to clean up after them. She was known for frequent fits of rage during which she had a tendency to throw food at singers. Her often cruel criticism left many, many students in tears after lessons. If she became unhappy with her students for any reason she would denounce them, summarily kick them out of her studio and ensure they were never cast again in another opera at the school. She was critical of absolutely everything and she would attack her students mercilessly. Tone, diction, breath support, attack of high notes, posture, expression, lyrical phrasing, foreign language skills, resonance, diaphragmatic breathing technique – nothing was ever right.

So the days that she would pick incessantly at mere trivialities, like what I was wearing, or how I looked, were some of the best days of my study with her. If she was reduced to the trivial, I knew I must have been singing gloriously. She would still insult me, claim my look was not professional, announce that I was getting fat, but I would rejoice. If there had been any weakness, any flaw, any imperfection in my singing she would have pounced on it like a hyena. I think now the only good things about my time in that studio were those moments – and the training she gave me for survival in Biglaw.

Biglaw is like that old, bitter opera diva in many ways. Biglaw is the Metropolitan Opera, the Major Leagues, Broadway or the Olympics and like these other elite realms, perfection is expected and getting there is excruciating. But be happy when partners criticize stupid, petty things like your omission of a period in the citation on page 54 or the fact that you used the color red to denote unfinished review batches on your tracking spreadsheet. If that is all they could find to complain about, you are probably doing pretty well.

If you enter Biglaw you know you are in for a refiner's fire of constant criticism, hellish demands, stupid assignments, unbending expectations, impossible deadlines, crushing workload and a frantic pace. You will always be chasing perfection and never allowed the time it takes to achieve it. The ever-present problem in Biglaw is how to find the motivation and discipline to take on every task, no matter how inane, as if it were your debut at the Met. In performance art, ballet, opera singing, theater, no performer can hold back from giving his or her utmost in every rehearsal. That is how you get to the opening night performance that electrifies an audience, be it an audience of twenty at the local nursing home or an audience of three thousand or more at the Met. Every rehearsal, every performance is life or death for the performer.

Biglaw is the same, without the built-in rewards of the art – including the satisfaction of delivering something precious to an audience. So how do you do it, how do you summon the motivation, in the face of all the things that will stand in your way, to give your all? Even if you are not consumed with a desire to take on more complex matters, determined to stick around at the firm long enough to make partner or anything of the sort, you still must find a way to give your all, take true ownership of every assignment – as if your client's life was in your hands alone – if you are to survive and succeed in Biglaw. It is a struggle every day. I have swallowed despair and fought an urge to chuck it all countless times and then turned to the task before me to give it as much as I could. Because the required motivation, energy and focus is hard to maintain every second of every day, you will make mistakes and this chapter – not surprisingly the longest in our journey together – will address how to survive them.

There are two realities you will need to understand in order to navigate Biglaw. First, as a junior associate you will be blamed for everything, no matter who is really at fault. There will always be something you could have done better. Second, you will make so many mistakes of your own early on that the first point will be almost irrelevant. Almost. Both of these realities are unavoidable, but there are things you can do to survive with your humanity intact, lessen the number of mistakes you make in the short run and mitigate the damage when mistakes occur.

Young associates have a tendency to isolate themselves and suffer alone. Don't do it. Your associate colleagues have invaluable information about how to navigate in your firm, how to deal with certain partners – from the one whose behavior is always borderline abusive to the one who demands everything in sixteen point type and highlighted in green. Use all of your fellow associates. Use your mentors. Many firms have ombudsmen, neutral partners you can go to and speak with on an anonymous basis. If you have made a mistake and are suffering in silence and feel you have nowhere else to turn, go to the ombudsman. Find someone to talk with. Many, many other associates are suffering along with you, at the edge of the cliff. No one has an error-free career in Biglaw. You do not have to go it alone.

A. The Blame Game

Biglaw associates have to practice triage on a daily basis under enormous pressure. The scale, scope and complexity of Biglaw cases dictate you will make mistakes. Lots of them. And many of them will not even be entirely your fault. Partners are geniuses at expecting you to read their minds and parse what they want as a final work product. Senior associates are excellent at only communicating part of what you needed to know to finish the assignment successfully, and then at blaming you for not knowing enough to ask them the right questions so that they would remember to tell you all you needed to know to begin with.

Partners and senior associates seem to share an irrebuttable presumption that you are a dumbass, that you are not committed to your work, that you are a slacker, that any mistakes you make are the result of negligence, sloppiness and stupidity rather than honest oversight or lack of experience. This likely comes from years of working with negligent and sloppy attorneys who hate their jobs so much they have lost the capacity to care what happens. Completely not your fault, but you will still have to fight endlessly against this presumption. For the first few years, you may never move beyond it. No senior associate will ever think, "Maybe I didn't explain fully and clearly my expectations, provide enough factual background, give enough information about the logistics of the review database." No partner will ever wonder whether perhaps he was not very good at managing the work streams of his massive, multi-district case or communicating about deadlines.

You know that if you are going to survive Biglaw with your sanity and self-esteem intact you need to develop a thick skin, that you will have to accept from day one that nothing you do will be adequate. Don't take it personally. Senior associates and partners will always be able to find ways in which you could have done more or done better or finished faster or wasted less time or money. Everything, absolutely everything, that can be blamed on you, will be. If there is a miscommunication resulting in some huge screw-up, it will never be the senior associate or partner who takes the blame. It is never that they were unclear or gave you confusing or partial information. Never that they failed to communicate their expectations for what the final work product should encompass and how to best accomplish the task. Never that they gave you completely impossible deadlines and not enough assistance to complete the task as perfectly as they expected. Never that they came back to you eight hours into the project with, "Oh, yeah, focus your search on the 9th Circuit only and don't worry about the estoppel issue," thus rendering your last eight hours of work a complete waste of time.

Never that their expectations for perfection are so screechingly high that no one could possibly reach them, not even Superman.

Rather, it will be that *you* did not understand the instructions and did not seek proper clarification, *you* did not follow up adequately, *you* failed to ask enough questions or the right questions to clarify the objectives of the assignment, *you* worked inefficiently and wasted time and effort, *you* did not delegate enough of the task to assistants to allow you to meet the deadlines. Even if you *did* proactively email a partner with questions and did not hear back from him, it will be *your* fault for not getting an answer. Why didn't you call to follow up and make sure the email was received and didn't fall under the radar? Why didn't you send another email after there was no response for six hours? Why didn't you know Partner X was in a deposition all morning and go ask the other partner on the team? Of course, if you had done any of those things you would have had your head handed to you for some other reason. It will never be the fault of those higher up the chain. That's just the way it is. It will somehow always be your fault.

You will always be wrong because when something goes wrong, which you know is a given, and the penetrating microscope of a senior associate with her rear end on the line is focusing on everything you did and did not do with the clarity of 20/20 hindsight – you will *always* be wrong. This is not just because you are low on the totem pole and blame flows downward. This is Biglaw: there are *always* more or better things you could have done. They will always be able to point to a failure of your understanding or a lack of your knowledge or experience or effort. It can be demoralizing never to be recognized for anything done well and always to be picked apart and informed by those micromanaging senior associates that "in the future" they are "counting on you" to "take ownership" and make sure that X is done right.

Say you are instructed to finish a thirty-page privilege log in one week. You sent samples of your proposed redactions months ago to the senior associate in charge and never heard back from him on whether he approved of your proposed priv calls. There are still thousands of docs to review for privilege and for which to write entries. Then you must go through the log to ensure consistency of methodology, of formatting and just to get rid of the typos. Never mind that this task is impossible. You have a week, and believe me, it better be perfect.

A sense of uneasiness can overtake you and become a constant sinking feeling in the pit of your stomach. Even when the priv log is off your desk it will not feel done and you can go from day to day simply waiting for the other shoe to drop, for the horrible mistake you did not catch to be discovered. You wait for your blackberry to light up with twelve panicked, accusatory emails about what has just gone horribly wrong. It can happen at any time, and it will happen quite a lot. There is no way you can avoid this entirely. No matter how hard you work, how much time you spend QC'ing, how diligently and carefully you work, horrible things will happen. And this uneasiness, this feeling of being shell shocked does not increase your ability to complete tasks with the necessary energy, attack and clarity of mind. If you embrace the concepts and the skills we have been talking about in this book, you will certainly lessen the number of times the shit hits the fan but you will never be able to steer clear altogether. What you can do is understand that this constant, low-level state of anxiety and stress is not your friend and will not improve the quality of your work. So for the sake of your work and in the interest of reducing mistakes you must take seriously techniques for reducing stress and interrupting the cycle of mistakes and blame by holding the big picture in your head and taking every opportunity to release the stress, even for the length of time it takes to walk out of the office and around the block.

Whatever disaster occurs, it will never be the fault of those *lower* than you in the Biglaw hierarchical chain either. If more-junior associates, staff attorneys, contract attorneys or paralegals under your supervision screw-up, it is your fault. You did not QC their work adequately, or you did not provide the needed guidance for others successfully to complete their assignments. Or you did not communicate the instructions, background, context or deadlines clearly enough. You did not delineate your expectations in a way that would allow your subordinates to understand the urgency of the project. You failed to anticipate obvious problems before they arose and did not work to prevent them. Unfortunately, it will never get you out of trouble to say, "Well, the paralegal totally botched the exhibits," or, "the duplicating office can't finish the copies before the FedEx deadline," or, "I'm not sure why the project attorney missed that totally damning, in-your-face, clearly privileged document." Your only course is to swallow the blame and correct the problem.

You cannot win. If you do spend ten hours QC'ing the work of staff attorneys to make sure no document is missed or inconsistently coded, you will be reamed for duplicating efforts, for doing low-level document review work you are too expensive to be billing for, for gross inefficiency and wasting valuable time. When client bills are being reviewed, from down the hall, through closed doors, everyone will hear the screaming. "You cannot read through every document that a staff attorney has coded! What are you thinking? If you had trained your people correctly or provided half-way decent feedback on their work early on, you should be looking at fewer and fewer of their documents over time. We cannot run this case by re-reviewing all of the documents repeatedly!" If, on the other hand, you do *not* spend ten hours QC'ing their work, you will be reamed for every hair's breadth inconsistency in coding that is unearthed in the senior associate's own QC of your work, every arguably relevant document missed, every potentially privileged document overlooked.

Or – another common example – on a new matter, senior associates will instruct you sternly to be over-inclusive in your review, if in doubt, to err on the side of marking a document responsive. Or to err on the side of coding a document potentially privileged so as not to let *any* privileged document out the door. They may share horror stories of that one privileged document out of 30,000 that was let through and the gruesome and permanent ramifications for a past case and then grimly intone, "This cannot be allowed to happen, ever! We cannot let privileged documents out the door!" They will excoriate you for the handful of relevant documents they find that you marked non-responsive. You will be treated to the faux question, "Are you having trouble grasping the facts or issues of this case," in a tone that means only a complete idiot would fail to grasp that this document is clearly responsive. But then, when the universe of documents to be produced swells to something unacceptably over-large and unwieldy from over-inclusive, cautious coding, they will lambast your lack of judgment, your inability to make proper decisions about which documents ought to be left out, your veritable "document dump" review techniques, your slapdash and rushed review pace (crazy deadlines notwithstanding). They will say, "If I wanted every document with the key terms on it marked responsive, I wouldn't need associates, I would have conducted electronic searches. I could have used a trained monkey (or a contract attorney). *You* are expected to bring judgment and intellect commensurate with your position in this firm to this case, not just be an electronic search machine. Perhaps we were mistaken in believing you had such judgment and intellect."

Even if you complete a task and do a decent job, you know there will be more to the story. There is always something you could have "fleshed out" in more detail, or something they will want you to "dig deeper" on, or an aspect you failed to incorporate in your analysis. There is always more to be done, new angles to follow up on, other issues to explore, or a better format or clearer organization of your findings. There is always that one horribly damaging document you should have caught. A writing instructor once said to me, "Biglaw attorneys, more than any other attorneys, ruthlessly hunt down ambiguity, weakness and flaw and drag them screaming into the daylight." So when Biglaw attorneys turn their focus on you and your work, and they will do so more often than you wish, you are going to be blamed for something.

Keep your focus on doing your best for every single assignment. That brilliantly-articulated eight-page email definitively proving beyond a shadow of a doubt that the mistake was not your fault? Never going to be a good idea – and you cannot take the time to write it. Okay. If it makes you feel better and you have time, go ahead and write but for heaven's sake do not even consider sending it. Take it on the chin, as it were, and let it go. If you let every little thing wound you, you will have a hard road. Concentrate on the work that is before you and on finding ways to break the cycle of stress, hold onto your humanity and retain some enjoyment in life. Force yourself to get out of the office and walk around during lunch. Set aside time to grab coffee with friends. Take a couple hours a week to take a yoga class. What you do is an individual matter, but you must give priority to the things that add richness and passion to your life.

B. Mistakes Will Be Made

Aside from all of the mistakes you will not make but for which you will be blamed, unfortunately, you will actually make plenty of mistakes of your own as a baby lawyer. Even though there is ample reason to know you know nothing on day one, things will be thrown at you as though you knew a great deal, with very little tolerance for ignorance or inexperience. Some of your mistakes will be unbelievably trivial – getting a deadline wrong because you simply miscounted the number of days when you put it on the calendar or forgetting a comma in a citation. Some of your mistakes will feel like the end of the world. You will email a newsletter from the Privacy group to the firm's major corporate clients, discussing routine developments in internet privacy law, and realize only after you hit the "send" button that you should have bcc'd all the recipients, so the clients would not be able to see the other mega-corporation clients on the list. Clients tend to be very sensitive about others knowing they are clients. You will let a horrible, damaging, obviously privileged document out the door that details litigation strategy for your case. You will miss a case obviously dispositive in your jurisdiction and it will come to light the night before oral argument. Even when you are diligent, cautious and do your best in all things, you will screw up. I will talk a little about avoiding mistakes to begin with, and then how to lessen the damage and ire you will face when you make them.

C. Avoiding Mistakes

No one can ensure that you will avoid making mistakes entirely, but there are habits of mind and ways of working that will reduce their number. Remember the keys to Biglaw professionalism we talked about in chapter six? Developing habits of judgment, prudence, precision and diligence, developing a practice characterized by careful deliberation, attention to detail, thorough and exhaustive preparation, it is this road that will lead to the fewest derailments. We will be reviewing all of the concepts we have been talking about in this book in this section.

From day one, junior associates are thrown into highly complex cases with very little of the experience and knowledge and few of the skills necessary to succeed. The number of times I have heard an associate exclaim, "Well, they didn't teach me that in law school!" is roughly comparable to the number of times I told myself I needed to make the time to write this book. My first week at the firm I was told to draft and file a minor motion, with no other explanation. Never having worked as a paralegal, I had no idea how to finalize and file a motion. A couple of mid-level attorneys helped me through it, and they told me something that day that has stuck with me over the years. The truth of it has been borne out on numerous occasions. "It's not going to matter that you didn't know anything and just started here a week ago. Your head will roll just the same if you don't get this right."

There are more ways for new associates to make mistakes than there are descriptions of ways to avoid them. You will probably trip over them all at least once. You will be thrown into cases full throttle and expected to catch up. You will begin working for attorneys who have been doing things in a minutely particularized way for decades and have complex and bizarre systems for running their cases – networks of cross-referencing spreadsheets tracking every little thing, which you should have known to update. Masses of specific, but to you unspecified, procedures for accomplishing every little task lurk in every case file. How would you have known that this partner expects weekly detailed spreadsheets on all work flows and ongoing projects? Or that she likes briefs to have a particularized, arcane format and hates (or adores) the Oxford comma?

So what do you do? What *can* you do? Knowing that mistakes are inevitable may reduce some of the stress that increases their likelihood. If you concentrate on developing the level of Biglaw professionalism you need to survive, you will have a positive map and goal before you as opposed to a minefield. This concept of professionalism we have been discussing throughout this book is not some lofty aspiration designed to guarantee a streamlined partnership track or a theme for a motivational poster designed to make you "be the best attorney you can be." If in no other way, it should engage your urgent attention simply as a matter of self-preservation. As we have said, in Biglaw, your level of professionalism is your shield.

You must develop the ability to analyze a brief at a glance and automatically see the weaknesses, omissions, poor support and other flaws. You must have a hypercritical eye to spot typos, organizational problems, inconsistent logic and factual errors in an instant. This critical focus will become how you *practice* law and it will be how you minimize mistakes. Always ask yourself what you have left out, what could be stated better or more concisely, how you could make your work product clearer. Learn to anticipate questions a senior associate will ask and address them in the first draft. Always check your work, double check it and then read through it again. Every assignment, no matter how trivial, must be attacked as if it were your moment in front of the Supreme Court. As in the performing arts, in the fifth Friday afternoon rehearsal of the tiniest part, you must give your all and put all of your energy and passion into everything you do. You must always be one hundred percent engaged. This will become second nature, the quality of your work will improve enormously and, over time, there will be fewer mistakes on your watch. And then one day, after eight or nine years, you will wake up and realize that you are a senior associate and that all of this is unconscious and automatic and that you bring this level of perspective and focus and care to everything you do and then you will find you have finally moved out of doc review hell.

Throughout this book I have talked about the kind of professionalism you need to develop and how to develop it. Like the hapless students of my *prima donna* voice teacher in the world of opera or an Olympic track star, you must strive and strain to reach a higher level of practice in Biglaw. Mistakes and fools will not be suffered lightly. There are a few basic principles, things we have been talking about all along, that may be helpful to review in terms of avoiding mistakes.

One good rule of thumb is to **err on the side of doing too much** whenever reasonably practicable within the usual constraints: time and money. Do more than is asked, spend a little more time making sure it is polished, well-organized and tightly constructed, and give more attention than is expected. When all that is asked for is "a quick email" summarizing main points or findings, make sure the email is clear, is impeccably organized, has your findings and conclusions immediately up front to leap out at the partner, contains bullet points with bold headings of the major issues and is thorough, well-supported and double checked. No one is interested in creative writing or flare – get your findings right up front, your conclusions or thoughts clearly expressed and your support easily understood. This does not mean you can take eight hours to draft an email any more than you can take eight weeks to make a document production a work of pristine perfection. What it does mean is that, on balance, you should take the time to ensure things are done right and done well.

You cannot do that if you allow partners and senior associates to pressure you into doing a sloppy job. **Do not cave in to pressure**. You know how much pressure you will be under. The terse, all caps emails every ten minutes howling, "WHAT IS YOUR STATUS?!!!!" will not be helping you to do anything properly or to avoid errors and will be sending your stress levels stratospheric. It is your job to focus on the task at hand and refuse to buy into it. If it is so urgent that you know no other matter could trump it, turn off your email notifications, get your head down and push through. They will roast you just the same if you slap off something half-assed. Fight the urge to please them in the short term and rush something out that has not had your full attention. You know it will not be their fault if you do a shoddy job under the pressure of their demands, it will be on you so you must take the time you need to do it right. If they will not let up, then push back and make clear the parameters of what you can and cannot do in the time allowed: "Okay, I can get this to you in an hour, but I will not have had time to QC the work of the staff attorneys." At least then they will have been apprised of the risks. It does not mean they will not blame you if there is a mistake but at least you will be able to document their acceptance of the scaling back of the assignment and of some additional risk and that will reduce the risk to you.

You must **give your best effort, always**. If you are a slacker, or regularly turn in sloppy, half-assed work, if you leave your task to the last minute and then try to rush through, if you are burned out and try to get by glazing over several hundred documents, coding them in a willy-nilly way, your days in Biglaw will be numbered. The only way you will survive all the mistakes you will inevitably make and the ones you will be unjustly accused of making is if you have done your damnedest to get it right at least most of the time. As a junior associate, you will still make numerous mistakes – large and small – even if you are busting your ass to get it right – so you better be busting it. If you can demonstrate that you are doing all that you can (and we get more specific about how to demonstrate that below), that you are committed to the team, that you are serious and determined, that you are proactive and tried to get it right, that you take real ownership of your work, that you will get it right next time, associates and partners will forgive you. They will still make your life hell, but they will understand that mistakes are unavoidable from time to time with all that you are responsible for doing. You will live to make more mistakes another day.

The Big Picture. Even though no one will offer it and all circumstances will conspire against your acquiring it, getting an understanding of the big picture of your case may inoculate you against some of the worst errors and omissions. Read the pleadings and background materials. When you get a new assignment, seek to understand with complete clarity what is expected of you and where your work fits in. How will your research be used? Is it going to be plugged into a brief, or used in a memo to the client? Do they want to find only a representative sample of this kind of doc, or do they want you to find every instance of it in the document universe? That will require a very different kind of review and you need to know it before you begin. Do you they want you to prove a negative, which takes even more time: look in the document production (over a million docs, likely) and tell me that there are *no* instances of X. That must be thorough and complete and will be incredibly time consuming and hard to accomplish with any level of confidence.

If you are not sure of anything – when it is due, how much give there might be in the deadline, what form of work product is needed, how long you should spend on the task – then ask questions until you understand. The biggest mistakes are often the result of incomplete information or misunderstandings. Do not ever take off running on some cloudy idea of what is expected – you will only waste time and more often than not find yourself having to redo everything. If you feel lost after discussing the case with the senior attorney, go back to your office and read all of the background materials you can find. Spend some time trying to absorb the facts and relevant issues and thinking about the case. It should orient you and make the information you have been given fall into place. But if you are still lost, reach out again and ask for more clarification. Even if you meet with ridicule and rebuke it will be far better than wandering around in confused darkness or pressing on blindly with the task doing untold damage in the process.

Also, when things are slower, ask to see the final work product to which your work contributed. Look at how much of your research and what parts were actually found useful by the senior attorneys. Read all the docs you found that they decided to include. You will rarely be offered this kind of valuable feedback from senior associates and partners but it is incredibly helpful for you to see what was taken from what you submitted and what was discarded, so you need to choose a moment when it will not be unseemly to ask and get this information for yourself. How else can you learn more about what might be relevant and important? Even though you will not often have time, or energy, to read things that are not part of your billable work, this is really the only way you will get feedback in many situations.

Communication Skills. Excellent communication skills are of paramount importance in Biglaw. Since in the beginning you will almost never make a decision without running it by a more senior attorney (see discussion below on recognizing when something is above your pay grade), you had better be brilliantly concise and clear in your communications. Everyone needs to be on the same page. When you are first given your assignment, always ask when it is needed and probe on this as much as you can without being obnoxious. Ask them what kind of work product they are expecting: a full memo, draft sections of a brief, bullet point emails, a chart, a quick discussion over the phone? Ask them how much time they are anticipating you should spend on the task. And right then and there in the initial discussion you should raise any potential issues you foresee – your time is going to be constrained next week on another case, you have already asked for this Friday off, or anything else you know of that may present a problem to completing your task. It is important to set the senior associate's expectations on what you can do right away, instead of coming in sheepishly a few days later and mentioning that you have theater tickets and will be leaving half of your work undone.

Since your job is to make it exponentially easier for senior attorneys to learn what you have learned, your ability to communicate is key. If you circulate a document that they saw last week and gave you changes and edits for, outline each change you made in response to their comments in an email, tell them what you added or removed, and anything else they need to know. If time permits, include a clean copy of the new draft along with a redlined version, showing all of the changes. They are not about to read it from scratch, trying to remember what it said last week and what they told you. Your job is a support function and you need to break everything down into quick, easy-to-digest bites.

Whenever an unforeseen problem comes up, you should immediately talk with another attorney to discuss a new plan of action, adjust the deadline or otherwise alert someone to the new situation. Problems come up all the time and the reaction will only get worse if you sit on something and do not communicate quickly with others on your team, whether it is a need for more time or for more information. It will be easy to think that you are bugging them, that this is too trivial, that you can surely figure this one out on your own but all you are doing is delaying the inevitable ire and increasing the chances for error. They will be much happier for you to get what you need to do something right than for you to bound off on some misapprehension and botch the project completely. Clarify, restate what you understand them to be asking for, send them a draft to show them the format you propose and let them provide input early on in the assignment. If you do not, you will work twenty hours, turn it in and get it thrown back at you because they wanted a table instead of bullet points, they wanted parentheticals instead of long blocks of text, they needed a focus on a different area. There will be something amiss. Trust me.

More problems are caused for young associates every day because of poor communication than anything else. It is indeed a very poor reflection on your intelligence if you allow fear of a poor reflection on your intelligence to prevent you from seeking needed information. If you do not understand, let someone know. If you still do not understand go to the senior associate. If an assignment will take longer, be more expensive or more complicated than originally thought, let someone know right away. If another case just exploded and is sucking you in for the next three days and you will have no time to turn to other assignments, let someone know. If you are confused or clueless about the case background, what is expected in your assignment, or anything else, let someone know. If you think you have found a better way to do things, let someone know. If you disagree with a call from the senior associate, let someone know.

Keep the senior associates updated on your progress regularly. Do not wait for them to ask where you are on a task – check in on a regular, periodic basis. They like to hear about the kinds of documents you are seeing, potential issues you may have flagged, holes in the document universe (holes are kinds of documents one would expect to see in a given case, with the custodians you have but that seem to be missing from your production). If you do not tell them, they cannot know what you are seeing, or how fast you are going. The more they know, the happier they will be. If you are going to miss a deadline, you need to let the senior attorney know as early as possible. Your clear and timely communication makes it possible for her to make the decision to extend the deadline or get you help. As we have seen, many associates and partners establish deadlines for you that have nothing to do with when the thing is actually needed so that they can have plenty of time for their edits and to allow for the possibility of emergencies coming up that will delay their attention – or to give them a week to procrastinate. But that is, after all, their prerogative. If any of these are the case, the deadline can often be pushed back. But none of this works if you do not communicate.

Of course, the usual caveats about judgment and prudence always apply: this does not mean that you email a senior associate every three minutes with status reports or piddling questions about every little thing. Good communication is not communication that buries its recipient in trivial inanities. Find efficient ways to ask questions. Instead of emailing after coming across a single difficult document, put aside a stack of thirty difficult or illustrative documents and then go and talk to the associate about how she would code them. Think through all the issues fully before you take something to the next level and remember to present your superiors with a concise summary of your analysis and conclusions and possible solutions, rather than coming to them only with a problem. In all of your communications be very careful to understand the level of the person to whom you are bringing your issue. You would not want to discuss vendor issues with a partner (about which they will have no clue at this point in their careers). One of the unpleasant consequences of such communication errors is to find yourself speaking to someone who cuts you off with a curt, "This is not my conversation."

Communication skills are especially important in juggling the competing demands on your time and meeting your deadlines. Many times you will be given an assignment with a flexible deadline. You are told it is not urgent and to get to it when you can. Weeks go by and you are pulled from one fire drill to the next on that and other matters. You never hear another word about the assignment you were to have addressed when you had the time you have not yet had until the day the partner shows up in your office out of the blue and wants to see the finished product. You need to protect yourself from a scenario like this by pressing for clear statements of deadlines when you receive assignments. If you have eight other more important projects you are juggling, list them for the partner and ask how *she* prioritizes them and which can get pushed aside if need be. Let her know at that time of other cases on which you are active. If you do this, then, at the very least, she will be on notice that you have a lot going on and will get to her less urgent project when other more important projects have been completed.

Take Ownership. You need to take ownership of your work. That means taking responsibility from day one to get your work done right. No one is going to hold your hand or call you up and remind you of that one thing you forgot whose deadline is looming. Whenever possible, you should be getting things in before their deadlines. You know how often things will happen that you cannot predict so staying ahead is always prudent. If necessary, get it in by the deadline. It is your work, your deadline. You own it.

So what is "ownership?" Senior associates love this word as much as many junior associates come to loathe it. Your superiors will beat you about the head and shoulders with it if you make a mistake, it will appear on year-end evaluations questioning your commitment or diligence, but what does it mean really? If your sense of ownership is questioned it is a sure sign that there is a perception you are not doing a good job. It is a dreaded word for junior associates. I received the following email recently from a friend who labors as a junior associate in another firm: "Sitting in team meeting right now. [Annoying senior associate] XX has used the word 'ownership' five times. I hate that word."

Ownership of a case, or of your responsibilities on a case, was explained to me once by a partner, thusly: if you showed up to work one day and everyone else on the team had died, and you *had* to get something done – file a brief, get a production finalized and out the door, manage a privilege review or whatever your task – you would move heaven and earth, on your own, to make it happen. Period. You would figure out a way to get it done. Even if you had never done a priv log, taken a deposition, figured out a thorough and efficient system for QC'ing the work of your contract attorneys, drafted a document summary of the key documents for a witness for client distribution or whatever the task at hand might be. Even if you had to sell your soul, lose a week of sleep, crawl through the mud. You would get it done. You would not pepper the senior associate with trivial question after trivial question, pass off responsibility to others, wait and do nothing while nothing got done, fail to follow-up when others dropped the ball, wait for the problem to go away or fix itself. You would turn yourself inside out to address and resolve issues and problems yourself. You would act as if the responsibility for the case were yours alone.

This does not mean you do everything yourself in a vacuum. Everything we have been talking about in terms of the need for clear, regular communication still applies. There is no tension between these two concepts. Ownership is the way you approach all that you do. You approach your case with that perspective, that level of commitment and the-buck-stops-here energy. But you still communicate and you still seek guidance and you must still recognize when a decision is above your pay grade – see discussion below. You check with anyone you can think of that might help (IT personnel, library resources, vendors), you research, you think of solutions. Then, and only then, you go to the senior attorney with the problem and your plan, your solution to the problem, your ideas about how to do things. Your ideas may be rejected out of hand – but that level of engagement and commitment is what is expected. You are a fully-engaged and productive member of a team. You are never passive, inert, zoned out. You do not run into a roadblock and hand it off to someone else, leaving him or her to deal with the problem.

Ownership certainly does not mean you go off on wild frolics of your own. You must still communicate and you must get senior attorneys to authorize your actions. But taking ownership means you are a full member of the team and you feel as committed to the success of the case as its lead partner and you show it. You work just as hard to learn about the case, to solve problems and give all of your time, talent and intellect to pulling it off successfully.

Showing ownership, or pride in your work, can be very hard to do under standard Biglaw conditions – constant criticism, micromanaging and pettiness, repetitive drudgery with no end in sight and work that seems anything but important or appreciated. Do you actually give a damn if one single document out of the millions you produced happens to be incorrectly coded? There will be days that you will not. But if you muster this ownership approach to your work, even if you fake it on the days you must, you will find that you will make fewer mistakes and your overall course will be much smoother. There will be times you will feel yourself to be perfectly capable of letting down that person who has been tormenting you for the last month but your own pride will keep you honest if you keep yourself fully engaged intellectually and own your work. You are getting paid the big bucks, and you are expected to show the level of commitment and zeal on your cases that is commensurate with a Biglaw associate.

Managing Your Work Flow. For junior associates, work flow is almost never consistent. By now you know the drill. Some days you are slammed, peppered every fifteen minutes with requests both trivial and not. Cases are so urgent, you feel like you have to email the team just to let them know you are running out for fifteen minutes to grab lunch. Other days, you flit along without hearing from anyone, with nothing to do, wondering whether your case settled and no one bothered to tell you. (It happens.) You could leave the office for the rest of the afternoon and no one would notice or care. And other times, it seems a mix of both. You sit all morning "organizing your files" or "performing administrative tasks" and then just when you are toying with the idea of going out for a two-hour late lunch, everything hits the fan and you are swamped with one fire drill after another. (Remember that partners and senior associates have a marked tendency to get around to thinking about your work sometime after four in the afternoon, when suddenly you will have a rush of follow-up assignments and checking in.) Deadlines can be arbitrary and sometimes meaningless. Routine assignments can suddenly become urgent or become irrelevant and be forgotten entirely. You will hear nothing about an assignment for two weeks, and then the partner will call, demanding to have it on his desk before you leave that day. If you are working fifty percent on one matter and fifty percent on another, very often each team will act as if it were entitled to one hundred percent of your time. It can be very confusing at first to balance and get through.

We have talked about the big cases, where there can be a large network of regular, steady work streams: various phases of privilege review; doc review, issue coding, production and other discovery issues; substantive research; building the factual part of a case; legal questions; a string of depositions or interviews to prepare for and various motions and responses. These may all have orderly schedules and you may be lured into thinking you can plan in advance how to balance your various cases. But it is never that simple. In the midst of your regular deadlines for finishing your doc review batch or your usual routine for QC'ing the review of staff attorneys, you will find yourself deluged with random demands. A partner will email out of nowhere, "I need the PowerPoint slide deck on criminal FCPA prosecutions over the last five years updated by three p.m." Or, "Why didn't document 194327 get included in the binder we sent to joint defense counsel?" Translated: "You will spend the next two hours backtracking and figuring it out, give me an answer that I'm satisfied with and let me know who I can yell at." Or, "The judge has moved up the deadline and we need to file this today." Sometimes, satisfying these demands will take over your entire day, leaving all of your regular assignments and deadlines at risk. If you know you need to prepare witness preparation materials for the vice president of your client's company by next week, start the day you get the assignment, knowing that Tuesday could disappear into re-reviewing documents you discover were missed in the first review and resolving technical issues and Thursday and Friday could be eaten up by some crazy fire drill completely unrelated to the case.

A key to managing inconsistent work flow is to make every effort to complete tasks as soon as they are assigned. Procrastination is tantamount to a death wish. Big mistake. If you wait until the last minute before something is due, even if you have calculated correctly and to the millisecond the amount of time required, which is impossible, you will always, always run into snags. You will begin a two-hour project with two hours to go, and something inarguably more urgent will land on your desk. Or – and here we return to that assertion of the impossibility of knowing how long a thing will take – you will quickly realize you will never be able to get through all of the documents you need to review in time. So you will rush through, breezing through handfuls of documents, and something key will end up being overlooked. Or you will wait until the day something is due, instead of doing it days early, and you will make the deadline, confidently handing it over to the senior associate at four p.m. on a Friday, with visions of happy hour dancing in your head. Thirty minutes later you get a call, asking why you did not draft a summary of the key documents while you were going along, why you did not include documents from custodian X in your searches, or whatever, and your weekend is blown.

You have to give the senior associates plenty of time to get back to you with follow-up issues, questions or new, related assignments. You will not escape them by waiting until the last second. You will just make yourself crazy. It is not that your work is deficient or that you are stupid. You simply have to leave time for them to evaluate your work. It will always raise questions for a diligent senior associate. "Why weren't there more docs from 2003 regarding the company policy change? And, about this new issue you saw in the documents, who was involved, when, why, how?" Or, "Please add a column in the spreadsheet reflecting the number of documents produced versus the number reviewed." Or even, "Please re-format this outline to use **BOLD CAPS** for the headings and ***bold italics*** for subheadings." There will always be tweaks, follow up, clarification, organizational comments, holes to fill or new issues that arise. Allow for that and your course will be much smoother.

Everyone at the top and at the bottom in Biglaw tends to underestimate the amount of time required to finish an assignment – partners because they want it yesterday and junior associates because they do not have enough experience.

It will always take longer than you think. And you know why, because there will always be something else. Always. Not because you have made a mistake necessarily but because in this practice everything is possible. The mistake is to fail to allow for contingencies. You are going to have to spend the endless hours to master the documents of your case, understand the context, spot hidden issues and organize the facts, all of which you will check, double check, re-check and confirm again. This takes time.

Another reason to get assignments off your plate quickly is to free up your own availability. If you are dying to get deposition experience and the *pro bono* coordinator calls you up out of the blue, you do not want a bunch of lingering assignments that could have been finished standing in the way. If you have been lobbying for months hoping to work with Partner X on trademark issues, I guarantee she will not call until you could not possibly take on another assignment.

The key to successful management of your workload is keeping things moving. It is like tennis: you want to get the ball back over the net. Say you cannot finish your task right away because something is holding you up. Find a way to keep the ball in motion. I try to bounce it back to senior associates as quickly as I can. Then, it is in their court and I can forget about it until they have the time to deal with it and come back with follow ups. I get it done and send it off and then at least can stop stressing about it until they finish.

Countless are the ways a junior associate can be tempted to procrastinate. The work is often boring beyond description. And it can feel endless. Just starting a project sometimes takes a will of steel. But the quicker you get through it, the better you off you will be.

Organization and Paper Trail. In everything you do in Biglaw, you should develop airtight organizational skills, not only to be effective and useful on your cases, but also to cover your own ass. All of the things we are talking about here as keys to avoiding mistakes and missteps – seeing the big picture, communication, taking ownership, managing your work flow – are important and basic but without superlative organization and meticulous paper trails you will be completely lost. Keep track of your deadlines, key documents and witnesses in a case and all of the important team communications. Go crazy building numberless, massive tracking Excel spreadsheets and work stream progress charts so that months after the fact, when a partner asks you if a binder was sent to local counsel regarding X important issue you can provide proof, along with dates, times, numbers of volumes, which custodians were searched for the documents in the binder, how many document productions were included, whether an updated binder with newer productions or custodians might now be required, in a matter of minutes. They will ask you which custodians were included – and they will expect you to know, so keeping close track of all of this as you go is key. You cannot possibly remember every minute detail about a case on your own. You will always be dealing with too much new information coming in and you will not be able to keep up with everything. Six months down the pike, when it becomes important, you are not going to remember a thing about why a decision was made to do something or who was responsible for something else. The purpose behind all the binders, spreadsheets, lists and endless waves of documentation is to master the facts and information of your case. And if we have done nothing else by now we have hammered home the point that this is Biglaw's *raison d'être*: only Biglaw can master all of the facts so well, and you must master the means of parsing those facts in order to thrive.

Developing a practice of organization is also crucial for your own protection. You need to be able to document your work. It is important to keep all communications that will permit you to track changes in instructions or new directions from partners. It happens more than I can say that months and months after the fact an issue will come up about why you are doing something a certain way, or a mistake will come to light and a partner will demand to know what the hell happened eight months ago to cause it. How did the contract attorneys you were supervising miss this bad document? Did you train them on the correct issues? You need to have the review guidelines ready. Did you QC regularly? You want to be able to anatomize the methodology, saying, "All documents were reviewed by at least two contract attorneys, then QC'd by a senior staff attorney and I personally viewed twenty percent of the responsive documents. We reviewed the docs marked 'Not Responsive' for error and did not find anything that would give us concerns about the coding."

You do not want to be floundering through five thousand email files trying to track it down. You will have emails with case directions segregated, you will have tracking charts, notes from meetings and clear documentation of the instructions you received, proof that your methodology was approved and proof of how you carried out those instructions. This will be important more often than I can say. Cases can be massive. In the rush to get things done, to meet deadlines, to respond to repeated fire drills, memories will blur. And when something goes wrong, you will want to be able to show that you were doing what was expected, that you were diligent in your efforts, that you communicated frequently with senior associates and that you did the best you possibly could to avoid problems. When a partner is yelling, "Why did you do this that way!!?!?," you need to have an irrefutable response to deflect all the anger that is flying at you. The more organized you become, the more you will able to protect yourself when things go wrong.

The same organizational skills will assist you in developing your practice from day one. Begin collecting samples of review guidelines you used for different cases, sample priv logs you have produced, good briefs containing general subject matter that might come up again in some other context or another case, ideas of how cases are managed and run. If you see a particularly useful way of organizing a spreadsheet to track a document collection, save a copy for the next case. As we have stressed throughout, lawyers very rarely seek to engage in creative efforts when it comes to nuts and bolts case management. Not reinventing the wheel is common sense and has nothing to do with taking the lazy way out and it certainly is not cheating. By now it should be crystal clear how inefficient it would be to try to come up with everything from scratch. The truth is the more you can cannibalize the good, the more effective you will be. Your speed will increase exponentially as you build a folder of templates and boilerplates you can compare, choose among and reuse.

Recognize What Things Are Above Your Pay Grade. All of these things we are discussing are interrelated but perhaps none more than this. If you want to avoid the most serious, career-threatening mistakes, make this understanding the ground note of your practice. In the beginning, just about everything is above your pay grade. If you are asked to draft a cover letter to send a DVD of documents to opposing counsel, you will probably think this is no big deal. Why not handle this yourself? It's a cover letter. You successfully managed more complicated tasks before law school. You are a highly-credentialed and intelligent person. You may even have had a successful career before Biglaw, in which you handled important matters on your own. So why can't you sign off on a cover letter? Why do you have to send it to a sixth-year attorney to approve? It seems ridiculous. Wrong. If you send that letter out, believe me, you will regret it. It is hard to accept how far this actually goes and this is a main factor in the endless frustration. In Biglaw, you are not even trusted to create labels for witness prep binders alone. Many senior associates want to make sure it is done their way but cannot spend the time to do it themselves. If you are drafting an email to send to the contract attorneys regarding certain errors you have noted in coding and providing guidance, send it to the senior associate first. She will have edits.

As ambitious, over-achieving individuals, junior associates tend to have a lot of confidence in their own decisions and abilities. There is a fierce desire to be independent that comes with the qualities of mind and the level of education necessary to get where they are. I often thought in the early years, "Why do I need to run every difficult document to code by a senior attorney? Why can't I just make a call here and go with it?" You know the answer: not in Biglaw. Let all of this go. Do not try to do anything on your own in the first few years. Senior attorneys, by nature, are nervous, risk-averse and believe that only they have the judgment, prudence, knowledge and experience to make good decisions. Anything you do alone will likely not be what they would have done, and thus, it will be wrong by definition.

If you reconcile yourself to this truth you will save yourself from future blame if something goes wrong. There is no point in putting yourself in the line of fire when you do not have to. Get everything you do, no matter how trivial, approved by someone above you. I felt ridiculous every time I sent for approval a cover letter that read, "Enclosed please find ten binders for witness X. Please call us if you have any questions. Sincerely, Partner Y." But lawyers are extremely anal, type-A sorts and Biglaw gathers the most extreme. Your senior associates will want to read that letter and approve it before it goes out the door in the first year or so. This passion for oversight can be more than a manifestation of obsessive-compulsive personality. Perhaps there has been a change you would have no way of knowing about in the client relationships and Partner Y is persona non grata this week. The letter should have been signed by Partner Z. Perhaps, unbeknownst to you, there is another binder to go out containing another sub-set of documents you did not know existed. Perhaps the contact person at the client company changed overnight. How would you know sending to the person you always send things to would be wrong this time? They will let you know when the time comes that they trust you to send a letter out without their approval. Until then, get it approved. If you are going to survive one month in Biglaw, you just need to do it.

And while it is true for the trivial, it is a billion times more important for calls that could have long-reaching consequences. Don't touch them with a ten-foot pole. Senior associates get very cranky if they are hit with a surprise. If you run a search and get four thousand docs, do not dive in and spend the next week going through them and then cheerily mention a week later that you are nowhere near making the deadline. Immediately email the attorney in charge and let him know. If a vendor calls and says that the amount for processing each gigabyte needs to be increased by five dollars – or even five cents – find someone else to approve it. Have a superior sign off on your plan before you do anything. If you need to make a call about how many staff attorneys to staff on a given matter or whether a document is privileged, and you find yourself pausing for even a moment to think about it, that is a sign to get input. Never make those gray area decisions on your own as a junior associate. You will get a sense later on – and we will talk about how to develop that sense below – and more and more of your calls will turn out to be correct. For now, you need to cover your ass and if you are looking at a document for even a moment and saying to yourself, "Well, I could code it this way, but it might be better coded this way . . . ," then put it aside until you have consulted with someone else, remembering, of course, to apply the points we talked about earlier regarding communication skills. Imagine the consequences if you were to code the next eight hundred documents under the same theory before the error were to be picked up in the QC. I would say that, early in my career, every single time I had that moment where I paused and thought I was not certain how to proceed and then made a close call without any outside input, I came to regret it.

We also talked earlier about a possible perceived tension between the concepts of communication and ownership and how to reconcile them. The same applies here. This is the tightrope every junior associate must walk. You must bring your intellect to your cases, take ownership, be engaged and involved, contribute your thinking, add real value to your team, not just mechanically follow orders and mindlessly scan documents. But in the beginning, you know so very little about Biglaw practice that it is not safe for you to make important decisions on your own.

And important decisions can be:

"Is this a privileged document or not really?"

"Should this document be coded for this issue even though it is discussing it outside the relevant date?"

"How should I set up the review platform for the contract attorneys – do we really need a check box that says 'Reviewed"?

"I've seen someone in a document talking about an issue that seems odd, although it isn't anything the partner said the case is about. Should I show it to anyone?"

You need to understand that, in the early days, you may come to the wrong conclusion more often than not. But that does not mean you should not struggle with the issues and formulate an answer. It means you must complete your own analysis and seek confirmation from a superior. You must still throw yourself into your cases and be responsible for getting your assignments completed. But getting the right guidance and realizing what things you should not be deciding alone is part of that process. Early on, I would advise asking a more-senior associate about every single question you have. After a few months, you might find there is a little less that you don't have a clue about or about which you have no prior experience to bring to bear. After two years, even less. But there are still days even now when I stop and think, "I'm not sure about this . . . . I wonder . . . ." I know at that point that the decision is above my pay grade and I do not want to make it alone. And all attorney have learned this. You will see senior associates pause throughout your case and put an issue on hold until they have had the chance to run it by the partner. They have learned what you will need to learn – there will always be things above your pay grade and it is important to learn what they are.

Transparency. Being transparent in your work habits is another counter-intuitive characteristic you need to develop to do well in Biglaw. It really goes along with leaving a paper trail and it is essential to your survival but, in the face of so much criticism, there is a natural tendency to want to be less and less transparent in your work, to try to hide the ball:

"If they don't know where I searched for the legal support, they won't be able to tear it apart and tell me to search other places or berate me for missing something obvious. They'll just assume that I did everything I should."

Wrong.

"I've already been trudging through this assignment for nine hours and I'm fed up and don't want to do anymore. If they don't see the search terms I used to find important documents about a certain issue, they won't be able to criticize me, tell me to do it all over again, and tear apart what I've worked so hard and so long to accomplish. Maybe it will save me just a little work."

Wrong.

It is completely natural. Every fiber of your being will scream out when you have to redo an already onerous assignment from scratch. "You mean you only searched in the Produced database and not the Review database? And only for electronic documents (emails, files)? Now you need to go back and search through all of the scanned hard copy documents because they have not been OCR'd and will not show up in your electronic searches. And you need to go to the other database and review all the docs you can find there." It is natural to want to try to prevent them from doing that to you. But the impulse is all wrong. In Biglaw, all of this will happen anyway: you will get criticized, you will be torn apart, your decisions to search this treatise but not that one will be questioned, your search terms will be ferreted out and then shredded. And you will have to do many, many things over. It is going to happen and nothing you do will prevent it. No senior associate worth his or her salt is going to accept anything (especially from a junior associate!) without question.

So let go of those self-protective impulses right away. Moving in the opposite direction is what will protect you. Remember what we have talked about in terms of communication, paper trail and recognizing what things are above your pay grade. No difference here. As you become more and more transparent, you force the senior associates to take more responsibility for your assignments and thus decrease the likelihood that you will be found completely inadequate and be forced to do it all over again. Before you spend seven hours searching for information with a flawed methodology – or even one that just differs from what your superiors might have chosen, no matter – let the senior associates know your planned search terms, which databases you are searching in, how many relevant documents you are finding initially, additional issues you are seeing that may complicate the matter, etc. Close your email with, "Please let me know if you have any additional terms to add." If you send them your search terms, they will likely suggest a few more that you should try. This increases your work on the front end but may radically reduce it overall. You have got to demonstrate that your efforts are broad, exhaustive, comprehensive and that you are catching important issues as they come up. You need to give them confidence in your work product and insulate yourself from criticism when something goes wrong. No better way to do that than to let them tweak the parameters. This is especially useful when you do not find what they wanted you to find. If they had no idea about your methods and you come back empty-handed, you will be redoing a lot of work. If they had input up front, there is a lot less they will feel the need to redo.

Sometimes junior associates fail transparency not out of self-protectiveness but out of misdirected zeal. For example, a junior associate decides that the production review batch from the contract attorneys that he is QC'ing is a mess – bad calls and sloppy coding abound. So he spends an additional six hours reviewing a batch of docs that the senior attorney expected would take two hours, fixing the coding himself, making sure he is confident that everything has been done properly before marking it approved on the spreadsheet and moving to the next batch. He diligently ensured the coding was correct. He did a good job. What could be wrong here? You already know the answer. Now the QC is not going to be finished in time, and the senior associate will not even know there was a problem until she is told, days later, that the deadline will not be met, that there are still several outstanding batches to be reviewed. And our misguided junior associate wasted six hours on one batch. At his billing rate, that is a pretty expensive batch of documents. He failed to report the problem to his senior associate before he went trudging back through the entire batch and wasted a lot of time. He figured the best way to ensure something was done right was to fix it himself and get on with the next. What she would have told him immediately, if he had brought the bad coding to her attention, was to send it back to the reviewers, with specific examples of missed calls, bullet point critiques of issues that were found, etc., perhaps schedule a follow-up call with reviewers to discuss the missed issues as a group and then to move on to his next batch while they redid the problematical one. Then he would have an opportunity to re-QC a portion of the corrected batch to make sure the reviewers understood the corrections and provide more follow up as necessary. Contract attorneys need feedback and careful supervision and, when there is a problem, you have to let them go back through the documents and do it over or their work will never improve. Yes, it would have taken an hour to draft the email and find useful examples of documents to attach with it, but that would have been one extra hour instead of six. Would the junior associate's coding be more reliable than a contract attorney's? Certainly. But he should have known from the beginning that he should not be doing something outside of his pay grade and he should have thought clearly about the need for transparency and communication.

Remember what we said about running a search and coming up with four thousand documents? Same thing: let the senior associate know. If they want you to proceed and review every one of those four thousand documents, fine, at least you are covered and your time has been authorized. But the greater likelihood is that they will come up with another way to get at the information you are searching for. And you will have protected yourself from later criticism. If they approved of your terms, where you were searching, and how you were going about things, you are covered. This is vital. When you have finished all of the searches and have not come up with the information they wanted, they will be satisfied only if they approved the methodology. Otherwise, you will be doing it over.

Let's look at this in practice. Say, for example, you are given an assignment to search the document universe of a case (your produced documents and the other side's produced documents, totaling over two million documents in all), to find out more about a certain issue that has recently become important. The partner wants to know if a certain person had any knowledge about the bad employment practices going on at the plant between 2006 and 2010, when the company was sued. Your task is to conduct searches to help the partner understand the issues, who was involved, whether the company has any potential liability and the extent of that liability.

Most junior associates make the mistake of simply doing the assignment with a focus only on the final answer (yes, they were liable, etc.). They spend hours and hours looking through documents, with greater or lesser degrees of success, running broad searches and trudging through the voluminous results, certainly reviewing docs they have already seen a few times. Focused on the question they have been asked to answer, they may take a few notes regarding the information they glean, but fail to note the doc from which they got the information, the custodian or date. Their efforts are random, duplicative, over-broad, haphazard and not documented in a way that can be replicated later by another associate. Thousands of documents later, they arrive at what they think is a pretty good answer and email the partner and the two senior associates on the team with a nicely detailed description of the players and the exposure: yes, some lower level supervisors engaged in the following behaviors, leading to some liability for the company, but no one in higher level management was aware of the problem. They throw in a random stack of fifty printed-out documents in support of their conclusions, with some flags on the most important pages. Period.

And then they are stunned by the barrage of further questions, some that will take hours and hours to hunt down, about who might have known what when and who might have done what when. "Why didn't you check employment records of custodian X from the human resources department?" "Sort your findings by date!" "Why is a document with Bates number 67,473 in this batch? Why were you searching in Bates ranges 55,675 to 74,834 when those ranges have nothing to do with this company?" And "Why didn't you review every single doc of employee X within the dates in question? She is key to this issue?!"

These are common mistakes you already know how to avoid. You know the partner needs to know she can rely on what you have done and you know why. She needs rock solid certainty if she is going to proceed on this basis and must therefore know your results can be duplicated. You would be prepared with immediate answers to questions about which terms were used in the database searches, how many documents came up in the searches, why there were no relevant documents for the year 2009, how you tracked the documents or saved them so that others could find them in the database. And you would never have handed a partner a stack of flagged documents you know she has no time to read. You would have known to draft a nice bullet-point summary of all of the relevant documents in chronological order, with the most important points boiled down to a sentence, the format and extent of which summary you would have run by a more senior associate well in advance of your deadline. The hapless junior associate who failed to record any of the necessary information as he was merrily reviewing documents, must go back and reconstruct everything, document everything, prepare his summary and it has to be ready tomorrow. It is a nightmare and one that was completely avoidable.

It is not that his conclusions were wrong or his analysis faulty. He took ownership, wrote a thorough and concise answer to the question posed. But he failed to understand his position and the larger picture of the case, did not communicate, flunked paper trail 101, lacked all caution with regard to managing his work flow, sought no guidance, provided no transparency – not quite every mistake in the book, but close. Your superiors are not going to take what you tell them as a given until they have satisfied themselves that your searches were thorough, exhaustive, that you understood all of the important issues and could not have overlooked any possible information. Remember, they will not presume any of this of junior associates at first. If you do not find something they thought you should find, you are going to have to defend your searches. You have to give them this stuff right up front. In all of your emails providing answers or findings you should have a paragraph of what you did to find the answer to the question posed. This lets them evaluate for themselves whether your findings are reliable and your search exhaustive. If they see additional avenues you might have pursued, they will send you back with follow up questions. If they do think you did a complete job, you will usually hear nothing. They accept your findings. But they will never accept what you give them without being able to see how you got there.

This applies to every phase of your work. When you have finished reviewing and coding documents for a certain task, for example, let your superiors know you QC'd ten percent of the documents reviewed by contract attorneys, provided them feedback and had them go back through X number of batches, then you performed a key word search on frequently missed items to follow up and see that your feedback was incorporated correctly. Only then will they know to what degree they can trust what you have done.

So in *all* of your assignments, as second nature and without thinking, when you deliver your findings and conclusions, you should begin with a statement of what you did, including where you searched, what you found, how much you found, where you did not look and why and whether there were holes or gaps that you yourself can perceive in what you found. They should be able to recreate your searches and come up with the same results. As in mathematics or physics or chemistry, your awesome discovery will only be accepted and believed when it can be duplicated by others.

Develop Your Spidey Sense. Finally, many mistakes will be avoided as you progress in your career by the kind of instinctual response that comes with experience. Senior attorneys talk about developing a "Spidey sense" and many brain scientists, psychiatrists, philosophers and pop culture gadflies have testified to the existence of the phenomenon. The kind of intuition I am talking about is one based on years of experience practicing law. You have seen it or done it before so when something comes up a little tingle tells you that something is wrong. A Spidey sense allows partners to look at a document or a problem or an issue in a case and in a single flash understand that something is going to raise a flag or be a problem. They will sense a hole somewhere, instantly understand that a proposed course of action will bring a challenge, allowing them to recognize where a problem is going to arise and how to avoid it. A search of custodian X only turned up three documents? Something is wrong. The staff attorney tells you that she searched for ten hours straight and only looked at forty documents? That can't be right. A privileged document has gone out the door. Do we claw it back, drawing the other side's attention straight to the document, or do we let it go and risk being vulnerable on other similar privilege calls because we arguably waived the privilege by producing that document? What kind of trouble will it bring if we make a second motion to compel production of documents with this judge? Is it worth the risk? They can make these calls.

This kind of leap is, of course, way, way, way above your pay grade, and will be for many years, but here is a more down and dirty real life example. I was sitting in on a call between a senior associate and a vendor who was to assist in the technical side of producing documents. The senior associate and the vendor were discussing the upcoming production when the associate said, "Now, when you produce the redacted documents, you need to ensure that the text underneath the redactions is not searchable." To me, this question came out of nowhere. How did she know to raise that issue? Who would imagine that something redacted would still be searchable? I later learned that the senior associate had been on a case in which documents redacted for attorney-client privilege were found – after they had been produced to the other side – to be searchable underneath the redactions. Very bad. And she had been on another case in which the opposite had happened. The vendor had completely eliminated the redacted text so that not only could the other side not search on the redacted text, but it had actually been removed from her own database, so she could no longer search on the text of her own privileged documents. So her Spidey sense was primed to tingle when she spoke with vendors about methodologies for producing redacted documents and she knew what questions to ask and where to probe. There is no mystery in this example, just experience and a good memory.

A Spidey sense kicks in when you are about to do something that will likely cause problems. It says, "Wait! Something's not right here." Or, "Wait, remember that time . . . ." It is incredibly valuable but unfortunately, only comes with time practicing law. You will develop a Spidey sense, too, but gradually. A Spidey sense is not that different from the alarm that goes off when you recognize something that is above your pay grade. In the beginning this is everything. As you develop you can begin to rely on more sophisticated alarm systems.

It is how senior associates know when you have not searched in all the right places just from looking at your results. It is how they know you missed some cases or there are holes in your findings just from a glance at your draft. They know because they have been in your shoes and done the work. They know the enormous time and effort it takes to do the assignment right, and they can spot it in a second if you have fallen short. There is no fast track to what a ninth-year associate knows without thinking.

The only way I can help you to get there faster is to urge you to pay attention. It comes from being in the trenches day after day, seeing what works; what goes horribly wrong; how senior associates deal with problems; how cases are run, organized and managed on a daily basis. It is the gratuitous end result of accumulated experience by a supremely attentive practitioner. And it comes from watching great lawyers practice law. If you want to develop it faster, then take an afternoon and go sit in a court room every once in a while, just to observe how it works, the arguments made, the way people interact, odd issues that arise and how they are resolved. If I have a case in a local court I will always try to go observe the judge's courtroom one day to try to get a sense of how she will be. Read the final briefs the partner filed. Read the other sides' if they are any good. Look through the evidence used at trial. Read deposition transcripts and notice lines of questions that were particularly useful. Try to get the partner's deposition outline and see how he prepared. Ask to attend interviews or depositions or client meetings on a non-billable basis, just so you can be there. It is great whenever you can watch good lawyers practicing law and it is the best way to develop a Spidey sense. Basically, throw yourself into the practice of law and try to absorb whatever you can as you go along.

High Quality Work Product and the Quest for Perfection. Finally, you will avoid a number of serious mistakes, pitfalls and frustrations if you take as a given that a quest for perfection is definitional in Biglaw. You already know Biglaw clients are some of the biggest, wealthiest and most powerful individuals and corporations in the world and you know what they expect. The kinds of legal problems these clients bring to Biglaw are the most complicated, large-scale and sophisticated problems anywhere and we charge accordingly so what this means for the young associate is that unbelievable levels of detail and perfection are expected of everything you do.

Remember that $100,000 privilege log we mentioned in chapter six? A friend recently finished a privilege log for a multi-national corporation in a large litigation that cost the corporation at least $100,000. A fifty-page priv log, which is relatively small as priv logs go, was worth $100,000 to that company. Of course no company paying that kind of money wants to see any error, no matter how small, insignificant or silly. And it needs to be polished and pretty as well. Junior and senior associates spent hours of their precious time debating how to format, how to deal with problematic documents, whether certain documents were privileged at all, which privilege descriptions to use, how to characterize various types of documents. The pros and cons of "reflecting legal advice" versus "containing legal advice" were given at least an hour. You can imagine hours and hours and hours of associate fun. Our clients pay for and expect the best legal services in the world and that includes not only the best legal minds, most brilliant legal analyses and arguments of the partners. It means the blood, sweat and tears of every single junior associate striving to make the best work product possible from the smallest witness interview binder to the most trivial email.

I recently sent an email to my contract attorney team – and I have sent many a similar email in the past. "Folks, please remember to use *bright yellow* highlighters in the witness preparation binders, not the darker yellow ones. The darker highlighters leave marks on the page when the binder is duplicated and the bright yellow ones do not. Thanks." Do I feel like a tiresome nag? Yes. But this is very, very important to the senior associates for whom I work. And I would rather irritate the contract attorneys than get another snitty email from a senior associate complaining about highlighter pens. And the sad truth is – it does matter. The senior associate is right. It has to be perfect. This is Biglaw.

I hate sending those nagging, yellow highlighter emails. Do I care about smudges on copies? No. Do I know the contract attorneys call me an "alien taskmaster overlord" behind my back? Yes. I do not enjoy going through eight drafts before I ask a senior associate to look at a memo, nor obsessing about Excel spreadsheet formats or colors of flags for a binder. It is horrible to spend so much of one's time as an associate focusing on things of minimal impact. But it would be a mistake to do otherwise. The competition in Biglaw is fierce. The fees are high. This is the level of perfection that is expected. Cue the Metropolitan Opera, Big Leagues, Olympics and Broadway metaphors. You cannot offer a merely competent performance. You must strive for perfection in everything you do. If you are here long enough, it will become an ingrained part of you.

I will leave to you the important philosophical and spiritual questions of whether obsessing about highlighter pens is worth it in the grand scheme of things. Perhaps you will wisely decide that it is not worth it to you. At least you will know, then, that Biglaw is not your path.

If you do go this route, you will make your share of mistakes in Biglaw. Sometimes you will not even know how you screwed up. You will write a memo for one partner who will think it is great. You will later turn in a similar work product to another partner who will think it is completely unacceptable. I know one associate at a Vault top-twenty firm who was once asked to draft a letter to a client for a senior attorney who had a bad reputation for crankiness in the best of situations. Thinking that she was being clever, proactive, steering clear of danger, avoiding duplicative efforts and utilizing existing work product to efficient ends, all highly prized skills in Biglaw, she found a similar client letter in the case files written by that same attorney. She reworked and updated the letter for the current circumstances and confidently sent it off to the senior attorney for his review, certain that she had aced the task. She shortly received the letter back, full of red marks and edits, with a snide email pointing out the various grammatical and stylistic flaws. My friend laughed all day – bitter laughter, to be sure – but she laughed. Would anything she had written for him have passed muster if his own writing was not up to snuff? Probably not.

Biglaw attorneys become so intensely focused on picking apart, finding fault, catching every error, that they are merciless, even with their own work. This story demonstrates why my best advice is to do what you can to avoid mistakes but grow a hide like a rhinoceros and learn to let it all roll off your back. You will seek perfection but not achieve it. You are not going to please senior attorneys most of the time. You cannot read their minds. You are going to make, sometimes idiotic, mistakes as a junior associate. And you will never be recognized for the disasters you helped avert, for the seventy typos you did catch in the brief, for the things you did right. You will only hear about the typo you overlooked, the one document that was missing its second page that you let go through in QC'ing a binder. It's just the way it is. You are not alone.

I have a friend who put it very well. "Some days, I come in the office and I feel like I can take anything. No one can get me down. Other days, I walk in and feel like I am going to crumble if anyone says anything negative to me at all. I've had all I can take." It will be this way for you. Some days, the number of bad mistakes, screw-ups, nit-picking sessions will be one too many. You will leave swearing you are going to start looking for another job the next day. You will feel like you are about to break. Other days, none of it will bother you, the world will be at your feet and you will be ready to take anything that Biglaw can throw at you. Sometimes the best advice is: just get through the day. Much is forgotten very quickly and you will find people have moved on.

D. Mitigating the Damage

Okay, so having done all you can to avoid mistakes, having given one hundred percent on every assignment, every time, still, inevitably, you will make mistakes. But there are some things you can do to mitigate the damage, many of them in the same litany we have just been repeating. First, as discussed above, communication skills are paramount. Contact a senior associate immediately and let him or her know what happened. This is the same, proven-effective damage control basic maneuver so frequently ignored by vulnerable politicians. So it must be on some level counterintuitive, but it is always the best course. Just think of those shame-faced politicians – delay makes it worse, hiding makes it worse and certainly lying is a nonstarter. It will be far easier for you if you fess up right away and take the initial blow of anger, instead of letting the anger grow through your inaction, denial or excuses.

The sooner your superiors know about the problem, the more can be done to address it before the problem metastasizes. And you know not to approach anyone with only the problem. You will always come prepared with possible solutions ready to offer. Senior associates are happiest when they can decide among several reasonable options and evaluate a number of possibilities, instead of having to generate something themselves, especially under pressure. Remember, your main job is still to save them time and effort. Help them by presenting as many options as you can. Do not dump your mistake in someone else's lap and expect him to invent the wheel while you stand there in a panic. Instead of simply, "I miscalculated the deadline to file our interrogatory responses and it is due tomorrow!!!" – it should be, "I miscalculated the deadline to file our interrogatory responses and it is due tomorrow!!! I have called the paralegal on the team to let him know we will have a late filing tomorrow and we will need all the time he can give; I have gotten two sample responses from a similar case I was on last year that we can start with; I have asked the staff attorneys to plan for a late night tonight so we can wrap up loose document searches; I will try to send you the rough draft by COB today; what else can I do?"

We are back to ownership. Taking ownership means owning your mistakes as well. If you realize you have just been through half the production and have been miscoding documents, let the senior associate know immediately so she can adjust deadlines, see if it is worth it to recode, make decisions about splitting up the extra work or getting more manpower. You will look far less incompetent if you discovered – and uncovered – the mistake on your own. If someone else finds your mistake – and someone will – then they will just think you are an idiot. Suggest targeted searches you will do to find the docs that were miscoded. Offer your ideas for quick ways to isolate the documents instead of going back through all of them from the start. Let them know you are willing to do whatever needs to be done. Forget about sleep and make sure the problem is fixed and the production is back on track.

And take heart: there are (almost) no mistakes you can make in Biglaw that cannot be fixed.

E. When and How to Push Back

When mistakes happen there will inevitably be criticism. "What do you mean you didn't review every, single document the staff attorneys reviewed and so this horrible document went unnoticed until thrown in our face by the other side?" "Why wasn't this production absolutely perfect?" "Why didn't you make sure those witness binders got out the door two weeks ago?" It is very hard for an inexperienced, junior associate to defend against perfect hindsight and searing scrutiny of her work, since there will always be more she could have done or better ways to have done it. It is laughably easy to look at what someone has done and see the zillions of ways it could have and should have been done better. And when something goes wrong in a case, that is exactly what senior associates and partners will do. How did this happen? Will it happen again? What breakdown in the process or work streams allowed this to occur? It is not solely that one glaring, disastrous document that is the problem. That bad document is evidence of an error in the methodology. Something broke down in the various work streams of paralegals, contract attorneys, staff attorneys, associates and partners and something got through the net. This is frightening to a partner, because if one thing escaped notice, who knows what else might be out there about to leap out at them. They do not like surprises.

But you know excuses are not acceptable. You cannot say you were too exhausted, too overloaded on other matters, too burned out to do your work effectively. It does not matter that you have a pounding headache or the Black Plague, or that your personal life is falling to pieces. No one cares. They want to know what went wrong and how to fix it. And how hard they should kill you. So you cannot make excuses but you can push back.

You have some small weapons and you should use them. Biglaw wants perfection, but it also hates waste of resources and your time is valuable. Why did that bad document slip through? "Because I was doing all I could do to train the contract attorneys, provide them with guidance and feedback, frequently QC their work early on in the review process by reviewing ten percent of what they reviewed, then less and less as time went on. The system I had in place was one approved by senior associates, and I followed it. It was never a part of the plan for me to review *every single* document, and so that one must have slipped through. I will have another training session with the contract attorneys and make sure they understand what we are looking for going forward." No one in Biglaw will argue that an associate should review every document that a staff or contract attorney has already reviewed. No senior associate wants to admit to a partner that they had a three-hundred-dollar-an-hour associate first-line review three thousand documents. You can push back when things are not perfect by pointing out what you did do. Give them every detail of your diligent efforts to avoid the problem, and you can remind them that the client would not have been happy having you do the entire review at your billable rate. You do the best you can within time and financial constraints, not free of them.

If you are given a crazy deadline, one you cannot possibly meet with a reasonable probability of a successful result – and there will be many such deadlines – put them on notice right away that you need more associates to help, that you have a pressing deadline on another case that will take some time, or that there are too many documents and if they want it fully QC'd and reviewed, you will need more time. They would never agree that you should do a less than completely conscientious job. If they do not agree to give you the help or the time you need to do it the way it should be done, push the responsibility for their expectations back on them. If they want to dream up a way for you to do it that they believe can achieve the requisite standard of perfection in the time they have given you, without any more support, let them dictate that to you. And, while the onus will never be on them if something goes wrong, at least you will be on record. You have to do the best you can, with the time and resources given. It is what makes Biglaw practice grueling, erratic and stressful. But my task here is to arm you with knowledge, not solve the many, many dysfunctions of Biglaw.

Chapter Eleven

Have a Life

So, the obvious question left at this point is: how do you make it work? We talk a lot about giving one hundred percent in all of your efforts and we have said the firm will take over ninety percent of your life, so where does that leave everything else? How do you maintain sanity, never mind pleasure in life? The bad news is I do not have any magical secrets and there are no easy answers. To be honest, this was a hard chapter to write. I struggle with making it work every single day and some days I lose. It is a big choice to enter Biglaw and you cannot have it all. Sometimes, I still wonder what I want to do with my life and whether I can make that work with a career in Biglaw. But I do have some surprisingly simple suggestions with profounder implications than you might think. If you have decided to be in Biglaw, these small victories for your sanity are important. And wrestling with the dilemma is a struggle worth having. If you simply let Biglaw run your life, you will lose much more than your intimate relationships, friends, health, hobbies and sanity. You risk losing your soul.

If I have ever met a single person in Biglaw with a normal life, I did not know about it. Most do not and those who cannot adjust their lives to Biglaw usually leave. I had coffee with a colleague early in my Biglaw career who was leaving her firm to go in-house. She had recently had a baby and explained that before the baby, she had always had just enough time for her husband and the firm. Many associates will tell you that there is room for one, and only one, major commitment in your life outside the firm. Those two things filled up her life, but she had enough time and energy successfully to give everything her husband and the firm needed to be happy. But with a baby, things were different. "Now," she said, "either I leave the firm or my marriage is dead." There was room for one other intensely demanding relationship along with the firm, but not two. She had time for the baby and the firm but her husband was left out and her marriage was at a breaking point. She believed that she had to leave Biglaw to keep her marriage from going under. It is a situation I have seen many times. The number of women in Biglaw who want kids but cannot fathom how to make it work is staggering.

The number of people with kids, but with a spouse at home, is large. Parents who seem to be able to make it work just happen to have a musician/writer/artist spouse at home. It is, still, harder for women than it is for men. Many end up leaving but I think more and more are trying to make it work. The number of people struggling to have time for spouses, children and other passions in the teeth of Biglaw's all-encompassing demands is roughly equivalent to the number of people in Biglaw. It is never going to be perfect, and sometimes you will be more successful than at others, but the following three things will help.

A. Strip Down

You need to become super-focused on what really matters in your life. Figure out what those core things are: marriage, kids, family, training for a marathon or 5K race, charity work, church involvement, community theater? Whatever it is, brush aside everything else. Jealously guard your time. You will only have enough for one outside passion, maybe two if that passion is not for a person, but you can succeed at making room. Do not ever throw away your time. Ever.

A partner once gave me this advice, which has had a huge impact on my daily life in Biglaw: if there is anything you can pay for to make your life easier, spend the money. This means house cleaners, dog walkers, grocery delivery, automatic bill paying through your bank, online shopping, restaurant delivery, nannies to drive kids to and from after-school activities. Take advantage of them all. Buy double the usual number of necessities like socks and underwear so that you can make it through the extended times when doing a load of laundry is an impossible oppression. If you can manage for three weeks, you will not have to worry about doing laundry every single weekend after a week of fourteen-hour days. Forget about doing any of this yourself, you do not have time. I started out using a house cleaner every two weeks and squeaking by in between. During a horribly compressed trial in my early life as an associate, I switched to having cleaners come every week and I never looked back. You are making the big bucks. Use them to make your life manageable.

I pay an enormous amount of money every month to park my car under my office building in the city. Yes, there is public transportation and, yes, I care deeply about preserving the environment. But when it takes me an hour to get home on the metro, when I can be home in fifteen minutes in my car, I cannot rob my daughter of those forty-five minutes. Often it is the difference between our having dinner together and not seeing her before bed at all. Similarly, I live as close to my firm as I can afford. I cannot give up an hour twice a day to live far enough to have a horse and stable in the back yard. For me, given my priorities and family responsibilities, I need to be close enough to be able to work from home when I need to and make it in to the office in fifteen minutes or less if I am suddenly needed. Your individual needs may be different, but what is important is taking the time to figure out what it is that your life revolves around. What is it that you need and what do you want? Then figure out what can go and how you can shuffle and juggle what remains to make that work with the demands of Biglaw. Do all that you can to organize and streamline your life.

It sounds fine in theory to pay for whatever you can to save yourself time. But I really mean everything and by time I mean increments of a tenth of an hour. You will feel stupid for paying $9.95 to overnight one tube of toothpaste and some soap when there is a drugstore on the corner. But you will do it. I order everything I can online. I know it feels wasteful and extravagant to order one thing you really need now – say your headache medication – and to pay twenty extra dollars for express shipping, when you could walk down to the corner and get it. You do not have time to waste feeling bad about it. There will be plenty of times when you will not have the energy or the time to walk two blocks or even downstairs. Do everything you can to make your life easier. Money helps.

Letting the less important parts of your life go means a shift away from other pleasant pastimes that may have filled a vacant hour in your life. You will not have a vacant hour. Enjoy window shopping on the weekend? Gone. Like to garden? Not anymore. Scrap booking? Nice try. You will have to let it all fall away. Cramming more demands, commitments or responsibilities – even if ordinarily they would be pleasant – in your strained life will only add to your stress and that is something you never want to do in Biglaw.

If it is not your central passion, you cannot afford it anymore. I used to feel bad every time I could not help out at my daughter's school fundraiser, every time I had to pass up all those other things I felt I "should" do. But there is no time and feeling guilty will make you miserable. Spreading yourself too thin with "shoulds" and "oughts" will add stress to your already bursting anxieties. Be wise and frugal about any new commitments you take on. Do not get that new puppy. Do not offer to have the full, extended family Thanksgiving dinner bash at your place this year – unless you have it catered.

Unfortunately, this means losing some things that made your life full and rich. It is hard to let them go, but one way or another, you must. I started running the summer after my second year in law school, to combat a quickly expanding waist line, the predictable consequence of too many summer associate events, and maintained it faithfully – about twenty-four miles a week – even through the bar exam. I love to run, but I stopped the third month at my firm and was not able to pick it back up for years. There was honestly no room in my life. It is said, and it is true, that the firm will take ninety percent – and it will not be cheated – so you really will have to fit everything else into the remaining fragments of time.

Be willing to delegate whenever you can and, indeed, rack your brain to come up with all the ways you can let others take care of the things they can. Lean on the support system you have in your life, expand it and let others help you.

But never let go of the things that remind you you're human. Nourish the non-Biglaw-lawyer in you – the you filled with creativity, humor and memories of your former self – by clinging feverishly to your passions and little pleasures. Fill the remaining ten percent of your life with as many of them as you can. I know I said never waste time but sometimes a person *needs* to watch trash TV and eat popcorn. Take a spontaneous weekend getaway (you know you cannot plan it) to someplace extravagant, sing in a local punk band, steal an hour to meet a friend for coffee, write a book on your Biglaw life – whatever keeps you alive inside. And strip away all the stuff that does not matter and often consumes so much of our daily lives. Much of your time in Biglaw will be dehumanizing, soul-killing and numbing. If you do not regularly counteract that effect, the numbness will consume you. Exhibit A: all the non-lawyers Biglaw has left in its wake and all the cold, reptilian lawyers you will encounter there, who checked their hearts at the door and never left the building.

B. Balance

You do not have to stay at the office until seven or eight p.m., a slave to the notion of potential face time, when you are not needed and things are slow. This ought to be obvious, and I know I have said it many times, but plenty of associates feel that they need to stay and look busy every evening, even throughout a month-long dry spell at work. Since you know there will be times when you will barely see the inside of your apartment for weeks, that there will be days and weeks and months when the firm will take everything you have and then some, you need to save up for those times. You can learn to ride the ebbs and flows. Some days, the balance gets thrown completely and I am forced to make painful choices. Either I don't see my daughter before she goes to bed in the evening or I piss off my team on an important assignment and risk getting written off as not being committed to my work. Understand that this will happen sometimes and there is no avoiding it, but if you do everything I suggest, you will make it work most of the time and that will be enough.

If you have been away for three weeks on a trial, holed up in a hotel in Marshall, Texas and working every single hour of every day, you will take a week off when you get back. Do not even think about showing up to the office to sit around in a daze. It is common not to see a trial team for more than a week after a trial ends. No one can give one hundred and ten percent 24/7, 365 days a year. One of the most important things to learn as a junior associate is to get out of the office when you are not busy and replenish your energy when you are given the chance. This means it is vital that you take all of your vacation time. Your firm will give you a month or more off – do everything in your power to take it all, every year. You will have to strategize, of course, and be prepared for disappointment but take the time when you can. Take long weekends here and there, but also take a good, long vacation at least once a year. You need to get away and be gone long enough to allow the impulse to check your Blackberry every five minutes to fade.

Another point about balance: you cannot possibly do everything and this applies to firm events and activities as well. There are countless "events" at Biglaw firms. My firm schedules massive weekly luncheons with an array of distinguished and fascinating speakers. We have training sessions, mentor events, practice group meetings, *pro bono* opportunities, continuing legal education courses, committee assignments, endless support groups for any subgroup imaginable, exercise classes, new associate welcome lunches, farewell to old associate lunches, and on and on. They range from profoundly useful training or networking events to complete wastes of time but at least some of them will be command performances for the management of the firm, in one sense or another, requiring your attendance. For example, firms often spend thousands of dollars buying tables at charity events – and then need placeholder associates to fill the seats so the tables do not look pathetic. I spent many hours as a junior associate in random training sessions, watching the hours pass and fretting about how I would manage to get my billable work done. My heart would sink lower and lower, as it gradually dawned on me how much longer into the night that four-hour training session would force me to work to complete my required ten hours of doc review for the day. Everything that takes time away from your billable hours will only delay what has still to be done – it will never free you from a single billable hour requirement.

You will need to exercise your judgment about all of these events and distractions. Learn which ones you should not or cannot miss. Ask more senior associates whether there is an unwritten expectation about how many times per year firm management will expect your attendance at a charity dinner or event. Is it at least once a year? Or more? Is it expected that you will participate in a committee? How many? Do your part, of course, but then do not do any more. And never feel pressured into attending more of these things than is customarily considered necessary. Remember that if you are billing heavily the burden on you is lightened. If I am keeping a full billable work load, I feel no pressure to show up at these kinds of firm events – even the ones that are billed as "strongly suggested" or "very important" in supporting the firm. At the end of the day, you are making the firm money only when you are billing, and it wants you to keep on doing that. This is not the Academy. I have never seen anyone get in trouble for billing too many hours, being antisocial about firm events and refusing to volunteer for committees. None of these things is billable. All of the lunch events and training programs can be great – you can learn about new practice areas, network with other attorneys, hang out and socialize during the day, and you may want to take advantage of them on occasion. In fact, you may want to load up if you are having a slow period so that you can show your loyalty and involvement with the firm and add value to the firm in other non-billable ways. But remember that the clock is ticking. Every hour you spend at a non-billable event is another hour you will have to make up in your billable life some other time. The clock never stops ticking. Of course you need to find the balance, break up the tedium and recharge over a pleasant lunch occasionally. It is part of keeping your sanity. But if you do have a family, a girlfriend or fiancé or other demands that you are trying to fit into your life, all of these events will literally steal the time that might have been for them.

Time in your life is a zero sum game, and Biglaw will not be cheated. If you decide to take a moment to breathe, go out for coffee, attend a diversity seminar or firm charity event, or whatever might help you balance your life, you can and should do that. But know that Biglaw will get its hours from you just the same. You will make them up – at three a.m., if necessary. And every second you allow yourself to do things that are not core, quality of life things, it insidiously drains away your life. When you have to bill ten hours, you will have to bill them one way or another. And all the time you spend at lunch will be time you are away from home later that night. There are twenty-four hours in a day. Let's say you need roughly eight for sleeping. That leaves sixteen hours in your day. If you must bill twelve hours on a given project, you have only four other hours for everything else: showering, eating, commuting, picking up the dry cleaning and loading the dishwasher – everything. One thing Biglaw will do for you is impress indelibly upon you how valuable your time is. If you waste forty-five minutes at a suggested firm event, you will have to start cheating your sleep and personal life time to make it up. It is so easy to let your time dribble away. So do take advantage of the lunches and interesting diversions and activities. Do relax, be sociable, make friends at work, break up the tedium. But remember that the clock is ticking and you will always have to make up your Biglaw hours.

C. Draw Lines

After you have decided what matters to you and you have whittled the less important things from your life and have attempted to achieve a balance of the things you want and need in your life, you should delineate your boundaries, draw lines where you must and stick with them in almost every circumstance. There will be exceptions, there are always exceptions, and more on that below. But you can establish boundaries in Biglaw. They will come at a price, but you can set them. If you must leave work by five p.m. on Tuesdays and Wednesdays for whatever reason (child care, book club, charity meeting, German language class), draw that line and stick with it in almost all situations. If you never work on certain days for religious reasons, make that clear right away with everyone with whom you work and do not give it up. If your best friend's wedding is coming up on a certain date and you absolutely will not miss it, draw a line in the sand months in advance.

But make them sacred. Do not give up your lines. If you start canceling important personal activities to finish a super important project here and there, if you allow Biglaw to disrupt and control your life, you will never get it back. There will always be a super important project. Always. Unless you are happy to dedicate your entire life to Biglaw, you will need to draw lines and stay firm in the face of subtle or overt pressure. The key is to communicate early and often to everyone on your teams. Remind them a month before your event, then a week and then the a couple days before and the morning of. In a big enough firm there will be other associates who can step in and carry the load while you are away. And you will do the same for them.

Of course, you understand by now, there will be times in Biglaw when it is all-hands-on-deck, when whatever is going on is so crucial and time-sensitive that you, and everyone else you work with, will frantically throw yourselves at your task for as long as it takes. You will cancel everything when this happens or face severe consequences. But the good news is that this is not the daily norm of Biglaw. It will happen – on some cases it will happen often – but it is not and does not have to be the norm. Do not be fooled or pressured into treating every urgent assignment as an all-hands-on-deck frenzy. You will quickly learn, or be told, when you are absolutely expected to stay. The best approach is to ask directly, "Do you need me to stay and cancel my Hawai'i vacation?" Clear communication will rarely lead you astray. Slipping into treating every important, time-critical assignment as a reason to give up your boundaries, will make those boundaries meaningless in the firm. If you abandoned your lines for X, you surely should be able to do it for Y. You will meet plenty of associates who have no boundaries – either because they never set them or they let them slip away – and they will generally not be among the sanest people you will meet. For the most part, if you are attuned to the differences between the important and the truly critical and if you are clear and consistent in your communications and your application of your own policies, you should be able to draw lines and keep them even through hectic and time-sensitive deadlines and demands. Your team will often be able to plan ahead and spare you if they know there is something you want to do – or that you always do – and you have communicated it clearly and well in advance.

It is more difficult to keep your boundaries when you are on case with a smaller staff and there simply is no one else to replace you, or when you become senior enough on a large case to be integral. Being integral on a case is really the best and worst of times simultaneously. If they cannot live without you, that means you are needed, your job is secure, you are receiving better assignments and more responsibility. But if they cannot live without you, they can't live without you. And often that comes to mean that you are at work alone, shouldering most of the load and the stress, while other associates are home living their lives. It is good to become important to the cases on which you work. But – unless your goal is to become a partner – not *too* important. If you want to have a life in Biglaw, not pursuing a partner track, but just getting through – then you will draw more lines and hold to them more firmly than other associates. You will do your best, always, on your cases, and become trusted and important. But you will also maintain your boundaries and not give them up. As we have said from the beginning you have to know what track you are on and what you want out of your time in Biglaw. Decide right up front whether you want to be the person that every partner runs to, at all hours of the day or night, for any reason whatsoever. If you do not want that position, then draw your lines and stick to them.

Biglaw is becoming somewhat more tolerant and flexible over time. There are many more options for flex-time, part-time and other alternative work situations than were previously considered possible. But your line drawing should still be done with judgment and prudence. As I said, it does not come without cost. There are any number of young, single associates who have nowhere to go and are willing to dedicate their entire lives to being at the firm, if need be, and will happily take your place. If you are not that person, and you make yourself too unavailable, you risk making yourself irrelevant. You already know the consequences of that. Understand, too, that some partners will be less tolerant of life-balancing efforts than others. Old-school partners will demand limitless availability and the ability to walk in and have you cancel all other plans on a dime no matter what, and will be very unsympathetic of your attempts to have personal boundaries. Drawing lines will have greater costs to your work with them – and they may simply decide not to work with you. So be it. You will make sure you have enough relationships with other partners to ensure adequate work flow. One way or another – unless you are a singularly driven individual with limitless personal discipline, single-mindedly focused on the firm above all – you can and must stick to your guns if you are to survive with your humanity and your love of the law intact.

In drawing lines, you cannot, of course, expect to work a nine to five day in Biglaw unless you are going part-time. But if your line drawing is reasonable, legitimate, consistent and you are always available for true emergencies, work long hours most days and you are willing to pay the professional cost of not always being in the office, you should be able to have the boundaries you need to make your life work.

In my early years at Biglaw I was a single mother for a time. It was a difficult time and I remember regularly wondering on the drive home if I was going to be able to make it work at all. I decided right away to do all I could to leave the office by five thirty every evening and then work from home after my daughter had gone to bed. I did not have a spouse who needed my attention and so this worked for me. Almost every day – of course there were exceptions – I left the office and spent the evening with my daughter, only to log on to my network after she went to bed and work as late into the night as I had to. One key to making this work was that I never asked for permission. I know I have talked endlessly about hierarchy and the need for communication but there is also an old Army truism that sometimes applies. Note that this is an expression used in a world as rigidly hierarchical as Biglaw: "If it is important enough, better to take action and face the consequences than to seek permission and be denied." I decided that my daughter needed to see me every evening at a reasonable hour and I made it happen. That goal was more important to me than winning Biglaw Associate of the Year. If I had asked if I could work from home regularly, or if I could leave the office so early, I feared I would be told no, and then I would have had to choose between defying my supervisors and giving up crucial time with my child. So I just did it and, for me, it worked. Another key was spending no energy on anything else. I worked and took care of my daughter. Full stop.

Other associates sometimes expressed some resentment. When they were hanging out all evening in standby mode to be available "just in case," it was easy to murmur, "What makes you so special?" I would get good-natured (and sometimes not so good-natured) jabs and comments. It was bearable and I had supporters at the firm, but my leaving was certainly noticed. And I always felt guilty every time I left the office. Each evening I would skulk quietly out of my office and then rush to the elevators, hoping not to run into any partners who would notice that I was leaving even before most of the administrative staff. In over two years I never got over the chagrin. I always knew I was breaking unwritten rules. I still feel the same sense of dread if I leave the office between five and six in the evening – even if I have been at the office since before seven in the morning. If someone sees me in the halls, I know they are wondering why the hell I am leaving at such a non-Biglaw time.

A very small handful of partners would not work with me at all simply because I was not guaranteed to be in my office whenever they wanted to see me there. In one instance, I was not included when a case I had been working on for nine back-breaking months went to trial out of state, even though I was the most senior of the junior associates on the team and had always received positive performance evaluations. The other associates had joined the case much later, and two of them were a year junior to me (remember, all this matters in Biglaw). The partner who broke the news was one I had once heard bitterly joke that she had not seen her three-year-old son in a month. She explained to me casually, but haltingly and without making eye contact, that I was going to be transitioned to a new assignment – one with no possibility of going to trial and a much shorter lifespan altogether as it happened. She sat across from me, in my office, telling me they needed my deeper experience on this other case and I looked back at her and nodded, saying, "Okay, no problem." But we both knew the truth. She was shunting me off the trial team after all that painstaking work and taking two more junior associates in what was, by rights, my place. They gained unbelievably valuable trial experience and I stayed behind, because at the end of the day she worried about my commitment to the team because of my family responsibilities. Line drawing does not come without cost. But at that point in my life, satisfying the demands of Biglaw, but only marginally, was what I felt I had to do to raise my daughter on my own.

One difference between a humane Biglaw firm and a cutthroat one can be seen when someone on the team has another obligation or responsibility. What happens when someone, in the middle of a mad rush to file a motion before a midnight electronic filing deadline, says, "I'm sorry, guys, but my mother-in-law is in town and I have to leave at 6:30 tonight." At a cutthroat firm, the associate would have quietly called his wife from his office hours earlier, backed out of the dinner and never raised the issue. But if you land at a decent firm, people will realize that you have obligations, that you give up enough, that you pull your share and will take the load for someone else one day and it will occasionally be okay for you to make that dinner with your mother-in-law. However, even at decent firms, there might be teams and groups that are not so humane. Beware if you are on a team or in a firm filled with the types of associates described earlier – those who have given up any semblance they might once have had of a personal life and damn well expect you to do the same. If you work on a team characterized by this single-minded approach and you decide to try to honor some of your other responsibilities, your life will be hell. You are damned if you do and damned if you don't. If you do not give up everything for any silly fire drill, you will be seen as less loyal, less dependable, less committed and you will be shunted off to grunt work. You will suffer, no doubt. For most people, the whole point of subjecting oneself to Biglaw is to learn from the best, to work up to the great, sophisticated work that takes place at the highest levels. But if you do give up everything, if you let them win, Biglaw will chip away pieces of the rest of your life one fire drill at a time until it leaves you, miserable and alone, with nothing in your life outside the walls of the firm.

So make a decision to draw lines if you want to have a life. Think about how you can make your life work, what you can give up, what you must not give up if you are to remain human. Be creative. More and more firms offer options like part-time work, flex time, onsite childcare options and alternative work schedules. I know one associate who has a sixty percent part-time schedule and leaves her firm at two thirty in the afternoon. Many others are on seventy-five percent part-time and leave at four thirty (but beware about going part-time: they will all say they seem to still be working enough for a full-time associate and are only getting paid less). Seventy-five percent of a sixth year associate's salary is not bad. I have colleagues who bring their young kids into their offices when they have to be there over the weekend. One partner leaves every afternoon his son plays soccer and then returns to the office in the evening. One friend never works on Sundays for religious reasons – ever. And she still has a job. One planned her massive, gorgeous wedding during her lunch hours for months. One performs in community theater on the weekends. One couple, both Biglaw associates, live an hour from the city and carpool together every day. The long commute keeps their marriage going during the times they barely have any other time to see each other. One new father came to work at six thirty every morning and left at five p.m. for months at a time. Another associate took a six-month "sabbatical" from his firm to follow his yoga instructor girlfriend to Australia. They all found their individual ways to survive Biglaw.

I have also seen many people fail, divorce, give up or remain miserable and harried far into their senior associate years. I have seen even more run screaming from Biglaw for their very lives and never look back. If, after understanding the truth about Biglaw you still decide to enter it for whatever reasons yours may be, know that there are ways that you can make it work, that you cannot have it all but you can survive. The trick in Biglaw is to fight every single day to retain your humanity, your kindness, your "Keep Calm and Carry On" attitude, in the teeth of stress, exhaustion and outrageous demands. Drawing lines of your own and respecting the lines and lives of others is one way to maintain a grasp on the person you were before you entered Biglaw. Whatever you do, do not allow yourself to become the sneering, micro-managing, oppressive, passive aggressive senior associate who assumes everyone will always cancel anything and everything for the firm. You will meet plenty of these kinds of associates. They will make your life miserable. But you should fight every day not to become one.

D. Be Kind

One final thought: be kind. There are more than enough assholes in Biglaw. There will be days when you will want to cuss out your legal assistant, everyone in the duplicating office and the other associates on your team. You will be faced with what feels like the absolute last straw that cannot fail finally to break the camel's back sometimes repeatedly in a single day. When you give what you think is a direct, clear instruction to a staff or contract attorney or a paralegal and the instruction disappears into the ether as if you had never uttered it and nothing happens or the simple task is misunderstood so thoroughly that it takes a team to undo what one person got wrong, do not let the pressure turn you into a screamer. Don't snap or berate. Always treat the staff with whom you work with respect and kindness. It is a choice, and you should decide from day one that you will be kind to others when everything goes wrong. You will make mistakes and so will the people around you. The key is to remember that they are people.

There seem to be two basic types of people: those who, when they receive abuse from above, unconsciously pass it on to those below and those who do not. Deep psychological inquiry aside, one difference appears to be the degree to which one is capable of getting between the impulse to lash out and its expression. Awareness of others as full human beings and basic human fairness help a lot. So do the regrets from moments of getting it wrong. I have a friend who, early on in her career, in the midst of truly horrific deadline pressure snapped at a technician who inadvertently turned off the power to her computer. He turned to her, with tears in his eyes and, in a thick Russian accent, said, "I am so sorry. And you, you never made a mistake, nothing?" She never forgot it and says the memory of that simple human exchange is enough to stifle many an unworthy impulse.

You will get binders back from legal assistants, after carefully and clearly explaining exactly what you wanted, asking them to: highlight the name of the witness and the date on each document, put the documents in chronological order, print with the Confidential legend at the top left, print with the Bates numbers on the bottom right, include an index with "Volume 1 of 5," put the witnesses names and job positions on a label, etc. But when you get it back, things will be wrong. Who knows why – everyone is under stress, everyone is trying to do a million things at once and things get screwed up. Do what you can to make it right. Send it back to be redone if there is time, so you do not waste your own time and so they can learn what they did wrong. Feedback helps ensure that it will not happen again. QC and double check everything you can within the time constraints. Delegate what you can and see if others have some free time to help get the project back on track and out the door by the deadline. Let those who got it wrong know it was not acceptable. But be kind.

None of this has anything to do with what one likes to think a lawyer does. By now it should be clear that your success for the first couple of years in Biglaw will have less to do with how brilliantly you can analyze a complex legal issue, how masterfully you can craft an argument or argue a motion or the breadth of your expertise on insurance coverage litigation and more to do with how successfully you navigate treacherous waters, manage and execute your many tedious tasks and project a competent image of professionalism.

So if you have made it this far, I am sure you see the conflicted relationship I have with Biglaw. Every day while writing this book I would tell my husband something that happened at work, or something a friend told me about another firm, and he would say, "That has to go in the book."

"But I already have ten glaring examples of Biglaw irrationality, injustice, inhumanity," I would think. Every day of my life could add to the picture of associate bitterness, frustration and exhaustion. Some days are better than others. But this is Biglaw. If you read this book and run screaming in another direction, I have done my job. If you read this book and find that you are thrilled by the challenge of endlessly preparing and laboring with no real end in sight, no big day in court to look forward to, no "thanks for your hard work" in the end, only worlds of criticism, but you feel that the benefits are worth it, well, welcome to Biglaw. My only purpose is to give you the information you need to take some power and control over your life and career.

If you choose Biglaw, throw yourself into it with abandon. Resistance is futile and will make you miserable. Rebellion will just get you fired. Give in to the Zen way of Biglaw: acceptance and flow. As Yoda says, "Do, or do not. There is no try." You must embrace your life as a junior associate, if that is what you choose. As they teach in twelve-step programs: "acceptance is the answer to all my problems today." It will still suck more often than not, but you will survive. If you stick around long enough, I can promise you it will get better. Remember what Janet Reno advised: build it right and then you will not have any need to fear.

They say a good final line of a poem is one that sends you back to the first line to reread the poem with new perception. Over and over again in this book we have come to the question: so where do you find the motivation you need to press on each day in the face of so many things capable of destroying your spirit? And all I can do is refer you back to the introduction. You have to know why you are here. And it has to be a reason strong enough to sustain you. I hope that, if you have read this far, you will have a better sense of what that means. Am I happy in Biglaw all the time? Do I skip down the halls whistling the Biglaw associate theme song (whatever that may be) like some jolly cartoon character? Far from it. Will I be here in five years? I have no idea. There are still days I am not sure I can pull it all off for even one more day. I have spent years here fighting despair and resentment, swinging from apathy to panic and back. But I have also gained more than I can express. Biglaw has shaped how I will approach the practice of law for the rest of my life and some of the lawyers I have met are just incredible. Am I a success in Biglaw? That depends on how you define it. I am still here. I have survived through some of the harshest economic times and I still have a job. I have made mistakes – some horrific – and managed to come back from them without having my career implode. I have been able to play a proactive role in my career path and chart more of the course I wanted. I juggle my work and my family with some semblance of balance and control. I have survived, so far, with my nerves and sanity mostly intact. I have learned a ton and gained invaluable skills. And one strong measure of success in Biglaw – I think there is a chance I will be able to decide when I leave Biglaw – on my terms, not the firm's. For me, for now, that's enough.

I probably have not spent enough time in this little book answering the question why all that I have described is true. I have tried to explain the underlying reasons that Biglaw is like this and why won't it change as long as Biglaw continues to make the claims it does about what the firms can deliver. But in the end I worry that the questions I address seem academic and that answering them won't actually help the first year associate survive or get any real benefit from the Biglaw experience. What I do know is that I have described, candidly and accurately, our common experience as junior associates.

The truth of my description can be tested. If you put any set of Biglaw mid-level associates in a room for a management training seminar, and ask them about the qualities of good and bad managers, you only have to wait a second. The anecdotes will start to fly with a pent up, sardonic fury that will stun: transparently false deadlines, passive-aggressive communication, the hoarding of substantive work by senior attorneys, poor organization, regularly holding an assignment until Friday at 5 p.m., no positive feedback ever, partners with no investment in the development and careers of associates, who provide no useful constructive feedback, no respect for the time and lives of associates, no clear communication on expectations, never giving the big picture of a case or involving junior associates and bringing them along, approaching any mistake as being the end of the world in scope, obscene demands for perfection and micromanaging. On and on.

I'm not just describing the ways in which Biglaw associates *think* the systemically bad managers for whom they work make daily life a struggle. What we experience mirrors facts about Biglaw that everyone knows to be true: the crushing work load it imposes on associates, the tedious nature of many assignments that naturally stems from the nature of the hierarchical Biglaw world, the breakdown of the loyalty and commitment the great firms once gave to associates' professional development. All of this makes for a recipe for associate misery. No doubt the more senior attorneys would tell a different story, but this is life as Biglaw associates experience it, even in a firm like my own where the pathologies of Biglaw are least controlling.

I have tried to describe this experience in this book. Is it an apologia, or an indictment, or a little of both? You must answer that. All that this book offers is a candid glimpse of Biglaw life, some insights about Biglaw professionalism that will protect you in Biglaw practice if you internalize them and incorporate them into your practice from day one, and the message that you are not alone. I started this book out of my own quest to find the value in the years I have spent in Biglaw. I had to make sense of the time that has slipped away — and assure myself that it has not been wasted. I came to the conclusion that what I have gained from Biglaw is indeed immensely valuable, however different my experience has been than my picture of what the training and development of a young associate's career should be. My husband has taken to referring — lovingly — to this book as a survival guide to an insane asylum. But you need to understand that it is what it is. It is Biglaw.

Index

Above the law, 66, 97, 102
Alternative work schedules, 69, 176, 178
American Lawyer, 3, 16, 75
Benefits of Biglaw, 64
Big picture, 46, 47, 52, 57, 121, 141, 146–147, 153, 182
Biglaw definition, 3, 13
Billable hour, 37, 40, 67, 68, 75, 84–96, 109, 173
Billing rate, 17, 19, 20, 38, 39, 89, 91, 159
Binders, 5, 22, 26, 29, 30, 34–36, 40, 50, 52, 55–57, 59, 61, 70, 71, 73, 77, 82, 90, 118, 151, 153–156, 164, 165, 167, 180
Blackberry, 37, 99, 102–104, 173
Blogs, legal, 66, 97
Boundaries, 111–112, 116, 174–179
Buckets, 124–125, 127
Case staffing, lean vs. heavy, 40, 106, 108
Client, 8, 15, 19, 23, 28, 36, 38, 40, 44, 57, 58, 59, 71, 74, 80, 83–84, 86–87, 92–93, 101, 135, 163–164
Commitment, 7, 9, 95, 150, 182
Communication, 23, 34, 35, 43, 46, 69, 71, 88, 93, 98, 100, 103, 116, 126, 130, 134, 139, 141, 147–149, 150, 154, 159, 161, 165, 175, 177, 182
Compensation, 65–68, 92, 97
Contract attorneys, 38–39, 40, 46, 50, 53, 55–56, 61, 86, 89, 92, 124, 128, 141, 142, 154, 159, 164, 167
Criticism, 8, 10, 21, 33, 61, 89, 137–139, 150, 157–158, 181
Demotivators, 33, 36, 37, 40, 58, 61, 88, 138, 181
Doc review, 14, 16–17, 25–26, 34–35, 38, 39, 45, 46, 47, 49–62, 71, 78, 84, 85, 87, 89, 92, 101, 110, 118, 121–135, 144, 151
Email, 15, 16, 42, 81, 97–104, 145, 147–148
Evaluations, 9, 26, 75, 93, 95, 102, 110, 149
Feedback, 7, 10, 25–31, 33, 61, 85, 91, 96, 102, 147, 182
Feudalism, 37–47
Flex-time, 176, 178
Flexibility, 69–70, 77, 118, 176, 178
Goals, personal, 6, 8, 10, 12
Golden handcuffs, 68
Hierarchy, 15–16, 18–21, 28, 30, 33, 38, 40, 43, 46, 49, 61, 131, 140–141, 177, 182

Information mastery, 23, 27, 29, 41–43, 45, 47, 50–52, 62, 70, 82, 83, 121–135, 154
Judgment, 11, 53, 59, 69, 71, 79–84, 86, 92, 93, 96, 97, 123, 124–126, 142, 143, 148, 173, 176
Junior associates, 4–5, 6, 7, 10, 15, 16, 21, 23, 27, 28, 35, 37, 41–42, 44, 51, 57, 62, 70, 77, 78, 82, 131, 132, 138, 148, 161, 163, 182
Land of Binderia, 40, 52, 56
Legal research and writing, 17, 30, 40, 41, 49, 83, 86, 151
Leverage, 40
Life balance, 15, 107, 118, 172–174, 181
Lifestyle firm, 15, 67
Lockstep pay structure, 66–67, 92
Merit-based pay structure, 66–67, 92
Meritocracy, 5, 37–47, 106, 108
Metadata, 73, 126
Mid-level associates, 15, 19, 52
Mistakes, 9, 17–18, 24–26, 28, 59, 108, 123, 127, 137–168, 181
Money, 6–8, 10, 13, 14, 22, 64, 65–68, 170–171
Nihilistic path, 9–10
Non-billable time, 84, 87, 91, 163, 174
Old school partners, 25, 34, 35, 176
Ownership, 12, 26, 61, 80, 95, 138, 140, 146, 149–151, 156, 157, 161, 166
Part time work schedule, 64, 69, 176
Partners, 23, 38, 69, 85, 90, 95, 103, 105, 106, 107–110, 116–119, 132–133, 139, 148, 160, 167, 177
Perfection, 18, 22–24, 28, 34, 36, 45, 70, 71, 81, 82–84, 137–139, 140, 163–165, 167–168, 182
Precision, 53, 79–84, 86, 92, 143,

Preparation, 15, 23, 36–37, 44–45, 55, 70–73, 80, 101, 121–135, 143, 181
Priv log, 35, 36, 44, 50, 59–61, 83, 118, 126, 140, 163
Pro bono, 8, 20, 64, 67, 74–78, 96, 115, 153
Prudence, 79–84, 96, 104, 148, 155
Reasons for choosing, 8, 64
Recruiters, 10
Reputation, 21–31, 37, 40, 90, 92–93
Salary, 15, 66, 68, 84, 92, 178
Senior associates, 15, 18, 43, 182
Side effects, 62–64
Skills, 5, 8, 15, 17, 22, 52, 64, 70, 75, 145–165
Spidey Sense, 161–163
Staff attorneys, 38–40
Student loans, 6, 7, 8, 64–65, 70, 75
Time entries, 85–91
Toxic teams, 112–119
Transparency, 124, 157–161
Trust, 21–25, 113, 176
Vacations, 13, 29, 92, 95, 103, 108, 115, 116, 173, 175
Witness preparation, 5, 30, 40, 50, 54–58, 70, 73, 82–83, 108, 152, 164
Workflow, 19, 151–153, 161, 176
Work-life balance, 118, 172–179
Write-offs, 90, 93